In Your Face

SEXUAL CULTURES: New Directions from the Center for
Lesbian and Gay Studies
General Editors: José Esteban Muñoz and Ann Pellegrini

Times Square Red, Times Square Blue
Samuel R. Delany

Private Affairs
Critical Ventures in the Culture of Social Relations
Phillip Brian Harper

In Your Face
9 Sexual Studies
Mandy Merck

In Your Face: 9 Sexual Studies

MANDY MERCK

NEW YORK UNIVERSITY PRESS

New York and London

NEW YORK UNIVERSITY PRESS
New York and London

Library of Congress Cataloging-in-Publication Data
Merck, Mandy.
In your face : 9 sexual studies / Mandy Merck.
p.   cm.
Includes bibliographical references and index.
ISBN 0-8147-5638-7 (cloth : alk. paper) —
ISBN 0-8147-5639-5 (pbk. : alk. paper)
1. Sex in mass media. 2. Sex in popular culture.   I. Title.
P96.S45 M47 2000
306.7—dc21   00-056253

New York University Press books are printed on acid-free paper,
and their binding materials are chosen for strength and durability.

Manufactured in the United States of America

10 9 8 7 6 5 4 3 2 1

Contents

Acknowledgments

This book was begun at Cornell University, where in 1992 I spent a semester teaching Women's Studies at the kind invitation of Nelly Furman and Biddy Martin. My thanks to them and their Cornell colleagues, particularly Shirley Samuels and Mark Seltzer, for hospitality, friendship, and the launch of my rather belated academic career. I also owe a debt of gratitude to the Program in Film and Video at Duke University, to which Jane Gaines invited me to teach cinema and queer theory in 1993. Here I must also record my great appreciation to Mandy Berry, Jennifer Doyle, Jonathan Flatley, Katie Kent, Michael Moon, José Muñoz, Janice Radway, Eve Sedgwick, and Ben Weaver, remarkable colleagues, collaborators, and friends. In spring 1994, I taught lesbian cinema and feminist theory in the Women's Studies Program at the University of Santa Cruz. To the program's then chair Wendy Brown and the students of "L Is For The Way You Look" go my thanks for an extremely instructive and entertaining term. My thanks as well to Judith Butler, Sarah Franklin, Carla Freccero, and Teresa de Lauretis for their kindness and support during my stay.

The greater part of this book was written while I was a member of the School of Cultural and Community Studies at the University of Sussex. My thanks to the School and to the Media Studies subject group for leave to complete it in 1999. Thanks also to the students, staff, and teachers on the MA in Sexual Dissidence and Cultural Change, particularly Jonathan Dollimore, Rachel Holmes, Andy Medhurst, Alan Sinfield, and Vincent Quinn for creating and sustaining a remarkable postgraduate program and the "Queory" seminar.

I must also thank my new colleagues in the Media Arts Department at Royal Holloway, University of London, for their support in the book's final stages. I am particularly grateful to my Head of Department Carol Lorac and our administrator, Elodie Gouet.

Many of the articles in this book began as conference papers. For the invitations that gave rise to them, I want to thank Jennifer Doyle, Jonathan Flatley, and José Muñoz; Nancy Hewitt, Jean O'Barr and Nancy Rosebaugh; Claire Kahane; Teresa de Lauretis; Lynne Segal; John Fletcher; Lynda Nead; Lisa Duggan; Yvonne Tasker; Allyson Polsky; and Paul Smith.

My thanks to Hannah Liley, Caroline Bassett, and Chris Townsend for intrepid picture research on this volume, to Esther Saxey for her patient preparation of the typescript, and to Cecilia Feilla at NYU Press for her editorial assistance. I am especially indebted to José Muñoz and Ann Pellegrini for commissioning it.

"Hard, Fast and Beautiful" first appeared in Annette Kuhn ed., *Queen of the 'B's: Ida Lupino behind the Camera* (Trowbridge, Wiltshire: Flicks Books, 1995); "Figuring Out Andy Warhol" in Jennifer Doyle, Jonathan Flatley, and José Estaban Muñoz eds., *Pop Out: Queer Warhol* (Durham: Duke University Press, 1996); "MacKinnon's Dog" in Nancy Hewitt, Jean O'Barr, and Nancy Rosebaugh eds., *Talking Gender* (Chapel Hill: University of North Carolina Press, 1996); "Savage Nights" in Mandy Merck, Naomi Segal, and Elizabeth Wright eds., *Coming Out of Feminism?* (Oxford: Blackwell, 1998); "The Medium of Exchange" in Peter Buse and Andrew Stott eds., *Ghosts: Deconstruction, Psychoanalysis, History* (Basingstoke: Macmillan/St. Martin's Press, 1999); "'Not in a Public Lavatory but on a Public Stage'" in Costas Douzinas and Lynda Nead eds., *Law and the Image: The Authority of Art and the Aesthetics of Law* (Chicago: University of Chicago Press, 1999); "The Queer Spirit of the Age" in Roger Luckhurst and Peter Marks eds., *Literature and the Contemporary: Fictions and Theories of the Present* (Harlow, Essex: Longmans, 1999). Where necessary, these articles have been updated for inclusion in this collection. My thanks to their respective editors and publishers for permission to reprint them.

And a final thank you to Nel Druce, for her forbearance.

Introduction

In Your Face

1. Sex!

October 9, 1998, was National British Sex Day. Noting its impending arrival, at the climax of autumn celebrations which also included National Good Sex Week, the critic Brian Sewall asked in the London *Evening Standard*:

Do we need a National Sex Day? With the retiring film censor arguing for greater free- dom in the field of pornography, with the age of homosexual consent bitterly debated in the Lords, with the introduction of Viagra to popular morning television, and the remorseless exposure of President Clinton's sexual preferences, no one of any age, any class or any occupation can now be innocent, for sexual awareness has, these past three months, advanced further and faster than in the past half century.[1]

One month later, in the U.S. weekly *New Republic*, Contributing Editor Lee Siegel expanded on Sewall's allegations about the sexualization of contem- porary culture. After condemning Hollywood, contemporary literature, newspaper editors, legislators, and the independent prosecutor Kenneth Starr for seeking (and apparently finding) a "more genitally obsessed nation," he trained his polemic on another target: "[n]owhere," he argued, "has the sexualization of reality proceeded so intensely and so relentlessly as in the seminar room."

What follows is an attack on "the contemporary academic obsession with sexuality and 'the body,'"[2] more specifically, the subsection of that inquiry known as Queer Theory and one of its leading exponents, Eve Kosofsky Sedgwick. Sedgwick became a *cause célèbre* in the American media early in the 1990s for daring to discern references to anal sex in the works of Henry James and—even worse—masturbation in those of Jane Austen. But most unforgivably, she has been known to refer to the anal and the autoerotic in the context of her own pleasures, and these confessions clearly unnerve Siegel. "A reveal-all-hurts-and-wounds style of writing,"[3] he calls it, accusing Sedgwick of playing the victim card in her admitted identification with the intense humiliations visited upon the sexually stigmatized. In a fulmination against what he takes to be her school, Siegel announces, "this cannot be literary criticism, and this cannot be life, and this cannot be sex. When we reduce our lives to 'bodies and pleasures,' we reduce bodies and pleasures to an ongoing debate about the meaning of our lives. . . . Sexualizing all of life," he concludes in an aphorism weirdly reminiscent of Mae West, "takes all of life out of sex. Poor life, poor sex."[4]

Criticism. Life. Sex. If not eternal, the triangle that Siegel decries is now a curricular commonplace, as a variety of critical studies engage with issues of gender, sexuality, and the body on the presumption of their relevance to the meaning of our lives. In this regard the academy seems, for once, in phase with the wider culture, whose interest in sex is, according to the Anglo-American press, unparalleled in human history. "Sex! Sex! Sex! And Sex!" headlines one British newspaper, over a column attempting to anticipate every conceivable banality churned up by the arrival of the U.S. sitcom *Sex and the City*.

Sex! It's a basic human right, like food, shelter and Prozac!
Sex! Now you can have it when you're on Prozac. As long as you're taking Viagra as well.
Sex! Good sex! I think we all known what I mean by that!

Sex! Bad sex! I've never had it, but I bet it's terrible, eh?
Sex! Can't live with it, can't live without it!
Sex! It's everywhere!
Sex! We're really very confused about it![5]

Where there's confusion, there's hope for academic enterprise, but even in the seminar room the study of sex is no more a simple matter than it is a pure one. In the fields that gave rise to this collection—characterized as "Women's Studies" and "Sexual Dissidence" in the rubrics of one British university's MA programs—what to study is itself a matter of some controversy. When the editors of *The Lesbian and Gay Studies Reader* rashly propose that "Lesbian/gay studies does for *sex* and *sexuality* approximately what women's studies does for gender"—that is, treat "gender (whether female or male) as a central category of analysis"[6]—Judith Butler replies by asking what they mean by sex. "Sex" as the supposed biological correlate of the cultural "gender" which designates women and men "female and male"? Sexual desire and practice? Sexual identity as a regulatory ideal unifying the physical and the practical? Or, in Butler's critique of what she sees as the imperial ambitions of the *Reader*'s politics, all of the above:

The editors lead us through analogy from a feminism in which gender and sex are conflated to a notion of lesbian and gay studies in which "sex" encompasses and exceeds the purview of feminism: "sex" in this second instance would include not only questions of identity and attribute (female or male), but discourses of sensation, acts, and sexual practice as well.[7]

This is not just a turf war between fledgling disciplines. At issue for both fields of inquiry is an unwitting androcentrism that would consign gender, and gender conflict, to the ladies' auxiliary of a "new" politics—one that purports to supersede sexual difference but may merely suppress it.

How new the politics of "sex and sexuality" are is itself a matter of debate. The sexual liberationism of nineteenth- and twentieth-century feminism, as well as the historical alliances and overlapping constituencies of the campaigns for female emancipation and homosexual rights, complicate the picture of a premillennial movement snatched from the womb of a feminism trapped in the obsolescence of its biologically ordained remit. Nevertheless, in the early 1990s, Queer Theory emerged to propose a new site for the study of sex—nothing less, in Sue-Ellen Case's term, than "ontology." Taking the homoerotics of religious mysticism and vampire legend as her models, Case argues that the "queer desire" they represent transcends the limits of a naturalized organicism to confound not only gender but generation as the norms of sexual organization. Without life, and life-giving, as its sanction, such sex cannot be assimilated to a principle of being defined in opposition to death. Undead, liminal, "hauntological"[8]—in Derrida's term—it declares its reality without recourse to the presumptive proofs of biological reproduction.[9]

If queer desire, in this account, can refuse the stake of organicized being, it has been similarly counterposed to any notion of a stable or coherent identity. In 1990, the United States witnessed the foundation of a Queer Nation which brought together an array of groups proclaiming dissident sexualities under a flag of political convenience and patriotic provocation. Although not without the constraints of the racial and gender dominance that had threatened previous alliances, nor those of the official nationality that the movement sought to pervert, the concatenation of such groups as LABIA (Lesbians and Bisexuals in Action), UNITED COLORS (definitely not Benetton's), ASLUT (Artists Slaving Under Tyranny), and HI MOM (Homosexual Ideological Mobilization against the Military) sought to multiply and diffuse the identities that had hitherto organized radical sexual politics. In London, with the demand "Queer Power Now," an anonymous leaflet in 1991 announced "There are straight queers, bi-queers, tranny queers, lez queers, fag queers, SM queers, fisting queers in every single street in this apathetic country of ours."

Across the decade, a term that once signified a perceived oddity which could indicate homosexuality became synonymous with sexual identities whose transitivity seemed intrinsic to their transgression. Thus, a current study of "Queer Theory and American Kiddie Culture" offers the now-generic definition of "queer" as the "disorienting" of "a legible, secure identity and position."[10] Moreover, the resignification of the term itself, from sexual insult to positive self-avowal, has been adduced as evidence for the instability of all identity claims, opening up a *mise-en-abyme* of "queering" that cannot be stabilized by an appeal to any self-identity, queer or otherwise. Most recently, this theme of mobility and multiplicity in sexuality has been engaged by transgender theory, albeit with caveats against a "queer utopianism" heedless of the specificity of sexual desire and contemptuous of those sexual identities invested in embodiment.[11]

Readers who may be wondering where the sex is in these sexual theories will not be consoled by a student essay I recently received, which drily observed that when battling heterosexual norms, "sex is not necessarily the best place to start." One of the greater paradoxes of what Lee Siegel imagines to be the academic sexualization of everything is a pronounced displacement of sex. Not, as he fears, in favor of some counter totality like the meaning of life, but rather to propose it as "meaningful only in its articulation with other aspects of self and social relations." The phrase is Biddy Martin's, from an influential collection of writings critiquing those theories that would make gender and sexuality "too determining and stable even in their putative instability."[12]

This situation of the subject as an effect of a competing array of identifications and attachments, external and internal, involves more than the mandated recitations of the most commonly cited identity categories—race, class, gender, sexuality, nationality—already described as a mantra back in the 1980s. Instead, it insists upon these aspects of the self as constituents of one's "sex"—anatomical, cultural, psychical, practical—and such sex as conversely constitutive of class, race, nationality, etc., as well as of less ethnicized interests and affiliations. If such a conviction amounts to the sexualization of reality, it is ironically at the expense of any definition of sex that would give it priority in the formation or processes of subjectivity. Yet, even more ironically, this decentered definition of sex is the one most commonly proffered by those who have made it such a prominent object of intellectual inquiry. Thus, in an "anti-encyclopedia entry" on queer theory, Lauren Berlant and Michael Warner consider its relevance to public policy, the mass media, money, biography, and jokes, without ever getting to sex.[13] In a similar vein, Robyn Wiegman sets out to "queer the academy" and ends up addressing that institution's status as a capitalist enterprise, extracting more and more research from its weary work force while marketing saleable identities to students under the aegis of lesbian and gay studies.[14]

II. Sex!

Concluding the defense case for President Clinton in his trial before the Senate, the Arkansas Senator Dale Bumpers rifled his dictionary of familiar quotations to summon up a H. L. Mencken aphorism on what Freud called negation. "When you hear somebody say 'This is not about money,'" Mencken once opined, "it's about money. And when you hear somebody say 'This is not about sex,'" Bumpers continued, "it's about sex."[15] The Senator was replying, of course, to the congressional conservatives who insisted that their judicial pursuit of the president was prompted by weightier concerns than mere sexual dalliance. Nevertheless, his choice of citation was a little risky, since another bullet point in the defense's submission was that the defendant told the truth when he claimed that his relationship with Monica Lewinsky was not sexual:

The President maintained that there can be no sexual relationship without sexual intercourse, regardless of what other sexual activities may transpire. He stated that "most ordinary Americans" would embrace this distinction.[16]

But then negation, as Freud and Mencken agree, is not about denial but about acceptance, about allowing expression to a thought under the cover of its refusal. Interestingly, in the light of what did transpire in the Oval Office, Freud assigned such affirmation to the erotic instincts—to the oral stage specifically, and the ego's impulse to take pleasurable things into itself. If that impulse could speak, he argued, it would say "I should like to eat this."[17]

All this would be mere maundering to Gore Vidal, whose own defense of Clinton embraced the president's distinction between sexual activities and sexual relationships and rejoiced that the age of Freud is "now drawing to a close":

One can argue that, yes, there is a sexual element to everything if one wants to go digging but even the most avid Freudian detective would have to admit that what might be construed as sexuality by other means falls literally short of plain old in-and-out.[18]

Here Vidal neatly conjoins the two sexual themes of Zippergate and its era—that "there is a sexual element to everything" and—with my addition of a question mark—"what might be construed as sexuality?" Sex is everywhere, in everything, but what is sex? (Or "the sexual"? Or "sexuality"? The contemporary commutability of these terms should by now be evident.) Throughout the Clinton scandal, commentators linked the perceived proliferation of sexual discourse to questions about what was meant by sex. To the headlines decrying "Smut," "Sheer Filth," and "Indecent Exposure," declaring "Sex Objection" and "We Don't Care a Fig Anymore" must be added *Time* magazine's anticipation of the "cunning linguistics" of Clinton's defense in an article headed "When Sex Is Not Really Having Sex."[19]

As an actual issue in the case for impeachment, the defendant's definition of sex became an obvious subject of inquiry. Also judged newsworthy, by American—if not British—standards, were the questions children were said to have asked their parents and teachers about the president's conduct. Immediately after the initial revelations, *Time* opened an article titled "Eager Minds, Big Ears" with the question (in boldface) "Mom, what's oral sex?"[20] Almost eight months later, *Newsweek* headed a piece on "How to handle your children's questions about the Clinton scandal" with "Mom, what's oral sex?"[21] Should we conclude that in the United States only mothers are asked such questions, the Portland *Oregonian* ran a political cartoon comparing the "Questions the President has to answer about the Lewinsky case" ("What was the nature of your relationship?" "Can you explain the dress?") with those directed at "Dad": "Dad, what's a sexual relationship?" and "Dad, what kind of stain?"[22] This theme of one nation under interrogation about sex—Mom, Dad, and the head of the First Family who, it was stressed, had enjoyed "sexual relations" with a woman young enough to be his daughter—did not carry over into Britain. Absent both the parental relationship with the president and the cross-channel scheduling of network news at the family dinner hour, the British media did not represent the scandal as a subject of children's curiosity nor—*pace* Brian Sewall—as a threat to their innocence. And unlike their American counterparts, they had no patriotic incentive to recuperate a sex farce in the Oval Office into a moral example for the young, reminding them—in *Newsweek*'s inadvertently comic conclusion—of "the bottom line":

Bad behavior has consequences, even if you're the most powerful man in the world.

As an answer to the question "What's oral sex?" this homily rivals any evasion in Clinton's testimony, but then *Newsweek*'s advice to parents eerily echoes the president's own strategy under cross-examination:

When the questions are about sex, keep it simple. "You try to be honest but in as short a way as possible, and then let the kids ask more questions," says Kenneth L. Kaplan, a child psychiatrist in McLean, Va. "If they ask what oral sex is, I'd give a very brief answer."

What that answer might be, Kaplan never revealed to *Newsweek*, in a fit of discretion we might describe as presidential. Meanwhile, to deal with those childish queries about the cigar, the magazine sought the expertise of no less than the president of the Sexuality Information and Education Council of the United States, who sagely replied:

"What I would say is 'There's an endless variety of behaviors people will choose to engage in sexually, but I am not prepared to discuss this specific behavior with you. I would rather talk about the really bad decision making this person has done.'"

This may be sex education, if that has never meant more than the attempted inculcation of some nebulous normativity, but sexual information it ain't. Instead, it sustains the enigma of "an endless variety of behaviors people will choose to engage in sexually," a vastly proliferated and yet wholly unspecified phenomenon.

Such commentary might be designated metasexual in its purported interest in the social issues raised by Zippergate, rather than its sexual content. Yet for all their rectitude, the newsweeklies' parental advisories on how not to talk about sex did nothing to limit the circulation of that talk (and clearly were not intended to). As feature material that fleshed out the initially sparse details of the scandal, the metasexual commentary was as sexual as its subject, a fact acknowledged in a *New Yorker* cartoon of a little girl reading a newspaper and declaring to a little boy, "I think oral sex is when they only just talk about it."[23] Frequently, the metasexual commentaries on Zippergate dispensed with the pretense of child welfare altogether and went straight to the sex, via disparaging references to the references to sex made elsewhere in the media. A typical example of the latter appeared in the Portland *Oregonian* shortly before the president's DNA test:

A Portland news anchor confided to me one of her accomplishments last week: writing an entire story about the President Clinton/Monica Lewinsky developments without using the word "sex."

Clearly no easy task and a lot more difficult when you consider that television news is hurdling new boundaries in the coverage of this story, where those two "S" words—saturation and speculation—have taken center stage. . . .

On Friday, a MSNBC [a U.S. cable channel] anchor's tease may have said it all: "For the next hour, we're going to be talking about Monica Lewinsky's dress."[24]

This second-order reportage was merely the most blatant means by which the "quality" media appropriated and developed their tabloid inferiors' coverage of the scandal. One of the most adept exponents of this tactic in Britain was the *Guardian* newspaper, an upmarket daily that specializes in ridiculing the agenda of the country's mass circulation press in feature sections with a virtually identical agenda. Throughout Zippergate, the paper distinguished itself with articles discoursing at length on the extent of sexual discourse everywhere else. Thus, one columnist opened an ostensible discussion of Tony Blair's Clintonesque "third way" (itself an object of salacious punning during the scandal) with complaints of being "sick of hearing, reading and watching sex. . . . So I'm declaring a sex-free zone. If you're looking for details of whipped cream, cigars or other unexpected sex accessories, pass on."[25] In the same issue, another commentator observed:

This seems to be the Year of the Penis, what with the president waving his about, Viagra all over the place and the telly schedule stuffed with sex. . . . And this tidal wave of information could act as a nationwide contraceptive. Sexual overload and fatigue could set in.[26]

Note that here it isn't the end of innocence, but the possibility of *aphanisis*, the overwhelming of desire by sickness or fatigue, that this "tidal wave" of sexual information is said to threaten. This dread, which the psychoanalyst Ernest Jones claimed to be more profound than the fear of castration, clearly animates Lee Siegel's invective against Queer Theory's "sexualization of reality" and its anaphrodisiac consequences ("Poor sex"). When invoked by the *Guardian*'s writers, it is more usually in an attempt to dismiss the latest round of sexual representations as boring, vulgar, and not really "about sex" anyway. Thus, a subsequent column lamenting advertisers' eroticization of previously "innocent" commodities, citing the rather surprising example of the English National Ballet, bemoaned the sexualization of this art form:

Because ballet is not about sex. It may have a sexual component but this is not the same as being "sexy" . . . nothing in our culture that appears to refer to sex really does. It is, by now, a totally sealed, self-referential discourse that constructs an alternative reality. The one thing it doesn't do is describe what we really do in bed.[27]

Here again "sex" is both ubiquitous and ineffable, different somehow from as sexual an art as the ballet, with its romantic narratives, fetishistic costumes, and passionate *pas de deux*, or even from the sex talk which, this writer also complains, "covers up our inability to have real conversations." The term's only appropriate reference is said to be that other reality, "what we really do in bed." At last the location of sex, if nothing else, is revealed—

a site unvisited by Bill and Monica where true intercourse trysts with true converse, but only in the absence of sexual discourse.

III. Sex!

If sexual discourse, in Foucault's description,[28] constitutes sex as a problem of truth—a perpetually renewable puzzle of proliferation and evasion, hiding and discovery—discourse as discourse is perennially accused of error. Sex talk will never get sex right because, as representation, it is bound to fail. And representation is bound to fail because it is intimately connected to sex. The fallibility of representation, that ancient theme in Western thought, is rarely without a sexual explanation. More than two thousand years separate the *Guardian* on representations of what we really do in bed from Plato on representations of the bed itself. Yet already in *The Republic* a painting of a bed, unlike its divinely created ideal form or the furniture made by the carpenter, is said to be far from the truth. And when Plato turns his attention from painting to the nefarious medium of poetry, he needn't get out of bed, since poetry is compared to "a face which relied on the bloom of youth for its charm" and its enthusiasts advised to renounce it like a "lover who renounces a passion that is doing him no good."[29]

Seduction by representation has also been central to the charges of religious iconoclasm, notably in the Mosaic opposition to idolatry—the worship of a visual representation as divine or divinely empowered—with strictures against the making of any graven image, human or animal, and the uttering of god's name. Book 14 of the Old Testament *Wisdom of Solomon* offers this cautionary tale:

> *Then the ambition of the craftsman impelled*
> *even those who did not know the king to intensify their worship.*
> *For he, perhaps wishing to please his ruler,*
> *skillfully forced the likeness to take more beautiful form,*
> *and the multitude, attracted by the charm of his work,*

now regarded as an object of worship the one whom shortly before they had
  honored as a man.
And this became a hidden trap for mankind,
because men, in bondage to misfortune or to royal authority,
bestowed on objects of stone or wood the name that ought not to be shared.
Afterward it was not enough for them to err about the knowledge of God,
but they live in great strife due to ignorance . . .
confusion over what is good, forgetfulness of favors,
pollution of souls, sex perversion,
disorder in marriage, adultery, and debauchery.
For the worship of idols not to be named
is the beginning and cause and end of every evil.[30]

The pre-Christian connection of idolatry with debauchery survived in medieval associations of blasphemy with obscenity, in the Sadean celebration of such conjunctions, and into the contemporary English common law (under which *Gay News* was successfully prosecuted in 1978 for publishing a poem about Christ's homosexuality). In each case, an error of religious representation—irreverence to or misattribution of the divine—is compounded by sexual transgression. This understanding corresponds to what W. J. T. Mitchell describes as the iconoclast's "twofold accusation" against image worship: "folly and vice, epistemological error and moral depravity."[31]

In his essay on that image-maker par excellence, Leonardo da Vinci, Freud suggests a possible origin for this association of idolatry with sex. Where contemporary civilization makes the genitals objects of shame and repression, he argues, primitive societies worshiped them as gods. Our earliest idols were thus sexual, exalted representations of the genitals as "the pride and hope of living beings."[32] The idolization of one particular genital is a central theme in Freud's psychobiography of the artist, which develops his earlier claim that the young boy regards his penis as far "too important for him to be able to believe that it could be missing in other people."[33] Discovery of the mother's missing organ, if combined with a perceived threat to his own, is claimed to result in the abrogation of female objects, and the homo-sexuality attributed to Leonardo.

Support for this interpretation is gleaned from Leonardo's memory of a vulture descending to his cradle and repeatedly striking its tail against his lips. In this vignette, Freud discerns not only a loving mother showering kisses on her child, but the phallic mother of infant fantasy and ancient re-ligion. A word in his own mother tongue, *mutter*, summons up an apposite deity, the Egyptian mother-goddess Mut, traditionally represented with the head of a vulture. Leonardo's adulation of the powerful maternal principle represented by such figures is said to give rise to the key image of Freud's analysis, a painting that portrays both the mother and the grandmother of a god with the young divinity himself. The doubled tenderness of the *Madonna and Child with St. Anne* is described as a "glorification of motherhood,"[34] and may refer to the artist's experience of both a birth mother and an adoptive one, but doubling in Freud's theory is also an unconscious method of pre-serving something under threat. As the allusions to fetishism elsewhere in this essay suggest, the painting's aura of blissful perfection can be further read as a defense of the maternal body and, by extension, that of her son, from any phallic deficit.

But if the study of Leonardo suggests that even the most sacred subjects (especially the most sacred subjects) are replete with sexual significance, Freud's central argument is that artistry originates in sexual sublimation. Leonardo's impulse to representation, in both painting and scientific draw-ing, is traced to the premature arousal and consequent curiosity of the child of an abandoned—and therefore unusually ardent—mother. This aetiology of image-making (and by implication all figuration, including language) seems to run counter to the logic of religious iconoclasm. Where the Mosaic tradition sees representation as a cause of sex, the Freudian account sees sex as a cause of representation. But the formula can also be reversed, since psy-choanalysis also stresses fantasy as the representation that initiates desire, while *The Wisdom of Solomon* speculates that the craftsman beautified his image out of a libidinally invested wish "to please his ruler."

This circular causation brings us back to the Clinton scandal, and the confusion over his alleged wrongdoing. In claiming that this consisted of "a terrible moral lapse of marital infidelity; not a breach of the public trust," Dale Bumpers attempted to distinguish adultery from crimes against society, and the Senate concurred. But in his own efforts to make that claim, Bumpers effectively conceded what he called "the question about lying," arguing merely that "to say constantly that the President lied about this and lied about that . . . was too much for a family that has already been about as decimated as a family can get."[35] Whatever the merits of the president's legal case, even his defenders regarded debauchery as inseparable from deceit; thus the impossibility of clarifying Clinton's culpability, let alone the larger question of representation and sex. Desire and deception go together: an indistinction that traditional iconoclasm, as well as most ordinary Americans, would apparently embrace.

IV. Sex!

In 1991, an article in the U.S. quarterly *Outlook* considered the strategic dilemmas of a political movement with an anti-identitarian identity:

Queer Nationals are torn between affirming a new identity—"I am queer"—and rejecting restrictive identities—"I reject your categories"; between rejecting assimilation—"I don't need your approval, just get out of my face"—and wanting to be recognized by mainstream society—"we queers are gonna get in your face."[36]

"In your face": somewhere between "negative equity" and "collateral damage," the phrase became a shibboleth of the 1990s. Cassell's *Dictionary of Slang* tells us that it originated on the basketball court, where the defender attempts to obscure her opponent's view by crowding in close. Transmuted by rap culture into wider currency, the phrase quickly gained an awkward salience. As rejection ("get out of my face") was succeeded by aggression ("gonna get in your face"), its usage moved from adverbial to adjectival, from an indication of position to that of a property. As a synonym for all that was outspoken, confrontational, unavoidable, the phrase retained and enlarged upon its original sense of a provocative physical proximity—bodily aggression with a sexual charge.

The symbolic uses of spatial behavior have long been a popular research topic in social psychology, entering public consciousness with Julius Fast's 1970 bestseller, *Body Language*. Formalized in the study of proxemics, the field quickly turned to the question of space and sexual politics. By 1975, researchers were attempting to compare "the apparent willingness of the liberated woman to encroach upon what has traditionally been viewed as male territory—bars, clubs, occupations and sports" with the presumptive reticence of "females with more traditional attitudes." In one such experiment, women university students defined as feminists walked farther toward a male stranger in a 7 x 16-foot windowless experimental room than their apparently nonfeminist counterparts. This data was taken as confirmation of the researchers' hypothesis that "feminists are more aggressive and experience less discomfort in invading a male's personal space than traditional women." But in apparent contradiction to these conclusions, the feminist subjects were more willing than their traditional counterparts to allow the male stranger to approach them (to an average distance of 17.5 inches compared with almost twice that for the other cohort)—a finding attributed to "their greater affiliativeness and openness."[37] Moreover, despite the use of a female "control" in the experiment, no account was taken of the comparative attitudes of the two groups to same-sex proximity—not in 1975.

Read a quarter century after its publication, this research seems comically naïve, not least in its bland presumption of a simple, singular division between feminist and nonfeminist women, a division that had not yet fractured under the pressure of age, class, ethnicity, or sexuality, or conversely disappeared in response to unanticipated alliances between the supposedly aggressive and assertive feminists and their shyer sisters. (The latter, it should be noted, were vastly more willing to approach and be approached by the female control than by the male in the study, whereas the "feminists" marginally preferred the proximity of the men.) Nevertheless, the experiment's portrait of the liberated woman, aggressive and affiliative, if awfully straight, does anticipate the contemporary phrase such experiments in spatial psychology effectively underwrote. Twenty-four years later, Lisa Jardine reached for it in a salute to another 1970s feminist, Germaine Greer, for her "attention-grabbing brand of stand-up comic, in-your-face assertiveness," which, Jardine argued, "taught us all to behave badly and take control of our lives."[38]

In your face: the libidinal charge in Greer's exhibitionist incitement to behave badly (and her converse criticism of the president for "fucking the faces of little girls") recalls us to the Oval Office, or the Oral Office as it has become known since Zippergate. There Bill and Monica re-enacted the scene remembered by Leonardo, for the situation in that fantasy, Freud tells us, "of a vulture opening the child's mouth and beating about inside it vigorously with its tail, corresponds to the idea of fellatio." To Freud, such a fantasy is inevitably passive in character, typical of women and homosexual men who play the women's part in sex. Nevertheless, he admits it is a "wishful" fantasy, derived from our earliest pleasure, when we "took our mother's (or wetnurse's) nipple into our mouth and sucked at it."[39] Here the origins of fellatio are posed as not only infantile but also profoundly active, that of the baby taking in and sucking at the nurturing breast. The assertiveness of this primal act of incorporation seems to belie the passivity attributed to those who would draw another into their face. Such an impression is reinforced by the figure Freud identifies as the emblem of this infant bliss, the suckling Christchild of renaissance painting, a babe in arms and yet a god.

The ambiguity that attends this image of pleasure is even more emphatic in another of Leonardo's works, a portrait that has been endlessly read as an erotic enigma. In 1910, Freud could quote the prototypically kitsch observation that "hundreds of poets and authors have written about this woman who now appears to smile on us so seductively, and now to stare coldly and without soul into space; and no one has solved the riddle of her smile, no one has read the meaning of her thoughts."[40] Nearly ninety years later, the smile of Mona Lisa del Giocondo was repainted in a new guise, a magazine cover image of "the woman of secrets who no longer has any. . . .

She is everywhere. She suits all interpretations."[41] Translated into our time, the face of "Mona Lewinsky" (figure I.1), as the *New Yorker* styled her, no longer represents a sexual enigma. Instead, she personifies sex *as* enigma, a riddle of ancient origin and no foreseeable resolution, still smiling into the twenty-first century.

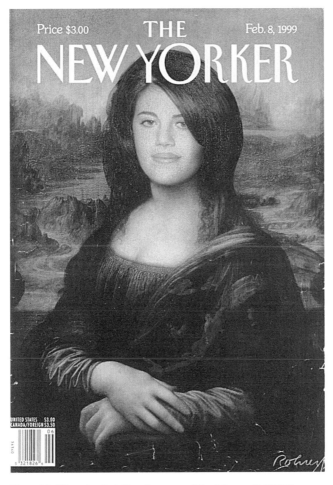

Figure I.1. "Mona Lewinsky" on the cover of the February 8, 1999 *New Yorker.*

17

PHANTOMS

1   The Medium of Exchange

Man has often made man himself, under the form of slaves, serve as the
primitive material of money.

—KARL MARX, *Capital*

The subject of this essay was the sleeper success of the 1990 film season,
the year's number-one box office draw in the United States, a similar hit in
Britain, winning Oscars for its screenwriter and supporting actress, and
bringing its theme song, the Righteous Brothers' 1965 "Unchained Melody" back into the charts. Like its supernatural successor, *Bram Stoker's
Dracula* (1992), with its slogan "Love Never Dies," this film was marketed
as a "date movie"—a "date movie," we should note, in which the hero is
posthumously penetrated, the heroine exhibits an enormous phallus, and
the two of them engage in a climactic act of inter-racial troilism with
Whoopi Goldberg. Furthermore, this is a film whose theme of untimely
death was sometimes read as an AIDS allegory, and one which subsequently attracted the attention of lesbian critics for what Terry Castle has
described as its "peculiarly homoerotic effect."[1] I am, of course, referring to
the yuppie elegy *Ghost* (written by Bruce Joel Rubin, directed by Jerry
Zucker). Judith Mayne's account of the film in *Cinema and Spectatorship* offers this synopsis:

Ghost tells the tale of a young couple, Sam and Molly, and the seemingly random mugging that kills Sam. As a spirit visible to the spectators but invisible to the rest of the characters in the film, Sam discovers that his best friend and co-worker Carl was responsible for his death, and he tries to warn Molly that her life may be in danger. When Sam discovers his murderer, Willie Lopez, who was hired by his co-worker, he follows him to the Brooklyn neighborhood where he lives and by chance encounters Oda Mae Brown, a phony psychic who turns out to be genuine, since she is the only human being able to hear (although not to see) Sam and communicate with him. He convinces her to visit Molly, and after a series of complications involving embezzlement, fraud, and disbelief, Molly not only believes that Oda Mae is in touch with Sam, she engages, through her, in one last embrace with him. At the conclusion of the film, the evil friend is dead and so is Sam, but each has gone his separate way, while Molly and Oda Mae are left in the land of the living.[2]

Unlike similar films of the ghost cycle of the period—notably *Always* (1989) and *Truly, Madly, Deeply* (1991)—*Ghost* offers no male substitute for the deceased loved one. This in itself tells us nothing about the film's attitude toward heterosexuality—indeed, it may attest to the couple's undying devotion, or at least to the film's refreshing disregard for the familiar thematics of working through grief, learning to love again, and so on. There are, however, significant other ways in which *Ghost* could be seen to suggest that heterosexual relations may be in crisis, or spent (a term whose ramifications I will pursue below), or in some sense *fantasmic*. Take, for example, the characterization of the two leads. Not only is Demi Moore's Molly—as an artist, intrepid interior decorator (her last name, Jensen, echoes that of the Danish Modern design group), and an apparent Shakespeare enthusiast—Sam's educational and class superior, she also spends a good deal of the film in the dark tailoring and gelled hairstyle of the metropolitan designer dyke. As for Patrick Swayze's Sam, he is both hunk and hayseed (his last name is Wheat), whose ducktail and tight trousers trail reminiscences of the actor's role in the 1987 *Dirty Dancing* (and a masculinity so overstated as to be suspect) into the Wall Street precincts of the bank where he works.

FIGURE 1.1. *Ghost:* Sam (Patrick Swayze) and Molly (Demi Moore) with her "masterpiece." BFI Films: Stills, Posters and Designs.

There Sam seems, both in class and professional terms, somewhat out of his depth, anxiously attempting to deal with Japanese clients while desperately crunching numbers in a vain effort to identify the source of the vast sums that have mysteriously appeared in the bank's computerized accounts. Meanwhile, Molly rises from the couple's bed for a nocturnal session at her potter's wheel that is so frankly masturbatory and so unmistakably phallic that Sam must collapse the clay column she straddles in order to initiate the film's only sex scene (figure 1.1). ("I hope it wasn't a masterpiece," he ruefully laughs, acknowledging that it was *precisely* that.) Is it surprising, then, that this waning principle of masculine eminence should be extinguished altogether at the moment Molly (sporting a leather jacket and a quiff) protests that he never says "I love you" and proposes marriage, and that this should occur after the couple attend a performance of *Macbeth*? But if this romance is "unmann'd" (to quote that play) almost from its outset, how did it achieve its remarkable success? How did it manage to sell what its British critics easily recognized as its refusal of "the robust assertiveness of the traditional male lead" (*Sunday Times*)[3] and its transformation of the heroine into "a ravishing boy" (*Scotsman Weekend*)?[4]

The first answer to this question, the one that originally prompted its lesbian rereading, is race. In her brief remarks on *Ghost* in *Feminism Without Women*, Tania Modleski proposes Whoopi Goldberg's Oda Mae as the film's most expressly liminal figure. The medium is the mediator in this movie because her racial difference, Modleski argues, can be read as sexual difference.[5] As she notes, Goldberg (who made her screen debut as a lesbian in the 1985 *The Color Purple* and played one again a decade later in *Boys on the Side*) has consistently functioned as the sexual other for her films' white characters, whether that otherness is represented as maternal (the literal "mammy" role in the 1994 *Corrina, Corrina* and the 1998 *Clara's Heart*) or as masculine (Goldberg as the only logical father for Drew Barrymore's mysteriously black baby at the end of *Boys on the Side*). In part, this masculinity can be conveyed by Goldberg's sturdy build, contralto voice, and broad face (whose ethnic connotations were registered with the cheerful racism of the British press in the *Daily Mirror*'s phrase, "a smile as wide as a frying pan").[6] In *Ghost*, this impression of expansiveness and solidity is directly counterposed to Swayze's ethereal pallor and pixie features, as well as to the delighted narcissism with which Sam dons the colorful suspenders of the Wall Street financier. (There is less distance between Sam and Vida Boheme, Swayze's subsequent drag queen character in *To Wong Foo, Thanks for Everything! Julie Newmar* [1995], than one might suppose.) Where the murdered Sam discovers his spectral state when a hospital trolley is driven right through him, Oda Mae's characterization is wholly within the traditional representation of the black subject as embodiment, physicality, even—despite her initial resistance to legitimate work—"the human body as labor," labor that will be invisibly transmuted into money.[7] Finally, in *Ghost*, as in the 1986 *Jumping Jack Flash*, an impression of masculinity is conveyed by presenting Goldberg's character as a total travesty in feminine clothing (an effect elaborated in the 1992 and 1993 *Sister Act* films when she is forced to masquerade in the cumbersome robes and veil of a nun).

The central comic scene in *Ghost* has Oda Mae impersonate a wealthy client of Sam's bank in order to withdraw $4 million which Carl has been

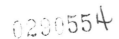

laundering for a drug ring—"laundering," in the sense of "whitening" and therefore legitimating, money being a densely impacted issue in this film. On the one hand, the drug trade is visibly represented by a man of color, Willie Lopez, and the black Brooklyn neighborhood where both he and Oda Mae live. On the other, the ghostly Sam's effective appropriation of Oda Mae's physical capacities to warn Molly and thwart Carl calls to mind the embodied black labor on which white wealth is founded, "slave labor" as Sam himself can joke when referring to his white friend's willingness to move furniture into his new loft. Fittingly, it is the black woman who foils Carl's efforts to cleanse the ill-gotten money of its criminal origins by claiming it herself.

The joke of the bank scene resides in the inadequacy of Oda Mae's performance as the holder of the account. Compelled by Sam to speak lines identifying herself with the appropriate name, account number, and social background, she veers between erroneous repetition and wild improvisation in what is virtually a textbook demonstration of colonial mimicry.[8] To be sure, Oda Mae's ludicrous efforts to impersonate a wealthy (and therefore "whiter") woman is itself an expert performance of a poor performance by a skillful comedienne. Yet, as with the British comic Lenny Henry's 1980s impressions of familiar black characters, Goldberg's rendition of a slum-dweller's awkward impersonation of a black bourgeoise opens her to charges of minstrelsy, with the black actress herself adopting blackface. Goldberg's film roles have frequently been slated for such stereotyping. Witness bell hooks' complaints about Goldberg's "sexist, racist" casting "as mammy or ho"[9] or Michael Atkinson's censure in the *Guardian* newspaper's *Guide*:

She's black and sexless like Hattie McDaniel used to be black and sexless, and it's no accident that Whoopi has played domestic maids several times, something I doubt you'll ever find Halle Berry or Whitney Houston doing. . . . Whoopi is the nineties version of a lovable minstrel performer: eager to please, inoffensive and thoroughly objectified.[10]

Even Goldberg's stage name has been indicted by Michael Rogin in his study of black representation in American cinema, which notes its allusion to

25

FIGURE 1.2. *Ghost:* Oda Mae (Whoopi Goldberg) in the bank with Sam (Patrick Swayze). BFI Films: Stills, Posters and Designs.

"Making Whoopee," the title song of Eddie Cantor's 1930 Jewish blackface western. Rogin also recalls her participation in a literal act of blackface, when she collaborated with her corked-up companion and co-star (of the 1993 *Made in America*) Ted Danson, in a much-criticized attempt to parody racial stereotypes at New York's Friars Club.[11]

Whether or not we bring these indictments to the bank scene, its comic effect depends on another trademark schtick of Goldberg's, her characters' discomfort in feminine clothing. Asked by Sam to wear "a nice dress," Oda Mae abandons her comfortably flowing (and vaguely African) garb for a tight skirt, pink jacket, and matching hat with high-heeled shoes (figure 1.2). Her attempt to pass is thus also marked as one of gender, a masquerade that is predictably (cue awkward walk in heels) unsuccessful. Moreover, the name under which the bogus account is registered is Rita Miller, which in combination with Oda Mae Brown gives us Rita Mae Brown, the lesbian novelist whose best-known character, the autobiographical heroine of *Rubyfruit Jungle*, is called "Molly."

So, the black woman can, by means of a racial difference historically connoted as the negation of female sexuality, "stand in"—Modleski argues—

26

"for the body of the white male."[12] This substitution is made explicit when Oda Mae appears with the spectral Sam at the door of the couple's loft to warn Molly that she's in danger. Having ventriloquized Sam's lines and provided him with his props, Oda Mae is finally allowed to enter the immense apartment. As the two women wait for the police to arrive, Sam and Molly express their desire to touch each other once more —a touch that Oda Mae reluctantly offers to facilitate. "You can use my body," she declares to a bewildered Sam, who eventually draws near and is dissolved into her. When Oda Mae opens her eyes and looks at Molly, a cut reveals a pair of white hands which are then clasped and stroked by a larger pair of black ones, adorned with vivid red nail polish. (The ambiguity of the shot contrasts the conventional handholding of the séance with the erotic implications of the gesture.) In a continuation of the same take, the camera cranes up Molly's bare arm past her bosom to track around until her face is revealed in profile, with her eyes closed and lips parted expectantly. Then a white hand reaches out to caress her cheek.

Where, in a previous scene, Oda Mae remained in vision during spirit possession, now (after the moment of homoerotic anticipation implied by the continuous take) she is safely replaced by Sam. So different is her difference (in a film where white and black egregiously signify heaven and hell) that she cannot compete for a leading role in the romance, but instead functions—as Judith Mayne points out—"to enable the fantasy of white participants."[13] (Never was a Supporting Actress Oscar so well earned.) At the crucial moment of contact, it is Oda Mae who is disembodied, who becomes the ghost, "a living subaltern ghost,"[14] or, in her own racier vocabulary, a "spook."

Here it should be noted that the ghost motif is virtually as old as cinema itself. There is now, of course, an entire library of spectral studies of the cinema, from Lotte Eisner's *The Haunted Screen*[15] to Gilberto Perez's study of "films and their medium," *The Material Ghost*.[16] But Gorky said it first, and most eloquently, after he saw the Lumière program at the Nizhni-Novgorod fair in 1896:

Last night I was in the Kingdom of Shadows. . . . Everything there—the earth, the trees, the people, the water and the air—is dipped in monotonous grey. . . . It is not life but its shadow, it is not motion but its soundless spectre.[17]

As if in recognition of its own peculiar "hauntology"[18] as the medium of exchange that transforms the pro-filmic event into an apparition, the early cinema produced scores of "phantom rides," in which cameras were mounted on gondolas, cars, balloons, funiculars, and especially trains, to provide the first eerily moving shots of the landscape; and it soon specialized in ghostly characters created by double exposure and superimposition. A comic genre was created to deploy these effects, the "trick film," whose extensive numbers include Méliès' 1897 *Enchanted Hotel* (in which the bewildered lodger finds his clothes disappearing, his boots walking away without him, his furniture collapsing); the British director G. A. Smith's 1898 *Photographing a Ghost* (itself now a "ghost film" remembered only in a catalogue synopsis); and a ten-minute 1901 version of *The Christmas Carol* entitled *Scrooge, or Marley's Ghost*.

And if the ghost motif dates back to the origins of cinema, the theme of racial substitution is nearly as ancient. Where the early cinema screened spectral rides by fastening cameras to moving trains, it also developed a much-repeated tunnel joke, in which a male passenger steals a kiss under the cover of darkness.[19] The joke begins with two white characters in the carriage, but by 1903 the transgressive theme is intensified, and the darkness of the tunnel duplicated, in the skin of the person kissed. The director of that year's *What Happened in the Tunnel*, the Edison pioneer Edwin S. Porter, is better known in the annals of racial representation for *Uncle Tom's Cabin*, in 1902 the longest American film and the first to use intertitles. Michael Rogin identifies this film as the earliest of four major "race movies" in the American cinema. (His other choices are *The Birth of a Nation*—1915, *The Jazz Singer*—1927, and *Gone with the Wind*—1939: an "entire cycle," he argues, "played out under white supremacy.")[20] Despite previous experiments with multiple perspectives in Porter's semi-documentary *The Life of an American*

Fireman (1902), *Uncle Tom's Cabin* has only one "point of view, and it is not an abolitionist one."[21] As Rogin observes, the film's emphasis is on the interracial harmony of the plantation (literalized in shots of dancing slaves) where Tom and Little Eva are paired in a primitive prefiguration of Shirley Temple and Bojangles Robinson.

Months later, Porter's *What Happened in the Tunnel* restages this interracial eroticism without the camouflage of childhood. The generic kiss is given a new twist by the race of its recipient, the black servant of its intended target. (The characteristic fade to black covers their exchange of seats.) When the indignant suitor discovers that he has kissed the maid instead of the mistress, both women laugh in shared amusement, but their reversal of his masculine presumption is emphatically racist.[22] (The level of the insult might be measured by an earlier version of the joke, the 1901 *An Idyll in the Tunnel*, in which the destination of the kiss is revealed to be a baby's bottom.) Eighty-seven years later, *Ghost* reworks this cinematic chestnut to affirm another cross-racial female alliance, even potentially to eroticize it, only to make the last-minute color adjustment that whites-out Oda Mae.

This dematerialization of the perverse possibility, its "apparitional" ontology, has been widely remarked in queer studies. The homosexual phantom offers heterosexual culture the advantage of its plausible deniability. Indeed, it could be said to enter eighteenth-century representation (specifically, a Gothic representation already disavowed by modernity) on condition of its incredibility.[23] But if the temporary "ghosting" of Oda Mae renders any union between her and Molly equally incredible—no more than the erotic fantasy that Modleski confesses to—neither can it save Sam. Having at last pronounced the loving declaration that he has avoided throughout the film with the term "ditto," he bids Molly a final "see you" and ascends into the white radiance of eternity. How should we read a romance whose titular ghost is the heterosexual hero and whose presiding spirit that of New Age credulity?

To answer this question, it is not necessary to forgo our consideration of either race or sexuality, but rather to situate it within the film's governing metaphors of commerce and communication. We should, as the anthropologist Jean-Joseph Goux advises, "put ourselves therefore resolutely under the patronage of Hermes," better known to us under his Roman name, Mercury, the divinity of exchange.[24] In his essay on "Numismatics," Goux develops Freud's observation on the unconscious association of the phallus with money (an association that the latter placed in the anal stage, and the infant's equation of the penis with the faeces and the faeces with the gift). Taking up Marx's argument that only those commodities whose value exceeds mere utility, which are not the object of immediate need (historically, gold metal), can achieve "the form of general direct exchangeability"[25] or money, Goux compares the medium of exchange with the privilege of the phallus, a privilege achieved, as Lacan famously argues, at the expense of any immediacy whatsoever. ("[T]he phallus can only play its role as veiled, that is, as in itself the sign of latency with which everything signifiable is struck down as soon as it is raised (*aufgehoben*) to the function of signifier."[26])

Commenting on the isomorphism of the money function with the phallic function, Goux maintains that "the phallus is the general equivalent of objects, and the father is the general equivalent of subjects, in the same way that gold is the general equivalent of products."[27] And, like gold, which can only become money when it is "*fetishized* and subsequently *symbolized* and *idealized*," the father can only fulfill the role of the Law, of the sovereign arbiter of conflict, "as long as he is . . . kept at a distance."[28]

What do we observe in the paternal register but that the mediation of the father is possible only to the extent that what functions as father is excluded from the world of other individuals, that is to say, is killed, functions only as the "dead Father," who rules only provided that he is separated from the group of people, that is, expelled into transcendence?[29]

If the commodity is only a social relation between men which assumes, in Marx's description, "the fantastic form of a relation between things," the patriarchal function is no less apparitional.[30] No wonder our money man must

FIGURE 1.3. *Ghost:* Molly (Demi Moore), Sam (Patrick Swayze), and Carl (Tony Goldwyn) debate the worth of the loft. BFI Films: Stills, Posters and Designs.

become a ghost. (Or, as one of the film's critics observed, "there is not a great deal of difference between a banker and a dead banker.")[31]

Ghost opens onto the white light of the past, the dust-covered upper reaches of Sam and Molly's new loft, in which it is just possible to discern the relics of a tailor's workshop—what may well have been, given the loft's downtown Manhattan location, a turn-of-the-century sweatshop. Its date might be ascertained by that of the Indian Head penny Sam finds there: 1898. The sequence of national expansion and expropriation commemorated by the coin's image of the defeated native is recapitulated domestically in the first seconds of the film. Having broken through a false ceiling to discover an additional story's worth of space, the yuppie couple (aided by Carl) claim all they survey and excitedly debate both its use and exchange value (figure 1.3).

This is gentrification as manifest destiny. It literalizes the theme of upward mobility, the trajectory that will eventually take the hero to heaven, and nationalizes his identity. Here I differ with Judith Mayne's reading of the film's racial inscription, whose "near-infantile" imagery of a white heaven and a black hell is permitted, she argues, by making "Oda Mae virtually the only character in the film who speaks of race."[32] Although no white character specifically refers to African Americans, Sam complains of his anxiety in pitching to his bank's Japanese clients in ethnically laden terms: "I can't very well tell them my Swedish pompom girl jokes." And far from going unmarked, Sam, Molly, and Carl's race is spectacularly displayed at the film's opening, when they emerge from the gloom of the unconverted loft in strikingly white work clothes and dust masks. (Their mock-Stakhanovite poses can be seen, however, as an attempt to appropriate an imaginary aesthetics of physical labor, notably muscular definition, from the actual workers who once labored in the loft.) This marking is particularly detailed with regard to the hero's status as a white middle-class American man. It is not difficult to see Sam Wheat, with his amber waves of hair, as Uncle Sam, the U.S. male (living just opposite the Post Office, working on a street draped in the Stars and Stripes). And like other white American men in the movies of this period, Sam is under siege—by Japanese businessmen, Puerto Rican muggers, phallic women, and, most of all, by his own destructive double, Carl, another fair-haired banker who attempts to take Sam's place with Molly.[33]

When the mugging commissioned by Carl goes wrong and Sam is shot, he becomes the victim of the injustice traditional to the ghost story. But it is through the everyday injustices that are the coinage of this story that Sam is able to take his revenge. Most significant is his domination of the reluctant black woman, whose body is possessed by this white man (to the tune of "Unchained Melody"), made into his medium of access to Molly, just after he demands that she give him money. In an attempt to verify his presence to the skeptical Molly, who has been warned by the police of Oda Mae's convictions for fraud, Sam expropriates the sum of a single penny. "Tell her it's for luck," he commands Oda Mae, recalling the couple's earlier discovery of the "good omen" of its nineteenth-century predecessor in the loft. Invisibly propelled by Sam, the penny rises up the surface of the door dividing the two women. On it is stamped the heroic image of another dead white man, Abraham Lincoln, famed for emancipating the nation's slaves and subsequently suffering his own assassination. (Moreover, Honest Abe is the prototypically unpretentious figure of the nation, "the pattern American" in Hawthorne's phrase, "directness and plainness and principle" in Leo Braudy's elaboration.)[34]

The image of this coin seemingly rising under its own power, indeed, that of a dead man's head ascending, conforms to the uniquely spectral status that Marx ascribed to the movement of money: "The independent existence of the exchange-value of a commodity is here a transient apparition, by means of which the commodity is immediately replaced by another commodity. . . . Hence, in this process which continually makes money pass from hand to hand, the mere symbolic existence of money suffices."[35]

Murdered for money, Sam becomes what money is—"a transient apparition," a ghost. ("In order, therefore, that a commodity may in practice act effectively as exchange-value, it must quit its bodily shape.")[36] If he will ultimately go to heaven because he is "good" (a moral distinction here characterized by an All-American artlessness—sleeping through *Macbeth*, cherishing his ugly TV chair, abjuring romantic declarations), he's also got the "goods" of an exceptionally prosperous life. In English, as Lacan reminds us in his seminar on *The Ethics of Psychoanalysis*, the meaning of the plural "goods" (i.e., property, wares, commodities) is opposed to that of the singular (i.e., something conforming to the moral order of the universe). This is not the case in French, he argues, which allows *les bons* both a moral and an economic meaning (the righteous *and* the valuable). Trading on his native tongue, Lacan moves from the compatibility of the economic and moral good in the French plural to their nonopposition in an ethics grounded in power. The philosophical basis for this ethics is Kant's *Critique of Practical Reason*, which challenges Bentham's utilitarian pleasure principle (that the law should be directed at securing the greatest good for the greatest number) by arguing that good defined as well-being, or pleasure, is merely an object of sensation, not of reason. In other words, feeling good is not necessarily good. On the contrary, Kant argues, in setting itself against our inclinations, the moral law often produces pain.

What has all this to do with our yuppie ghost? Let's look at *the good*, which Bentham would describe as *the useful* in its beneficial capacities (use-values, in Marx's terms) and at *goods*, which are private property, good not in their utility (although they may well be useful) but good as objects of personal ownership, and therefore of power. "To exercise control over one's goods is to have the right to deprive others of them," Lacan warns, quoting Proudhon's "All property is theft." "The domain of the good is the birth of power."[37] Following Kant's ethical observation, that the law is not founded on good, but the good founded on the law (the law isn't there to do you good, but you're only good if you obey it), Lacan argues that the moral law separates good will from any beneficial consequence. In that respect, the law is empty, grounded in no use or pleasure except the *jouissance* of its own exercise. Or, as Molly replies to Sam's question about what all their loft space is *for*: "Just space."

This ghostly space is the founding unit of value in this story, the reason people buy lofts, the nothing for which they toil, the *ex nihilo* that secures their signifying chain. It is both the origin of ambition and its merciful release: the white-out into which Sam blissfully merges at the film's conclusion. Where that other famous banker of the cinema, George Bailey, gratefully chooses castration over extinction at the end of *It's a Wonderful Life* (1946), the already "unmann'd" Sam finally accedes to oblivion—perhaps because, unlike George, he is required to surrender so little in the move from one very large space to another.[38] Where George is schooled in the slogan under his father's portrait—"All you can take with you is that which you've given away," Sam tells Molly as he rises aloft, "The love inside—you take it with you."

How appropriate, then, that Sam characteristically—and, as he insists, sincerely—expresses this love with the word "ditto" (a term of acquiescence to which Molly finally acquiesces, and echoes, in her reply to Sam's parting declaration). "Ditto," an Italian dialect past participle of *dire*, "to say," has been employed in English since the seventeenth century to say something without saying it, to say, literally, that whatever it is has already been said, is "the aforesaid." And "ditto," of course, is typically represented by two dots or quote marks enclosing . . . white space.

If this makes it the ideal signifier for the exhausted endearments of the Hollywood romance, it also corresponds to the purely mediating function that Goux ascribes in a later essay to the "post-traditional phallus."[39] Where the ancient predecessor of that phallus functioned as a token of exchange, the badge proudly worn by the young male initiated into the incest taboo and its compensations (renounce your kinswoman and receive a bride from another family), now, Goux argues, the phallus is only *logos*, a signifier of entitlement, but no guarantee of it. (Just being a man won't get you a woman, although it might, as Goux points out, permit you to apply for a "*mortgage on a possible, though entirely indeterminate woman.*")[40] The reference to finance is not beside the point: As Goux stresses, the cessation of the formal exchange of women between clans (like that of barter in general) made the phallus even more like money, a signifier of value in the abstract, exchange value.[41] Underwriting it, Goux reminds us (echoing Lacan echoing Kant) is the law, which the subject must obey because it is the law, not because it offers any reward for that obedience.

Detached from the utility of reciprocity, the phallus takes on the talismanic significance of "pure mediation,"[42] "just as the financial sign is nothing but the indefinite inscription and circulation of a debt by means of accounting"[43]—the ghostly millions that appear and disappear from Sam's computer screen. As for speech, it too is subsumed in the aforesaid of "infinite substitution," "ditto" in reply to "ditto."

This returns us to the peculiar success of this troubled romance. Its ending, and that of Goux's essay on the phallus, leaves me with a morbid interpretation. If Sam's early retirement is just another example of what Goux calls the "accelerated entropy" of our age, we might regard his ascent into heaven as a manifestation of a masculine death drive, the ultimate upward mobility of the male professional, the final sacrifice required to redeem the moribund prestige of the phallus.[44] The attraction of *Ghost* might then be not that of a love which unites its central couple beyond the grave, but the

35

annulment of all such entanglements, and most of all—in the case of the white male subject—that of the self.

As for *Ghost*'s medium, a final postscript: The success of this film and the subsequent *Sister Act* (1992) briefly made Whoopi Goldberg the highest-paid actress in Hollywood, a remarkable achievement for a black performer and an extraordinary one for a black woman "known to be combative and unglamorous."[45] If her character in *Ghost* is connotative of the congealed labor represented by the African American subject, she soon became that apotheosis of the commoditized individual, the bankable star, reputedly the first actress able to "open" a movie. Although Goldberg eventually yielded this primacy (to Demi Moore, among her successors), she remains a key figure in Hollywood while retaining her "outsider" image. This precarious position is perhaps best represented in her hosting of the Academy Awards, in 1994, 1996, and 1999, a mediating role that has not traditionally gone to a movie star, but to a stand-up comic-cum-talk-show host (from Johnny Carson to David Letterman to Billy Crystal) capable of the required monologues and ad libs. (Goldberg has hosted both TV charity specials and her own TV talk show.)

Before the 1996 Awards ceremony, Jesse Jackson, noting that only one of the 166 nominees was black (short-film director Diane Houston), urged those attending to wear the Rainbow coalition ribbon in protest against the under-representation of African Americans in the film industry. Quincy Jones, the Awards' black producer, readily concurred. Goldberg did not. Instead, she compered the proceedings in a ribbonless black velvet dress by Donna Karan and diamond jewelry said to be worth . . . $4 million. Her opening monologue ridiculed the plethora of ribbons donned at the ceremony for political causes (including one she designated as being for "gay rights," presumably the AIDS ribbon), remarks that can, of course, be read as criticizing the sanctimony of those who wear their loyalties on their lapels, and then only once a year. "You don't ask a black woman to buy an expensive dress and then cover it in ribbons," she added, neatly declaring her own political loyalties in the process.[46] This combination of hipness and conservatism seems totally consistent with Goldberg's cynical and sentimental role in *Ghost*, which can be seen to refute the old Hollywood stereotype of the superstitious black subject, rolling her eyes at some imagined specter, while ultimately endorsing New Age belief—albeit in a spirit of nothing very much at all. You may not laugh, but I suspect that this expert mediator did. All the way to the bank.

2 Figuring Out Andy Warhol

The resemblance of my title to D. A. Miller's monograph *Bringing Out Roland Barthes* is as fortunate as it was, originally, fortuitous. Miller's essay is perhaps best known for suffering the very extrusion of the homosexual hermeneutic that it regrets in Barthes's criticism. Commissioned as an introduction to the University of California Press's translation of *Incidents*, the posthumously published memoirs of the critic's cruising days in Morocco, *Bringing Out Roland Barthes* was ultimately brought out, but not bound with, its ostensible subject, at the insistence of the Barthes estate. Having now read this semi-detached preface (literally tied to its text in an apparently unironic gesture of fetishistic disavowal), I am happy for Miller to introduce *my* remarks, since they, too, constitute an inquiry into the relation between a body of work and the practice of gay sexuality.

Nevertheless, the writing of Roland Barthes may seem a rather perverse place to start. Doesn't Miller himself acknowledge that "however intimately Barthes's writing proved its connection with gay sexuality, the link was so discreet,"[1] whereas Richard Dyer salutes Warhol as perhaps "the most famous openly gay artist who ever lived"?[2] Then again, Miller describes Barthes's "most invidiously written texts" as "phobically sacrific[ing] homosexuality-as-signified" while "happily cultivating homosexuality-as-signifier,"[3] yet we know that the postmodernity of which Warhol is so celebrated an avatar has put an end to all such binary nonsense, indeed to semiotics itself: "The era of signs is rapidly fading. We have already entered the age of the figural," writes D. N. Rodowick in an essay whose epigraph concludes "Campbell, Campbell, Campbell, Campbell."[4]

So why bring up Miller's Barthes? Because, quite simply, Barthes's criticism is not the only one that might be accused of sacrificing to what Miller calls the "deity of general theory as fixed as ever in its white-male-heterosexual orientation."[5] Whether you endorse this Straight White Male characterization of Theory (and I'm not sure I do), the reproach is difficult to ignore. For out as Warhol may have been, gay as *Blow Job* (1964), *My Hustler* (1965), and *Lonesome Cowboys* (1968) may seem, his assumption to the postmodern pantheon has been a surprisingly straight ascent, if only in its stern detachment from any form of commentary that could be construed as remotely sexy.[6]

Thus, in typical terms, David James describes "the withdrawal of sensuality" from Warhol's early pop paintings, the lack of a "personal inflection" in his prints, the "draining" of "presence from his images of media personalities," and their "flattening of fleshly or psychic depth." And when he arrives at the films, this ascription of superficiality is matched by an appropriately abstract, almost taxonomic, rendition of their ostensible subjects: "marginal subcultures," "sexual deviants," "irregular sexual practices."[7] So widespread is this account that it styles frankly gay criticism as much as its Straight White Male counterpart. The gay British critic Emmanuel Cooper's study of homosexuality and Western art tells the familiar tale of Warhol's "avoidance of 'content' in his graphic work" and of "any mysterious meaning or classical interpretation." This opens Cooper to the familiar problems of explaining the flagrantly homosexual imagery in Warhol's films, a difficulty resolved in equally familiar fashion by eliding signification with affect.

Thus, *Blow Job* is said to make the audience "a dispassionate voyeur, led to assume all but being given little explicit information." And this is followed by a description of Warhol himself, in his "life and friendships," avoiding "direct communication and the expression of feelings."[8]

Most surprisingly for a gay critic, Cooper assigns this antihermeneutical commitment to the figure of the drag queen, recycling in the process the oldest Holly Woodlawn line in the book. Replying to Geraldo's quizzing on his ABC show in 1976 ("What are you? Are you a woman trapped in a man's body? Are you heterosexual? Are you homosexual? A transvestite? A transsexual?") Woodlawn answered, "But darling, what difference does it make as long as you look fabulous?" Now, Camille Paglia may dig out the same anecdote in defense of her disaffection with identity politics,[9] but it isn't difficult to demonstrate that drag does make a difference and that this difference is quite legible in Warhol's work.

Before offering such a reading, I want to turn back to an aesthetic precursor of Warhol, one whose representations of a very similar milieu were also recuperated, this time to modernism and *its* repudiation of "systems of significance."[10] The poet Frank O'Hara was no great friend of Warhol (like the one-time lovers Jasper Johns and Robert Rauschenberg, he loathed his notoriously "swish" demeanor), but he shared Warhol's involvement in the New York art world and its large homosexual constituency. A curator at the Museum of Modern Art and author of an influential study of Jackson Pollock, O'Hara (who once signed a letter "yours in action art") drew knowing comparisons between his poetry and the aesthetics of abstract expressionism: "Perhaps the obscurity comes in here, in the relationship between the surface and the meaning, but I like it that way since the one is the other (you have to use words) and I hope the poem to *be* the subject, not just about it."[11] Critics who took O'Hara at his word (and by the early 1970s, some years after his death and the posthumous publication of his collected poems, there were many) were nevertheless stuck with what Helen Vendler called "the sex poems": "We may regret the equableness and charm of our guide and wish him occasionally more Apollonian or more Dionysian (the sex poems aren't very good, though they try hard and are brave in their homosexual details), but there's no point wishing O'Hara other than he was."[12]

I am indebted for this review of O'Hara's criticism to Bruce Boone, whose pioneering study of 1979 (in the very first issue of *Social Text*)[13] set out to reconsider the poet's successive canonizations as a modernist, refusing "ideologies, causes and systems of significance,"[14] and then as an early deconstructionist—presence "stripped of . . . ontological vestments, . . . without depth [and] underlying significance."[15]

Boone traces this "programmatic misinterpretation by euphemism"[16] to the understandings of camp represented by Susan Sontag's famous "Notes" on the subject, in which the affection with which camp is said to behold human failings somehow sets it against any kind of engagement and, of course (after thirty years we should see this coming), *Against Interpretation*.[17] This might explain how critics could miss the patent elegy of O'Hara's famous "Lana Turner Has Collapsed," but how devoid are these lines of "significance"?

> *Then too, the other day I was walking through a train*
> *with my suitcase and I overheard someone say "speaking of faggots"*
> *now isn't life difficult enough without that*
> *and why am I always carrying something*
> *well it was a shitty looking person anyway*
> *better a faggot than a farthead*
> *or as fathers have often said to friends of mine*
> *"better dead than a dope" "if I thought you were queer*
> *I'd kill you."*[18]

It may be, as Boone concludes, that the "dominant group"[19] just don't get it ("it" being the flitty parataxis that here calls the speaker's manhood into question). Or, as I think more likely, since gay critics schooled in a certain tradition produce similar readings of Warhol, questions of sexuality—or, more precisely, questions of homosexuality—may simply not register in the discourses of chance, process, form, materials, distance, and

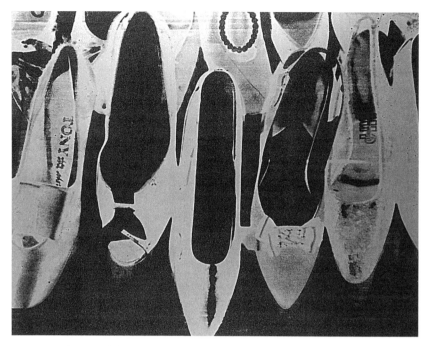

FIGURE 2.1. *Shoes (Parallel)*, Andy Warhol, 1980. © Copyright The Andy Warhol Foundation for the Visual Arts, Inc./ARS, NY and DACS, London 2000. The Andy Warhol Foundation, Inc./Art Resource, NY. Reprinted by permission.

disciplinary critique that articulated postwar criticism and then stimulated, and in a sense shrouded, the experiments of both the poet and the painter. Although this aesthetic would eventually spawn a second (left) and third (feminist) avant-garde, enlarging in the process to include both the aesthetic object and the class or gendered subject, it still clings to Warhol in something very like its original form.

What then of postmodernism's attempts to claim Warhol for its own concerns—the erosion of designation, dissolution of categories, loss of subjective coherence? One of the most influential investigations of these features, in contradistinction to those of high modernism, is Fredric Jameson's reading of Warhol's *Diamond Dust Shoes*. This 1980 series is of sufficient importance to Jameson's *Postmodernism* to provide both the volume's cover image (in color) and a central object of comparison (another painting by the same title in black and white). Jameson reads this second *Diamond Dust Shoes* (officially titled *Shoes (Parallel)*—figure 2.1) against one of Van Gogh's many shoe paintings, the 1887 *Pair of Boots*, which hangs in the Baltimore Museum of Art. One image is said to offer a place for the viewer, an initial content susceptible of painterly transformation, and a consequently hermeneutical project "in the sense in which the work in its inert, objectal form is taken as a clue or a symptom for some vaster reading which replaces it as its ultimate truth."[20] The other image, Jameson argues, refuses "even a minimal place for the viewer," as well as any putative connection between its ostensible content and a social or symbolic context. The first is said to accomplish a utopian transformation of its "drab peasant object world"[21] through the vivid color of oil paints; the second, to strip away any possible gloss from its potentially glamorous subject by reducing it to the ghostly black and white of a photographic negative.

In offering some footnotes to this very suggestive reading, I want to seize on three important opportunities that it presents. The first is Jameson's Benjaminian conviction that the extensive reproduction of the Van Gogh *Boots* will reduce the painting to wallpaper unless its "initial situation" is reconstructed, "somehow mentally restored." And that "situation" (defined as both content and raw material) is immediately identified with the hard life of the peasantry: "the whole object world of agricultural misery."

How does Jameson infer this world? In part, his subsequent remarks suggest, through recalling other paintings by the artist, the "backbreaking peasant toil" of, for example, *Women Picking Green Sprouts in the Snow*, 1890, and the faces "worn down to skulls" in the 1885 *Potato Eaters*. But there is also a famous precedent for Jameson's description in Heidegger's discussion of "a well-known painting by Van Gogh" in "The Origin of the Work of Art." Ironically, this account of a "pictorial representation" of "a pair of peasant shoes" begins by denying them any discernible context. "From Van Gogh's painting," Heidegger complains, "we cannot even tell where the shoes stand." The painting offers neither background nor ground of any kind— "not even clods of soil from the field or the field-path sticking to them." "And yet," in a remarkable turnabout, Heidegger suddenly takes off from a description of the "worn insides" and "rugged heaviness" of the shoes into an unabashed evocation of an exhausted peasant woman trudging across a windswept field on a winter's evening in an atmosphere charged with want, fear, and impending mortality.[22]

Heidegger's setting of this scene, which Jameson again describes as a "recreation" of a "whole missing object world,"[23] takes us to his second point, the *work* of art. The philosopher's definition of art as "the setting-into-work of truth,"[24] illustrated by a work of art said to be about work ("the toilsome tread of the worker"),[25] is appropriated to Jameson's account of the shared materiality of agriculture and oil painting. But if this materiality participates in some "equipmental being," the utility that Heidegger perceives in the Van Gogh boots, Warhol's shoes are deemed quite useless.

In the third of his observations, Jameson pronounces *Diamond Dust Shoes* mute ("I am tempted to say that it does not really speak to us at all"), ineffectual ("Nothing in this painting organizes even a minimal place for the viewer"), and lifeless ("a random collection of dead objects"). The accusation becomes one of fetishism, "in both the Freudian and Marxist senses," the latter alleging the shoes' commodified indifference to mere use value, the former consigning them to a perversion explicitly contrasted with Van Gogh's "heterosexual pair." The citation for this final observation is Derrida's own commentary on Van Gogh in *The Truth in Painting*.[26]

Taking these three points in order, I want to ask whether Warhol's painting would necessarily resist the hermeneutical treatment that Heidegger and Jameson give Van Gogh's. Those who seek, for example, an "initial situation" for *Diamond Dust Shoes* will find a number of accounts. Bob Colacello maintains that the series began as an advertising assignment for the designer Halston:

Victor Hugo sent down a big box of various styles to be photographed for the ad campaign of Halston's shoe licensee, Garolini. Ronnie turned the box upside down and dumped the shoes out. Andy liked the way they looked spilled all over the floor. So he took a few Polaroids and had Ronnie take a lot more. The diamond-dust idea was stolen from Rupert Smith, who had been using the industrial-grade ground-up stones on some prints of his own. He was foolish enough to tell Andy where to buy it and foolish enough to be surprised when it turned up as Andy's art. "Oh, it fell on my painting and stuck," said Andy.[27]

Warhol himself noted in his diary entry for July 24, 1980, "I'm doing shoes because I'm going back to my roots."[28] But which roots? The elegant shoe illustrations of his 1950s commercial art? Or the serigraph style of the 1960s? By 1979, when Warhol was commissioned to redo his best-known pop paintings for the *Reversals* and *Retrospectives* series that accompanied his autobiography, *POPism*, his reconsideration of the latter movement was under way, culminating in the stripped-down post-pop of another set of shoes, the black-and-white ads for the "Pumas" ("$24.99 pr.") and—shades of Van Gogh—*Work Boots* of the mid-1980s.

But if this return to footwear could allude to the graphic styles of two earlier eras, the jeweled appliqué of *Diamond Dust Shoes* was also very eighties, the 1980s of the deficit-funded Reagan budget (subject of a painted Warhol calculation c. 1983–84), the infamous 1981 *Dollar Sign* series, and, most surprising perhaps, the 1980 portrait of the German artist who would attend the *Dollar Sign* opening, the *Diamond Dust Joseph Beuys*. This diamanté tribute to the Marxist who employed "poor" materials and autographed Deutsche Marks with "Creativity = Capital," like Beuys' own portraits of Warhol from the same year, reflected their mutual interest in the exchange value of the artwork—and of the artist. (Warhol also did a diamond dust Georgia O'Keefe in 1980.) But while he agrees that Warhol's Coca Cola and Campbell's containers "explicitly foreground" this commodity fetishism, Jameson deems his shoes merely to *be* fetishes, stranded stand-ins for some irretrievable significance: "There is therefore in Warhol no way to complete the hermeneutic gesture and restore to these oddments that whole larger lived context of the dance hall or the ball, the world of jetset fashion or glamour magazines."[29]

Yet when we turn to another Warhol biography, not coincidentally titled *Loner at the Ball*, we learn that in 1980 Warhol asked his assistant Rupert Smith (Rupert Smith of the diamond dust) to buy large quantities of shoes in

45

the Jewish wholesale district where he lived. "They often had sidewalk sales," Smith recalled, "and one time I bought two thousand pairs of shoes for Andy; they were all really odd, either four quadruple A, petite little Cinderella feet, or they were Drag Queen shoes, size 13 quadruple D like Divine boats!"[30] (That's Divine with a big, indeed, quadruple D—the John Waters star.)

Now, if Jameson will allow Heidegger the "delirious dramaturgy"[31] of his reconstitution of the peasant scene ("the silent call of the earth, its quiet gift of ripening corn . . . the fallow desolation of the wintry field"),[32] I should be permitted to summon up the tackiness of a sidewalk display in the garment district, where outsized remnants of some previous year's fashions stand racked for wholesale, party pumps with bows and sling-backs, one shoe from each pair. Yet this remaindered footwear is also precious, dusted with diamonds, a jeweled allusion to Dorothy's ruby slippers and through their color and magical powers to Moira Shearer's *Red Shoes* (1948), and always, of course, to the glass four quads of that other "loner at the ball," another pair that get separated in the course of the story, leaving behind a lost lure for a pursuing prince or for Proustian remembrance. (Decades before *Diamond Dust Shoes*, Warhol moved from fashion illustration to fantasy with a series of jeweled shoes, drawings dressed with lace and gold leaf, ladies' shoes dedicated to the likes of Truman Capote and, yes, Judy Garland. One such print, the title page of a portfolio dated 1955, is headed "A la Recherche du Shoe *Perdu*.")[33]

Who would wear such shoes? Cinderella and the Drag Queen, Rupert Smith tells us, sizes four and thirteen, the ingenue and the ugly stepsister, femininity and masculinity, brought together by work. Of which, two venerable citations:

I'm fascinated by boys who spend their lives trying to be complete girls, because they have to work so hard—double time, getting rid of all the tell-tale male signs and drawing in all the female signs. . . . It's very hard work. You can't take that away from them. It's hard work to look like the complete opposite of what nature made you and then to be an imitation of what was only a fantasy woman in the first place.

When she takes off her shoes late in the evening, in deep but healthy fatigue, and reaches out for them again in the still dim dawn, or passes them by on the day of rest, she knows all this without noticing or reflecting. The equipmental quality of the equipment consists indeed in its usefulness.

The first passage is from *The Philosophy of Andy Warhol*.[34] The second is from the philosophy of Martin Heidegger, the section of "The Origin of the Work of Art" that discusses Van Gogh's shoes.[35]

Heidegger's conviction that the wearer of these shoes is a peasant woman may be even more perverse than my assumption that Warhol's would be worn by a drag queen. As Derrida points out in his review of the dispute between the philosopher and the art historian Meyer Schapiro (who thought the shoes in the picture were Van Gogh's own), there is no way to ascertain the gender of their wearer or even, for that matter, whether Van Gogh's various paintings on the subject portray *pairs* of shoes at all (although Derrida does think the Baltimore image may be "perhaps a pair").[36] Resisting the temptation to restore the "Old Laced Shoes" in another Van Gogh painting to some unified bipedal subject, Derrida muses on the "strange, worrying, perhaps threatening and slightly diabolical"[37] possibility of two *right* or two *left* shoes. And in a comparison of the earthy utility of Van Gogh's flats to the fetishist's single stiletto, he observes: "It is perhaps in order to exclude the question of a certain uselessness, or of a so-called perverse usage, that Heidegger and Schapiro denied themselves the slightest doubt as to the parity or pairedness of these two shoes."[38]

And what is the "perverse usage" to which the *Diamond Dust Shoes* will be put? Not the traditional purpose of the fetish proper, substitute for the woman's missing penis, but rather the dick's disguise, the equipment that some boys employ in the hard work of "trying to be complete girls." In this respect, as Derrida points out after Freud's observations on the bisexuality of dream images, the shoe is an ideal transitional object: "Could it be that, like a glove turned inside out, the shoe sometimes has the convex 'form' of the foot (penis), and sometimes the concave form enveloping the foot (vagina)?"[39]

Of course, the transvestite has often been named the central figure of Warhol's work, from Stephen Koch's 1973 positing of his drag queens as "the pivot of a conundrum about being and appearing"[40] to Jean Baudrillard's "Transpolitics, Transsexuality, Transaesthetics," in which he proposes Warhol himself, "like Michael Jackson," as a postaesthetic "mutant": "an androgyne of the new generation, a sort of mystical prosthesis or artificial machine which delivered us from sex and aesthetics, thanks to its perfection." True to form, this deliverance is attributed to indifference—indifference not only to aesthetic valuation (e.g., Warhol's famous declaration that "all art works are beautiful") but to sex, as designation and as affect, "an indifferentiation of sexual poles and an indifference to *jouissance*, that is to say, to sex as pleasure and joy."[41] Something like this is also suggested in Jameson's reading of *Diamond Dust Shoes*, whose reversed-out photo negative is seen as a "deathly" apparition, an intimation, indeed, of the "waning of affect in postmodern culture."[42]

I want to conclude these remarks with this specter, the same ghost that Derrida claims to haunt Van Gogh's shoes, those foot-shaped supports of some invisible wearer, explicit personifications, whose worn leather (unlike wooden clogs) displays "*face-on* . . . individual traits, wrinkles."[43] Finally, there's the painting's representation of the shoes, the "ghosting" that all pictures perform in doubling their subject.

In her reading of the 1963 horror film *The Haunting*, Patricia White describes a representational strategy that renders homosexuality as a haunting invisibility, a "process whereby the apparition of lesbian desire is deferred to manifestations of supernatural phenomena."[44] Diana Fuss takes up this theme in her introduction to the collection in which White's essay appears, noting its authors' "preoccupation with the figure of the homosexual as specter and phantom, as spirit and revenant, as abject and undead."[45] The ghost that haunts heterosexuality is its uncanny double, the illicit desire necessary to define legitimacy. The liminality of this figure, as Fuss and others have observed, reflects its ambiguity as a term of exclusion which nonetheless confers interiority. If the term functions as a "negative image" for the straight world, it is nevertheless not nothing, no more than a photographic negative is nothing. In a subsequent study Terry Castle has invoked Freud's "On Negation" to argue that the homosexual phantom gains entry to representation by virtue of its deniability: its ghostly appearance allows the culture both to register and to refuse its existence.[46]

If we turn this "spectral analysis"[47] to shoes whose magic purpose may be travesty, we find, as Teresa de Lauretis describes the butch-femme roleplay in the 1987 film *She Must Be Seeing Things*, that they show "the uncanny distance, like an effect of ghosting, between desire (heterosexually represented as it is) and the representation; and because the representation doesn't fit the actors who perform it, it only points to their investment in a fantasy."[48]

This doubling (of desire and its representation, girl and boy, straight and gay) is uncanny precisely because it refuses Baudrillard's transcendence. Drag fascinates in its simultaneous display of contradictory sexual meanings, not in their resolution or dispersal. It no more transcends gender than Michael Jackson's surgically altered appearance transcends race. Instead, we might describe cross-dressing, with Severo Sarduy, as "the coexistence, in a single body, of masculine and feminine signifiers: the tension, the repulsion, the antagonism which is created between them."[49]

In an analysis that exerts a powerful influence on Marjorie Garber's *Vested Interests*, Sarduy defines drag as "probably the best metaphor for what writing really is": sheer inscription, the mask without the face.[50] The opacity that renders it impossible to identify a true gender beneath the makeup and the mustache may also be discerned in Warhol's painting. Despite its "glacéd X-ray elegance" (in Jameson's evocative phrase)[51] it fails, unlike the shoe shop machines that irradiated American feet in the 1950s, to reveal the bare bones of the matter. We see only the shoes, glowing eerily in the dark. If, as Jameson argues, that "depthlessness" suggests a "mutation" in an object world "contaminated" by its contact with advertising, it does not divest it of meaning. Shoes are, after all, clothing, and clothing in art, as Derrida insists, is more than the fig leaf of form, draped over some material body. The radiance of another man's garb, for example, may alert the wary male spectator to the hazards of homosexual contamination.

By what I take to be coincidence, Baudrillard has christened the latest stage in the "microphysics of simulacra," that of the image in infinite series, as "the irradiated stage of value." Here, too, the consequence of this "chain reaction" is disease, "a sort of epidemic of value, a general metastasis of value."[52] Baudrillard diagnoses this epidemic as the "diffraction" of meaning: "We cannot read ['works of art'] any longer; we can only decode them according to more and more contradictory criteria."[53] Yet, despite the centrifugal rhetoric ("physics," "particle," "acceleration," "trajectory"), his discourse turns inward, cohering in the all too legible figure of the drag queen. Transvestite or transsexual, this exquisite artifact is named the spirit of our age, since s/he fulfills the body's postmodern destiny: "to become a prosthesis."[54]

Shoes are clothing at its most prosthetic, not only reinforcing the feet but retaining their form, "ghost-limbs" in Derrida's description.[55] They stand without us, but the pathos of their erection makes us want to fill them all the more. Thus, our desire to restore Van Gogh's *Boots*, and indeed Warhol's *Shoes*, to some original owner. If this is impossible in any case—art being, as Heidegger finally concludes, "by nature an origin"[56]—it is doubly so in drag. The transvestite explicitly resists such restitution, defying its opposition of appearance to reality, phantom to flesh. How can you, s/he asks with withering contempt, even try to identify the original of an imitation of what was only a fantasy in the first place? (And as for the original of a *representation* of an imitation of what was only a fantasy . . .)

Like the drag queen, the copy without an original has become emblematic both for queer theory and for postmodernism. That isn't altogether surprising, since the first is closely related to the second, and both come equipped with a genealogy of contamination, mutation, and pathology. But neither is it a matter of indifference. Despite Baudrillard's best hopes for "the triumph of a medley of all erotic simulacra," this "topsy turvy" age is not yet upon us. The "epidemic" he writes of has not been a proliferation of competing (and therefore mutually nullifying) values but one of "signification"—the homophobic signification still hegemonically constructing AIDS.[57] (Witness Baudrillard's own embarrassing elision of drag, mutation, and disease.)

This is not to deny that *Diamond Dust Shoes* (silkscreen of a photographic negative of a commercial display) radiates seriality and simulation. The resemblance of these dozen shoes to one another (and to previous generations of the image) emphasizes an internal correspondence that abstracts the figure from the ground.[58] The consequential self-referentiality is indisputable, but not in a way that resists interpretation. On the contrary, the circuitry of reference, the simulacral shadows, disclose a very vivid specter, still waiting to be laid by postmodernity. In outing this figure, in ascribing significance to simulation, I offer you no deliverance, either from aesthetics or from sex.

3 *Hard, Fast and Beautiful*

Florence Farley is a keen tennis player just out of Santa Monica High School. As she practices her strokes against the garage door, her mother Milly trims the dress she is sewing for her. Florence's practice is interrupted by a young man looking for a stray dog. He identifies himself as an assistant at the local country club and asks to use the telephone. Florence recognizes him as a former schoolmate, Gordon McKay, and introduces him to her mother, who inquires about his family and offers lemonade. Gordon declines, but invites Florence to play tennis with him at the club.

That evening, Milly rejects her husband Will's advances and complains about their neighborhood. As the couple prepare themselves for bed, Milly declares her ambitions for her daughter, but Will defends their homely circumstances. Florence enters and holds an excited conversation about her prospective match with Gordon. To her mother's disappointment, she reveals that he is not wealthy, but a student working his way through college. Will reminds Florence that her forthcoming match is "only a game." "Well, sure," Florence replies, "but maybe I can beat him."

Florence does beat Gordon, who suggests that she should play doubles with him at the club. She begins to win local matches and is soon asked by the club pres-

ident to represent it at the national junior championships in Philadelphia. When Milly refuses permission for Florence to travel there without her, she too is offered an expenses-paid trip. Before they depart, Gordon declares his love to Florence with an engraved pendant in the shape of a tennis racquet.

At the junior championships, tennis agent Fletcher Locke is impressed by Florence's ability and inquires about her to a colleague. Milly overhears and contrives to introduce herself to Fletcher by pretending not to understand the tournament draw sheet. Florence wins the tournament but defers to her mother in the post-match interview. Milly tells the press that they will "just go home and be ourselves for a while."

Florence, now wearing an expensive tennis outfit donated by a manufacturer, is picked up by Gordon after partnering a wealthy local woman. When Gordon reproaches her for accepting $50 in payment, she protests that she is not endangering her amateur status. Meanwhile, her mother brushes aside Will's objections to a new car and declares that she has already bought one on a deal arranged for Florence. Fletcher Locke flies to California to persuade the Farleys to enter Florence in the national championships. Milly conducts the negotiations as Will stands awkwardly by. Before leaving with her mother, Florence reconciles with Gordon and accepts his proposal of marriage.

Florence plays in several preliminary tournaments and loses one because of her weak backhand. Fletcher drills her on it exhaustively and impresses Milly with the prospective rewards of her daughter's success. As her sick father listens to the radio broadcast and Gordon watches from the stands, Florence wins the national championship. After the match, Milly suggests that Florence marry Gordon on tour in Europe, where he can work ghostwriting newspaper articles for her. Gordon angrily ends their engagement.

Florence tours Europe over the winter and then wins Wimbledon. After a drunken night out in London, she reveals to her mother that she now understands her unpopularity with the other players. She berates her for accepting illicit payments and separating her from Gordon. In Paris, Florence takes control of her affairs, refuses to endorse a shoddy racquet, and ends her tour to return for the U.S. championships.

There she responds to a journalist's questions about the amateur game with a sarcastic endorsement of the values of family and fair play. A telegram arrives with news of her father's illness, and Florence defies Milly to fly home on the eve of the final. Weak in hospital, Will is tender with his daughter but dismissive to his wife, telling her to "beat it." Exhausted from her flight, Florence struggles in the final, but ultimately wins as her father listens to the broadcast. Gordon is also watching from the stands and arrives to rescue the dazed victor from a barrage of press questions about her intended retirement. He abruptly escorts her from the stadium, but Florence turns back to hand her mother the trophy, saying bitterly that she has "earned it." A panicked Milly appeals to Fletcher to intervene, but he is already approaching a new protégée. As darkness settles over the stadium, Milly sits alone in the stands.

Contemporary reviews of the fourth film directed by Ida Lupino, *Hard, Fast and Beautiful* (1951), were quick to acknowledge its dual interest in mother-daughter relations and in tennis "shamateurism." Some, such as the *Motion Picture Herald*, saw no contradiction in these themes:

Ida Lupino directed with fine focus on feminine values this stirring contemporary drama, which shows in highly exploitable fashion how commercialism invades the amateur sports field without the knowledge of innocent contenders. With Claire Trevor in a polished portrayal of an over-ambitious mother of an amateur tennis champion, brilliantly played by Sally Forrest, the production is powerful in its appeal to the distaff element.[1]

Others complained of a generic misfit in the combination of maternal melodrama and social criticism:

The film ignores most of the opportunities for satirical comment on the occasionally odd interpretations of amateurism in sport and concentrates on a rather novelettish study of the relationship between mother and daughter.[2]

The apparent incongruity of the film's title was noted by *Time* ("a title that conjures up visions of a wanton wench on the marquee"), but not its possible linkage with the spectacle of the athletic female body (". . . turns out to apply to nothing more alluring than a tennis ball")³—let alone with the phantasmatic figure of the powerful mother. Where the film's source, a 1931 novel by John R. Tunis, had foregrounded the dilemma of a *Mother of a Champion*, its screen adaptation was titled with a trio of adjectives ostensibly suggesting sex.

To those familiar with Lupino's oeuvre, this suggestion comes twice as hard—echoing the 1943 Warner Brothers melodrama, *The Hard Way,* in which her character exploits the beauty of a younger sister to escape a tough mining town for show business. As Jeanine Basinger reminds us, the three words of that title are superimposed, not over the mean streets of the sisters' origins, but on the torso of an unidentified woman, "a set of breasts, shoulders, and fingernails"⁴ meretriciously adorned with jewels, orchids, and fur.

In the scenes that follow, we discover that this expensively clad figure has parlayed her sister's "natural resources" into Broadway stardom. But the *Hard Way* to Broadway requires the destruction of both women's marriages, as well as the career of a rival actress. The maternal function performed by the older sister in furthering her sibling's success is very like that of the brothel madam, enriching herself by supplanting affective relations with those of commerce, by becoming—in the crudest sense—"hard."

Nine years after *The Hard Way* came *Hard, Fast and Beautiful* and its remarkably similar story of a mother whose ambitions for her daughter threaten both her own marriage and that of her child. This time, however, Lupino was the director rather than the lead, and the daughter's career not show business but sport. Between the two productions Simone de Beauvoir published *The Second Sex*, with its observations on the mother's idealization of the daughter "she regards as her double,"⁵ as well as its provocative comparison of the cinema star and the courtesan—the latter "perhaps less a slave than the woman who makes a career of pleasing the public."⁶ But if the female performer could already be identified with the prostitute, *Hard, Fast and Beautiful* extended *The Hard Way* to the woman athlete, whose amateur status becomes an object of the economic pressure seen to bear down on all aspects of American life.

Such pressure is pervasive in the maternal melodrama, whose struggling heroines typically strive for "something better" for their daughters. In *Hard, Fast and Beautiful*, Milly Farley recalls this aspiration in her opening voice-over, addressed to the teenage girl hitting tennis balls against the garage door:

From the very moment you were born, I knew you were different. I could see things in you that no one else could. And I knew that somehow I was going to get the very best there was out of life for you. Listening to you drive that ball used to drive me crazy. That's because I always wanted something better for you. And I made up my mind to get it, no matter what I had to do.

Milly is not visible until, at the end of her second sentence, the scene changes to her trimming the fabric of Florence's evening dress. As Ronnie Scheib[7] and Wendy Dozoretz[8] have stressed, the dissolve from the athletic daughter to the ambitious mother, busily fitting the dress to its "dummy," suggests that Florence's youthful energies will be brought under maternal identification and control. But the mutuality of their endeavors is also indicated by what the girl is aiming *at*—painted numbers at which she directs the ball, just as her mother tailors the dress to the requirements of the dummy and the paper pattern. From the outset, sport in this film is no more an act of spontaneous physical exuberance than sewing.

Like her mother's housework, the daughter's tennis practice is performed in an ostensibly free domestic space which is revealed to be as rigorously delimited as the chessboard that stands at her father's side when he listens to a radio broadcast of her match. The Farley home is divided between the contending parents, who even sleep facing apart on twin beds whose central headboard barrier could almost parody the Hays Code restrictions on conjugal intimacy. When, early in the film, they retire to their separate beds while discussing Florence's future, a close-up centers the headboard to split the screen, and the couple, as each speaks and reacts antagonistically to the other. Similarly, Florence and Gordon are twice separated in their initial encounter: by the picket fence that surrounds the Farley property, and by the cuckoo that suddenly emerges from its own little clock-house to fly between them. Finally, the garage door against which Florence rallies is divided into squares whose numbers anticipate the figures that will be offered to her in illicit payments. To hit each number as she calls it out, Florence adjusts her stance to "angle" her shot—just as her agent will play the "million angles" of financial opportunity opened up by her tennis success.

Thus, despite postwar aspirations for a suburban haven away from the pressured environs of the workplace, with sport as a form of recreative play on its grassy lawns and paved driveways, the opening scenes of *Hard, Fast and Beautiful* mark out its domestic mise-en-scene as one of contention and commerce. The frustrated Milly Farley has married at seventeen to escape privation, only to end up in a cramped house in Santa Monica with an unmarried daughter and a husband unable (and seemingly unwilling) to earn their way out to the classier precincts of the Pacific Palisades. In the face of Will Farley's apparent economic passivity (his employment is never seen or discussed), Milly takes over the paternal function—albeit in the vicarious manner with which she choreographs her daughter's personal life and career.

This pseudo-economic role seems the only one available to a woman in Milly's circumstances. Unlike her most celebrated cinema antecedent (and near namesake) *Mildred Pierce*, the diminutive "Milly" does not move formally into the sphere of commodity production by, for example, becoming a dressmaker or restaurateur. Instead, she seems to welcome commerce into the home, greeting the nephew of a prominent figure as a potentially advantageous match for her daughter, then the local businessman and country club president when he arrives to ask Florence to tour with the club's team, and finally the entrepreneur Fletcher Locke when he seeks permission to enter her in the national championships.

If this vicarious economic activity demonstrates the difference between the working woman of wartime and her housewife successor, it is not the argument of this film that the latter is exempted from commodity relations.

On the contrary, Milly's dependence on Will encourages her to be constantly "at" him to improve the family's fortunes: in order to keep house she must be able to purchase the goods of postwar expansion. The key commodity here is, of course, the car (to which the title *Hard, Fast and Beautiful* might also apply), the new car that Florence's success will enable Milly to buy in the face of her husband's objections.

This is the California that inspired Theodor Adorno's *Minima Moralia* (written in Los Angeles during his 1940s exile there and published in the year of this film's release), whose habitations are described as "factory sites that have strayed into the consumption sphere"[9] and whose "leisure" pursuits are equally industrious.[10] Modern sports, Adorno cautions elsewhere, "seek to restore to the body some of the functions of which the machine has deprived it. But they do so only in order to train men all the more inexorably to serve the machine."[11]

To dramatize this striking convergence of work and play, industry and domesticity, there could be no better sport than the seemingly genteel game of tennis. The modern competition has evident precedents in the ball games of antiquity and the sixteenth-century development of "real tennis," but their Victorian successor was launched as an unabashed commodity by its devisor, Major Walter Clopton Wingfield. Lawn tennis, or "sphairistike" (as Wingfield christened it in a Greek locution freighted with a mercantile culture's fantasy of the nobler ideals of ancient athletics), was introduced at a party given by the Major in 1873. By the following year, this gentleman-at-arms in the court of Queen Victoria had patented the game, its name, and its equipment (nets, posts, rackets, and balls), which were sold in a boxed set exclusively from Messrs French & Co of Pimlico for the not inconsiderable sum of five guineas.

The price suggests the intended market for Major Wingfield's product: the middle class, enriched by industry and recently possessed of country houses with extensive lawns. More athletic than croquet, but sufficiently gentle for the ladies, tennis became the new pastime of the new class, with a dress code (white outfits from the 1880s), an absence of physical contact, and a disdain for time limits that wholly obscured the onerous labors on which its players' fortunes were founded. But if this sport was predicated on an almost willful detachment from its material circumstances, the detachment that notoriously endows the commodity with its fetish character, it would not be so for long.

With the rapid rise of national and international competition came the prospect of full-time play, *paid* play on the exhibition circuit, which the legendary French champion Suzanne Lenglen pioneered as early as 1926. Lenglen's decision to turn professional was regarded as scandalous in many quarters, but she replied with a telling criticism of the amateur rules, under which, she complained, "only a wealthy person can compete, and the fact of the matter is that only the wealthy people *do* compete."[12] Consequently, top amateurs, including the American star who supplanted Lenglen, Helen Wills Moody, were increasingly offered newspaper contracts and couture clothing, and more covertly rewarded with appearance fees for entering particular tournaments and with "expenses" beyond the tiny maximum permitted by the amateur authorities. "The only way now open for an amateur to avoid professionalism," wrote Wills Moody in 1931—twenty years before *Hard, Fast and Beautiful* and thirty-seven before tennis finally went "open"—"is for him to be rolled in cotton wool and moth balls between tennis seasons."[13]

This contradictory combination of amateurism and professionalism— "shamateurism" as it became known—provoked particular difficulties for women players. If amateurism is understood as a form of devotion, an engagement in a pursuit for the love of it, tennis was also tailor-made for another form of love, the courtship rituals of the Victorian bourgeoisie, for whom its "matches," in twos and fours, were ideally structured. The latter gave the ladies an unprecedented entry into the sport, with the first women's singles championship played at Wimbledon only a decade after Major Wingfield's party, and three years later in the United States. But the culture that offered women an invitation into what became the pre-eminent professional sport of their sex would also inhibit their athleticism. As one commentator recently observed in a report on the current women's tour:

I was constantly reminded of the balance that women were forced to strike between their ambition and society's expectations, between their determination to be unique— i.e., number one—and their wish to be "normal," between their desire to excel and their fear of losing their femininity.[14]

Two years before *Hard, Fast and Beautiful*, a player for whom the title might have been devised, Gertrude "Gorgeous Gussie" Moran, pushed those contradictions to their limits. Moran had reached the semifinals of the U.S. nationals in 1948, but she was more famous as the glamour girl of the tour, dating movie stars and releasing details of her 37-25-37^1/2 measurements. For her 1949 Wimbledon debut, she asked tennis couturier Teddy Tinling for "something feminine." His revolutionary creation was ultra-modest by today's standards, a white dress of satin-trimmed rayon hanging a few inches above the knee. Beneath it Moran wore the voluminous "panties" of the period, but edged for the first time with a tiny ribbon of lace. The result was a press sensation, record attendance figures, and an official Wimbledon rebuke to Tinling for "unnecessarily attracting the eye to the sexual area."[15] On the eve of *Hard, Fast and Beautiful*, women's tennis did indeed have—notwithstanding *Time*—"a wanton wench on the marquee," and the film acknowledges this. In an allusion to the scandal, it includes a locker-room scene in which Florence's first opponent at the national junior championships shows off *her* lace-trimmed panties to another player, who pronounces them "real wild." The incident, like the film's title, portrays tennis as an undeniably sexual spectacle.

Florence Farley enters this world as the classic ingénue—eager, unsophisticated, guileless. As her boyfriend Gordon points out after their first match, she has *no backhand*. Florence will acquire this stroke under the tutelage of Fletcher Locke, described in the film as "a combination coach and promoter—if you know what I mean." (Milly knows, but innuendo is a language that Florence has yet to learn. The indirection with which Fletcher is introduced underlines the deviousness that is his stock in trade.) A series of brief scenes, punctuated with montages of Florence's tournament play, establishes the links between her coach's financial con-tortions (accepting "backhanders" in exchange for Florence's favors) and her increasing expertise.

The series begins with Milly's voice ("It was hard, Florence, all the way, but my dream for you was coming true") over a montage of the girl in action at tournaments in New Jersey and Pennsylvania. (Lupino herself—in cap and dark glasses—is recognizable in a cut to a tournament audience.) After a loss to a reigning champion (in which the frightened Florence is literally marched on and off court by Fletcher and her mother), she is coldly in-structed to "work" on her backhand. The next scene shows Florence, in a dark practice shirt, hitting backhands until a pan left reveals Fletcher shout-ing criticisms of her technique and insisting that Florence "do it until it's au-tomatic." When the exhausted girl protests (in an echo of her mother's re-proaches to Will) that she has been "at it and at it," the coach concedes a rest. A dissolve to a dark evening bag hints at the financial rewards of this forced labor, rewards that Fletcher outlines expansively to a smartly dressed Milly in the swish surroundings of a cocktail bar: "Hotel chains all over the world! Press syndicates! A million angles, and they all work!" The action returns to a brief scene of another tournament, and then to Fletcher drilling Florence again on her backhand ("Now let's do it until it's mechanical") while he sits and smokes. Two tournaments later, the series ends with a telling bedroom scene in which the pajama-clad Florence sets aside the letters she has just written to Gordon and her father, dons an elaborate hat with a dark veil, and strikes poses in the mirror.

Here we see Florence becoming, as Gordon will accuse her, "more like your mother every day." A marked departure from the sportswear she has favored, the glamorous hat is the first garment to have anything in com-mon with the gauzy evening dress Milly has been preparing for her daugh-ter since the film's beginning. The coy femininity with which Florence tries it on before the mirror is also that of her mother—a mask assumed as surely as Milly's own disguise of nail polish, dark glasses, and elegant clothes. (In the absence of greater production values in this low-budget film,[16] the clothes that Milly continually sews, packs, recommends, or poses in function not only as the film's central status symbols, but also as figures of deception, clothing as *costume*, the concealment of the "real self" which the popular wisdom of the 1950s endlessly counseled teenage girls like Florence to "be.")

In her analysis of another woman who assumed an exaggerated femininity to conceal her guilty appropriation of the masculine prerogative, Joan Riviere famously refused to exempt any "womanly" behavior from the function of what she termed "masquerade."[17] It is not surprising that a film as interested in performance as this one, a film that is set next door to Hollywood and whose central character is clearly modeled on the pushy "stage mother," should foreground the performative aspect of femininity. What *is* remarkable is the connection it draws between the playing of this role, the playing of competitive sport, and work.

Florence learns her backhand, that difficult and deceptive stroke, by sheer, repetitive work. If modern sport, as Adorno argued, trains the weekend enthusiast to serve the machine, this film insists that the serious competitor must *become* a machine to win championships. The strangely mechanical quality of tennis, the metronomic tick-tock of its strokes and its comically "coercive"[18] swivel of the spectator's head to follow the ball, depend on abilities that must also become "automatic." Like the cuckoo that springs from the clock to interrupt her first tête-à-tête with Gordon, or the wind-up dog she toys with as she later berates her mother, the practiced Florence becomes something of an automaton—*hard, fast, beautiful*—machinelike in her strength and her speed, but also in a kind of patent prettiness. Where a more conventional story might have taken her athleticism as a departure from femininity, Lupino's film insists on the relation between the two.

Florence's mastery of the backhand is matched by her acquisition of other skills of indirection. (Her strategically delayed announcement to Gordon of their European wedding plans is one example. So, in a subsequent scene, is her newfound command of sarcasm.) The most emblematic of these skills is femininity, "womanliness" as a masquerade learned as mimetically from Milly as the high follow-through is from Locke. Florence's hat and veil, her beaded gown and elaborately decorated décolletage, are the costume of a new role, a form of simulation achieved through practice. In Florence's case the labor involved is sometimes made explicit: she can have the beaded gown, her mother explains, if she will just "pose for a few publicity pictures." Both sport and dressing up, those quintessential leisure pursuits, are revealed to be work. Together, these two forms of labor combine to produce the spectacle of the woman tennis star—athlete and erotic object. (The two terms are fatefully united on the engraved necklace that Gordon gives Florence: "I love you champ.")

However obscure to *Time*, the sexual discourse in this film is at the heart of its condemnation of commodity culture. As de Beauvoir argued in *The Second Sex*, the division between any female performer and the prostitute is at best uncertain:

All occupations in which women are on exhibition can be used for gallantry . . . frequently a woman who goes before the public to earn her living is tempted to trade more intimately in her charms.[19]

If we (as de Beauvoir wryly notes of the misogynist Henri Millon de Montherlant) attempt to exempt female athletes from this objection ("by the independent exercising of the body they can win a spirit, a soul"),[20] the commercialization of sport makes them as vulnerable as any celebrity to the lure of treating "not only their bodies but their entire personalities as capital to be exploited."[21]

In *Hard, Fast and Beautiful* this function is significantly divided: Florence is exploited, not by herself, but by her mother. The taint of prostitution is displaced onto Milly, who conducts the film's financial transactions and keeps as much information as she can from her daughter. And unlike Sally Forrest, who brings the bruised innocence of Lupino's earlier heroines (the unwed mother in the 1949 *Not Wanted* and the polio victim in the 1950 *Never Fear*) to the role of Florence, Claire Trevor had her greatest successes in the role of a prostitute (for which she won an Academy Award nomination in the 1937 *Dead End*) and the barroom "moll" (her 1949 Academy Award-winning performance in *Key Largo*).[22]

Yet these apparently differing roles—of the naive competitor and her controlling mother—have been aptly described as "two aspects of the same woman,"[23] a splitting that enables the double entendre of the film's title: the virtues of the strong, swift athlete and the vices of sexual experience and desire. At their most polarized, these are the characteristics of an extreme virginity and an extreme promiscuity—of impenetrable chastity and unfeeling corruption. They are also, and not insignificantly, figures of a transcendent masculinity and a grossly carnal femininity, the absence of the latter which—as de Beauvoir argues—leads de Montherlant to exempt the female athlete from the opprobrium in which he holds women. Finally, in psychoanalytic terms, these ostensible antinomies are simply different stages in the sexual development of women.

In Freud's narrative of this development, children of both sexes share a phallic phase prior to puberty, in which "the little girl is a little man"[24] with a clitoral focus of erotic pleasure and a primary attachment to the mother she endows with a phallic perfection. In order to achieve "femininity" (in order to become the mother rather than desire her), the girl is faced with two tasks. She must transfer her erotic sensitivity from the (active) clitoris to the (passive) vagina and her object choice from the maternal to the paternal. This double move is said to originate in the girl's successive discovery of her own "castration" and that of her mother, with the former failing bitterly blamed on the latter:

The turning away from the mother is accompanied by hostility; the attachment to the mother ends in hate. . . . the more passionately a child loves its object the more sensitive does it become to disappointments and frustrations from that object.[25]

So profound a repudiation of the mother, and its psycho-functionalist defense, has attracted extensive feminist criticism, not least Wendy Dozoretz's elegy for "The Mother's Lost Voice in *Hard, Fast and Beautiful*":

By the end of the film, the mother's place is totally subsumed by Gordon and Mr. Far-
ley. They assume the positive characteristics of both mother and father, leaving no
need for an actual mother. Accordingly, Mrs. Farley's voiceover disappears halfway
through the film, a typical occurrence in films with female narrators. Furthermore,
Gordon literally replaces Mrs. Farley as Florence's voice.[26]

Countering Freud's account with a Chodorowian analysis emphasizing the
durability of the girl's early attachment to her mother,[27] Dozoretz attributes
the film's savage demolition of Milly Farley to the ideological imperatives of
postwar familialism (under which Tunis's original story was revised not only
to separate the ambitious mother from her daughter, but also to marry the
latter off to Gordon).

Without denying the force of this reading, it should be noted that the
film's denouement is hardly the "happy ending" that the RKO executives
prescribed.[28] As at least one dissenting review complained, "Mom seems to
be in for a beating in Hollywood these days."[29] And the severity of Milly's
punishment is nowhere compensated for by Florence's nuptial joy. Instead,
the daughter grimly confers the championship cup on the mother who
"earned" it and disappears with Gordon from the screen. Far from representing some happy domesticity, the film's final shots stay in the stadium, where
the abandoned Milly sits in the gathering darkness.

This humbling of the mother is not specific to *Hard, Fast and Beautiful*
or to its era. As Ann Kaplan has observed, *Now, Voyager* (1942) offers a precursor to Milly in the oppressive mother of Charlotte Vale.[30] Although Kaplan does not discuss Lupino's film, the similarity is notable. Like Milly, Mrs.
Vale speaks for her daughter and separates her from a lover, and, like her, she
is in turn demoted through the double agency of a younger suitor and an
older paternal figure, Dr. Jaquith. (Kaplan notes that Dr. Jaquith personifies
the psychoanalytic ideology that later texts—including *Hard, Fast and Beautiful*—will simply assimilate.) Kaplan traces *Now, Voyager*'s subordination of
the mother to its opposite—the phallic power attributed to the female parent in early childhood, and its phantasmatic revival as women entered the

U.S. work force during World War II. The monstrous Mrs. Vale is merely the obverse of the adored mother. The daughter's fear masks her desire, a longing that is made explicit in Kaplan's final film example, *Marnie* (1964) and recapitulated in that recent epitome of the woman's film, *The Piano* (1993).

The "arrested desire for the mother" takes us back to *Hard, Fast and Beautiful* and the complex connections it establishes between professionalism, prostitution, and the maternal object. The film's manifest transgression—accepting money for amateur competition—is repeatedly associated with sexual misconduct. When Gordon is offered employment ghosting newspaper articles for Florence, he replies, in one of the film's most conspicuous euphemisms: "What you're asking me to do is become something there's a name for, and it's not for me."

The name for the profession Gordon rejects is clearly not "ghostwriter" but "gigolo," the paid male sexual companion he fears becoming if Florence, rather than he, is the family breadwinner. Gordon, the poor relation of a wealthy family and temporary skivvy for the "impossible" club president ("What a way to make a living!"), is appalled by such a prospect. "Do I look like a ghost?" he demands indignantly. And, indeed, the film posits masculine subordination as potentially lethal. Florence's father, who has accepted the secondary status that Gordon refuses, becomes sicker and sicker during his family's absences, until he lies in hospital listening to his exhausted daughter struggling to retain her national championship. As the radio announcer comments "The champion is fighting for her life," and Fletcher declares to Milly, "She's fading fast," a cut to the hospital matches the father with Florence much as the film's earlier sequence identified her with her mother. But it is Milly herself who is the film's ultimate ghost, and its most vivid figure of prostitution.

The equation of the mother with the prostitute is the theme of Freud's study of the compulsive attraction to women of ill repute. There he attributes this apparently bewildering passion to the Oedipal child's discovery of parental intercourse, and his (sic) jealous realization "that the difference between his mother and a whore is not after all so very great, since basically

FIGURE 3.1. *Hard, Fast and Beautiful:* Florence (Sally Forrest, left) accuses her mother Milly (Claire Trevor) of playing "it dirty for money." BFI Films: Stills, Posters and Designs.

they do the same thing."[31] This apprehension of maternal infidelity comes late to Florence Farley, for whom Fletcher and Milly form a far more sexual, and more secretive, couple than her parents. The high point of their conspiratorial romance occurs in the scene discussed earlier, when Fletcher regales a raptly attentive Milly with the aphrodisiac prospects of Florence's European earnings—a scene whose erotic tenor is signaled at its opening by his intimate foray into Milly's handbag in search of a lighter, and at its closing by his oleaginous compliment on her appearance.

Fletcher's wooing of Milly to ensure Florence's agreement to the tour underlies the convergence of economics and erotics in this film, a convergence that does not exclude its primary couple. At their climactic confrontation, Florence returns drunk to her London hotel suite at 4 A.M. and accuses her mother of deliberately separating her from Gordon in order to play "it dirty for money" (figure 3.1). As Milly anxiously attempts to calm her daughter and help her undress for bed, Florence decries her situation in terms that further sexualize both her exploitation and the filial bond that facilitated it: "Then I'll finish the tour. I'll play the game the way you play it, for money.

You've made our bed—now we'll both lie in it." Here the circuit of erotics, economics, and athletics is closed, for to be "on the game," in the venerable English usage with which the London-born Lupino could not have been unfamiliar, is to be a prostitute.[32]

If the mother's breast is, in Freud's evocation, "the place where love and hunger meet,"[33] the prostitute has been described as the point where "sexuality and exchange value coincide."[34] To Walter Benjamin, the prostitute represented the way in which "[T]he commodity attempts to look itself in the face. It celebrates its becoming human in the whore."[35] The cinema has had its share in this personification, from *Pandora's Box* (1929) to *Pretty Woman* (1990). However, as Mary Ann Doane has observed, the figure of the prostitute is far more common in art and literature than on film. Neither censorship nor notoriety wholly explains this scarcity, since the movie tart is almost invariably endowed with a heart. Yet, ironically, this rehabilitation of the prostitute may correspond with her obsolescence as a character. For *the* task of the cinema, in Doane's view, is to effect what she represents:

The humanization of the commodity. Perhaps this is why her literal representation in the cinema is unnecessary as such and the fascination with the figure of the prostitute declines in the twentieth century (in comparison with the obsessions of the nineteenth). The process of characterization now endows the commodity with speech, with emotions, with a moral psychology which strives to give the lie to both alienation and commodification.[36]

What is striking about *Hard, Fast and Beautiful* is its resistance to this project. Far from rendering commodification in any way congenial, it stresses its depredation of American family life. Intimacy is invaded, play is proletarianized, and the female body bartered twice over—in athletic competition and sexual spectacle. Worse still, the prostitute returns, not as a golden-hearted heroine, but as a *mother*. The fact that she sells not her own services but those of her daughter underlines the parasitism of an already vicarious enterprise, while the sexuality that she deploys to do so makes her both adulterous and incestuous.

That all this happens in the unlikely setting of a sport story only serves to emphasize the pervasiveness of exchange relations in this film. As its ending suggests, there is no other place to go. ("You can't fly home again, Milly," Will declares from his sickbed, calling to mind the domestic conflagration that greets the errant ladybird in the rhyme.) Florence disappears into an unrepresentable marriage with Gordon. Will sickens (and, in some critics' extrapolations,[37] dies). Fletcher pursues a new protégée. And Milly sits motionless in the dark stadium, arms folded iconically across her breast, her white garments and fair hair lit with a ghostly pallor.

Ironically, the film's intransigent (*hard and fast*) condemnation of commercial culture precludes the feminist endings that have been desired for it. Florence will no more be allowed "career and marriage," in Dozoretz's wish, than Milly will be permitted to finish her narration. In the first instance, the film's denunciation of exchange relations militates against the representation of emancipatory employment as effectively as it does that of domestic bliss. (When Florence and Milly finally return to Will, it is to a hospital, not to their home.) In the second instance, the termination of Milly's voice-over halfway through the film can itself be attributed to the commodification of culture.

The narration that the film, as a women's picture, conventionally offers the mother (unlike Tunis's novel) and equally conventionally rescinds before the end (like *Mildred Pierce*), is not assigned to Will or Gordon. The first may sum up Milly's moral failings from his hospital bed ("You never gave love . . ."); the second may speak for Florence at her final press conference ("That's enough. Let's go home"). However, the narrative functions that Milly initially performs are assumed by the radio commentator who broadcasts Florence's matches. As the film's action shifts from the domestic sphere to a series of national tournaments, it is he (in an on-camera role for an actual sportscaster of the period, Arthur Little, Jr.) who establishes time and place, recounts many of the film's most dramatic moments, and ultimately calls the score. In a move that appropriates Milly's story, while obliterating her enunciation, the mother's voice is literally *mediated*.

The formal advantages of this device are obvious. Writing the match commentator into the diegesis is an easy way to tell a sports story, and also to transform existing tournament footage intercut with shots of Forrest into some semblance of actual competition. But the move from the maternal to the media also consigns this story to the world of commercial spectacle—the stadium strewn with discarded programs and newspapers that Milly, in a fate redolent of Dante, cannot leave.[38] There she sits, no longer a housewife, but no career woman either. Unable to return to a private life despoiled by commercial imperatives, but stranded in the public arena, Milly is the casualty of her era—one that both incited and proscribed maternal ambition, and then turned the consequences of that conflict into its own statuesque (and manifestly commercial) spectacle, the sorrowful mother of melodrama, *hard, fast and beautiful.*

4   The Queer Spirit of the Age

When do people begin to speak of a "spirit of the age"? Writing in 1831, John Stuart Mill maintains that the expression is no more than "fifty years in antiquity. The idea of comparing one's own age with former ages, or with our notion of those which are yet to come, had occurred to philosophers; but it never before was itself the dominant idea of any age."[1] As Reinhart Koselleck was to argue 150 years later, "[the] triad of Antiquity, Middle Ages and Modernity have only fully come into use . . . since the second half of the seventeenth century. Since then, one has lived in Modernity and been conscious of so doing."[2] With this consciousness of time comes the anticipation of futurity, and an "exultation" (Mill's word) in progress. So much so, insists Koselleck, that temporality in the eighteenth century accelerates, robbing "the present of the possibility of being experienced as the present"[3] to escape endlessly into the future. But if the Spirit of the Age that first claims to have such a spirit is, historiographically, *proleptic*, it is also, and in an importantly related way, *spiritual*. The German "geist der zeit" shares etymological connections with godhead ("der heiliger Geist," the Holy Ghost, Third person of the Trinity) and other phantoms and spirits,[4] including perhaps the most heavenly of all, alcoholic spirits. Thus, the Spirit of the Age is at once temporal and spectral.

This combination is clearly observable in William Duff's 1767 *Essay on Original Genius*, an English treatise on what its author describes as "the philosophical spirit of the times."[5] Poetic genius is Duff's interest, and his ghostly evocation of the work of the imagination (a precursor of better-known Romantic meditations on the subject) reminds us that the term "genius" encompasses both creative power and supernatural presence (witness the Romans' "Genius loci," or guardian spirit of the place). Arguing that the "truly Original" poet, "finding no objects in the visible creation sufficiently marvelous and new . . . naturally bursts into the ideal world, in quest of more surprising and wonderful scenes,"[6] Duff describes the author as spirit-raiser, calling

shadowy substances and unreal objects into existence. They are present to his view, and glide, like spectres, in silent, sullen majesty, before his astonished and intranced sight. In reading the description of such apparitions, we partake of the Author's emotion, the blood turns chill in our veins, and our hair stiffens with horror.[7]

The reader's tumescent reaction to these apparitions, like that described by Freud in his essay on the Medusa, suggests that specters can also be sexy.[8] The shadows summoned into existence by creative genius bespeak erotic possibilities hitherto unacknowledged. Among these is the eighteenth-century phantom whose proleptic relation to our own time has been brilliantly evoked in a study I very much admire and occasionally disagree with, Terry Castle's *The Apparitional Lesbian*.[9]

The lesbian, Castle argues, enters literature as a ghost. Eighteenth-century fiction registers the spectral appearance of the female couple, but the apparitional ontology of the pair (their "hauntology" in Derrida's pun)[10] enables the Enlightenment to consign lesbianism to a Gothic already disavowed by modernity. Invoking Freud's essay "On Negation," Castle concludes that this strategy permits the fictions of the period both to acknowledge and to deny the phenomenon of female homosexuality as "only" a phantom. But if the ghost is, in the French term, a "revenant," whose first appearance is already a return from the dead,[11] Castle's ghost differs from its counterparts in coming back from the future rather than the past. The specter of the Enlightenment is, in her account, an anticipation of her em- bodied sisters—the lesbians of today. The final chapter of *The Apparitional Lesbian* moves from phantom to flesh, from the eighteenth century to the twentieth, and from fictional characters to a real-life performer, mezzo so- prano Brigitte Fassbaender in the operatic role of Richard Strauss's *Der Rosenkavalier*.

Significantly, Castle's homage to Fassbaender's homoerotic rendition of the role moves altogether out of the realm of spectrality. In her avowed proj- ect of reincarnation "[t]he dead are indeed brought back to life." "Used imag- inatively—repossessed, so to speak—the very trope that evaporates can also solidify. In the strangest turn of all, perhaps, the lesbian body itself re- turns."[12] But this embodiment has its price. The staged ghostplay in the opera's final act, the device by which the hero frightens his rival and gets the girl, must necessarily disappear, and with it, a thematically crucial scene of sexual indeterminacy. This reply is about my refusal to give up those ghosts.

The homosexual haunting of heterosexuality (as the late-nineteenth- century term of exclusion necessary to confer legitimacy on those enclosed within the straight and narrow) was noted by many critics in the 1990s. Where Diana Fuss, like Terry Castle, laments the abjection of the homosex- ual implicit in its phantomization,[13] Teresa de Lauretis stresses the political productivity of the apparitional in her analysis of the 1987 film, *She Must Be Seeing Things*.[14] Among the fantastic sights suggested by the film's title is the central couple's butch-femme roleplay: "exciting," declares de Lauretis, "not because it represents heterosexual desire, but because it doesn't; that is to say, in mimicking it, it shows the uncanny distance, like an effect of ghosting, be- tween desire (heterosexually represented as it is) and the representation."[15]

The conflict represented by these varying views—between a desire for a recognized identity so often figured as embodiment and a desire to flout such identities by satirical mimicry or resignification—could be said to character-ize contemporary lesbian and gay politics. Where Leo Bersani argues, in his insistently titled *Homos*, that "resignification cannot destroy; it merely pres-ents to the dominant culture spectacles of politically impotent disrespect,"[16] others have taken the very temporality of the term "queer" as evidence to the contrary. It is now common for theorists to begin their books with a position on this question, albeit one that may attempt to appropriate the best of both worlds. Readers of the queer collection on Andy Warhol, *Pop-Out*, will see de-tailed accounts of the artist's homosexuality repeatedly juxtaposed with de-scriptions of how his work problematizes any such identity. Even more in-corrigibly, the anti-identitarian tenure of the work is frequently adduced as evidence of the opposite in life (you can tell Warhol is queer by how indif-ferent he is to such labels), a low trick to which my own contribution to the volume might plead guilty.[17]

For Castle, on the contrary, lesbian identity is as real as it is physical—"sensual," "fleshly," "carnal"—and therefore its retrieval from phantomiza-tion becomes a literal matter of life and death. The first beneficiary of this at-tempted rescue is the author herself. Her study opens on a self-portrait of the academic with writer's block, stuck in the ambitious account of eighteenth-century spectrality which ultimately became *The Female Thermometer*.[18] She suddenly finds herself drafting something very different—a memoir of a liv-ing lesbian, a striking butch called Ed, encountered in her California child-hood. "Scandalously energised" by "the growing realization that is was pos-sible to write about something other than vapor" (the very physical Ed, first met in a YWCA locker room), Castle sets aside her "big book" for something more personal.[19] And more polemical. *The Apparitional Lesbian* is prefaced with an unashamedly square rebuke to "younger lesbian and gay scholars trained in Continental philosophy (including a number of the so-called queer theorists)" who question "the very meaningfulness of terms such as *lesbian* or *gay* or *homosexual* or *coming out*."[20]

We know who she means. Indeed, it is one of the ironies of the milieu that Castle excoriates that those of us who would insist upon the unstable, ambiguous, indeed "phantasmatic" character of the signifier "lesbian" would be equally certain that she is referring to Judith Butler. And so, when we turn the page, it turns out to be—Butler at her most provocative, on the "non-self identical status of [the] 'I' or its 'being lesbian'":

What or who is it that is "out," made manifest and fully disclosed, when and if I reveal myself as a lesbian? . . . To claim that is what I am is to suggest a provisional totalization of this "I." . . . But if the I can so determine itself, then that which it excludes in order to make that determination remains constitutive of the determination itself.[21]

Castle disagrees. The irritating younger theorist brings to mind a (presumably still younger) graduate student, who pesters her in class with endless questions about the meaning of the term "lesbian":

Was a lesbian simply any woman who had sex with women? What then of the woman who had sex with women but denied that she was lesbian? What about women who had sex with women but also had sex with men? What about women who wanted to have sex with women but didn't? Or wanted to but couldn't? And so on and so on, to the bizarre hypothetical case of a physically handicapped married woman, unable to have sex with her husband (or anyone else), who considered herself heterosexual, yet unconsciously desired to have sex with women. Inevitably, I responded to such questions by saying I used the term in the "ordinary" or "dictionary" or "vernacular" sense. (A lesbian, according to Webster's Ninth, is a "woman characterized by a tendency to direct sexual desire toward another of the same sex.")[22]

I want to begin with that student—not just for her questions (which seem all too familiar these days) but for her youth, or at least her junior status in comparison to her teacher's. For the apparition is a matter of time, of two times in Derrida's account, then and now, past and present. ("It *begins by coming back.*")[23] And this dual temporality may have some bearing on sexual, as well as spectral, signification.

Castle's literary history of lesbian identity reverses the conventional order of biography. Her lesbian starts as an eighteenth-century ghost and ends up alive and singing, from the stage of the Munich Opera House, in a 1979 production of *Der Rosenkavalier*. Unlike Defoe's Mrs. Veal or Diderot's Mother Superior, unlike Anne Lister or Janet Flanner, the German singer Brigitte Fassbaender is neither fiction nor history. Instead, like the vividly remembered Ed, whose recollection frees the blocked author from her world of phantoms (and the scholarly closet), Fassbaender is "something other than vapor." (Given the butch style she shares with Ed, one wonders whether a certain masculinity, as well as the admitted love of pasta which ultimately led Fassbaender to abandon trouser roles, enhances this impression of solidity.) If, despite a career of intensely realized travesty roles and controversial recordings of traditionally male parts in German lieder, Fassbaender wasn't exactly out when Castle wrote her tribute, many of her fans were. And in admitting to be among the most devoted of these, Castle outs herself as that most embarrassing of lesbian lovers, a "diva-worshipper." *The Apparitional Lesbian* gives way to the embodied lesbian, doubly embodied in the persons of the author and the artist she admires for performing the love of women so passionately.

Does it matter that this is performance, that Fassbaender's enthusiasm for women is (as Castle is careful to point out) revealed onstage, indeed that Castle has never seen her perform "live," but only as an electronically produced simulacrum? Not, perhaps, to that younger theorist who regards matter as performative. Nor, I think, to Castle's student inquisitor, who might smugly observe that her teacher's definition of a lesbian is elastic enough after all to extend to an actress who plays love scenes to women with apparent enthusiasm, but whose personal sexual preference remained, until recently, unstated. But if this ambiguous figure seems an interesting choice with which to rematerialize the apparitional lesbian, the opera on which Castle concludes her study is even more so. Hugo von Hofmannstahl and Richard Strauss's *Der Rosenkavalier* is undoubtedly a lesbian cult classic, in which not two but three women sing their love for one another at its heart-rending finale, but it is also an extended observation on the instability of that passion, and of time and identity itself.

Set in a "half-imaginary, half real version of the Vienna of 1740,"[24] the 1911 opera opens after a night of love between Marie-Therese, the Field Marshal's wife, or Marschallin, and her young cousin, Count Octavian. Their morning after is disturbed by an unexpected arrival, and, fearing the return of the Field Marshal, Octavian disappears to disguise himself as a chambermaid. The visitor is revealed to be the Baron Ochs, a rustic relation of the Marschallin, who seeks her support for a financially advantageous match with Sophie von Faninal, daughter of a newly ennobled, and very wealthy, bourgeois. While the lecherous Baron interrupts his appeal to pursue her striking young maid around the room, the amused Marschallin nominates Octavian as the bearer of the customary silver rose of betrothal. Only later, as she reflects on the unseemly union of the middle-aged Baron and his young bride, does the Marschallin come to realize that her own lover will some day forsake her.

In Act II, Octavian presents the silver rose to Sophie and they immediately fall in love. Enraged by Ochs's oafish condescension to the Faninals, Octavian challenges the fortune-hunter to a duel, which is quickly averted by Sophie's father, furious at this threat to his ambition for social elevation. In the subsequent plot to deliver Sophie from her disastrous engagement, Octavian invites the Baron to an evening's rendezvous, signing the invitation as the Marschallin's maid, Mariandel. The third act sees Octavian attend the assignation in disguise and eventually expose Ochs's philandering to Sophie's father. When the Marschallin is summoned to vouch for her disgraced relation, she sees that Octavian and Sophie are in love and gracefully gives way. At the opera's end, the Baron has been dismissed and the two lovers are united in a final duet.

The anachronisms in *Der Rosenkavalier* are deliberate and thematic. The establishment of the bourgeoisie is backdated to the opera's ostensible setting in the mid-eighteenth century, while the score includes references to the later classicism of Mozart, nineteenth-century waltzes and modernist discords, "to give the music, like the drama, a sense of the layering of history."[25] Baroque and Beardsleyesque, the work was designed by a founding member of the Vienna Secession, Alfred Roller, who inflected its rococo sets with a Jugendstil sensibility. Moreover, the telescoping of time is a central theme in the opera, most famously in the Marschallin's moving soliloquy as she gazes into her mirror and contemplates the fate of Sophie at the end of Act I:

> *I too can recall a young girl,*
> *who was ordered, fresh from the convent, into holy wedlock.*
> *Where is she now? Yes, look for the snows of yesteryear!*
> *I say that lightly,*
> *But how can it really be,*
> *that I was once little Resi*
> *and that one day I shall be an old woman?*[26]

And when Octavian comes to say good-bye, she warns the youth of "the frailty of everything earthly" in the face of time:

> *At times I hear it flowing—inexorably.*
> *At times I get up in the middle of the night*
> *and stop all the clocks, all of them.*

The passage of time preoccupied Der Rosenkavalier's librettist, Hugo von Hofmannsthal, throughout his writing, from his *Tercets on Transcience*, published at the age of twenty ("my Self held back by nothing/ Stole across to me from a young child")[27] to his libretto for Strauss's *Elektra* eight years before *Der Rosenkavalier*:

> *Where has it all gone to, where?*
> *It is not water that runs away,*
> *It is not a thread, that runs and runs*
> *from the spool, it is I, I!*[28]

In each instance, age renders the subject a stranger to herself: no more recognizable than a "silent dog" the *Tercets* lament, while the Marschallin wonders how the convent girl can become an old woman and still be "the same person"? And if identity threatens to fracture under the weight of time, it is also imperiled by passion. *Der Rosenkavalier* begins with Octavian marveling to his mistress in phrases that will seem strangely familiar to readers of queer theory:

> *You, you—what does it mean, this "you"?*
> *This "you" and "I"? Do they have any meaning?*
> *They are words, mere words are they not?*
> *Say so! . . . this "I" is lost in this "you" . . .*
> *I am your boy, but when sight and hearing*
> *forsake me—Where is your boy then?*

Where indeed, since the singer of this extraordinary knowing passage is a woman, cast in pastiche of Mozart's Cherubino, another boy played by a soprano who must, in the course of the story, disguise himself as a girl. In writing "a role for a young and graceful girl dressed up as a man,"[29] Hofmannsthal could plead the sanction of convention (albeit a very dated convention) as well as the prestige of his eighteenth-century predecessors, Mozart's librettist Da Ponte and the French playwright who created the original Cherubino, Beaumarchais. And so most critics continue to do. (The Lacanian scholar Michel Poizat has recently offered an ingenious psychoanalytic reading of the sexual indeterminacy of the high voice, connoting juvenile masculinity, mature femininity and an ethereal mediation "between the human and the divine, the angel.")[30] But at the same time we find critics complaining, of one of the most popular works in the repertory:

> *It seems distasteful that Hofmannsthal should have cast so sexually virile a figure in a female role, particularly in the opening scene which demands overt demonstration of the most passionate love—it is seldom that the two actresses involved manage to avoid suggesting a repellent sort of lesbianism as they hug and caress one another, crooning torrid endearments.*[31]

Does this settle the ontological question? Is the lesbian phantom finally made flesh? It seems likely that Hofmannsthal, an extensive reader of Freud whose library included *The Interpretation of Dreams, Totem and*

Taboo, The Psychopathology of Everyday Life, and—most importantly for this opera—the *Three Essays on the Theory of Sexuality*,[32] was aware of the implications of what he called his "psychological comedy." As for his audience, they were already familiar with the Eulenberg scandal of 1907, in which the German press was filled with accusations of homosexuality in the nation's military, diplomatic corps, and nobility—including Eulenberg himself, a princely favorite of the Kaiser famous for composing a suite of "Rosenlieder." So widespread was this scandal that it provoked complaints in the Reichstag about the "many hundreds and thousands of people who earlier hadn't the foggiest notion of the things now being discussed in public [who] will, after having been enlightened about these things, be tempted to try them out with their own bodies."[33] In a similar vein, one critic of the period was moved to condemn both Strauss's hugely successful opera and the erotic perspective of the young Viennese.

But if *Der Rosenkavalier* could be said to bring female homosexuality "into focus" (to borrow Castle's phrase), that recognition nevertheless depends, however paradoxically, on ambiguity. There is no lesbian character here as such, but a young man played by a woman, a role whose sexual ambiguity is deliberately underlined by having the character disguise himself as a woman. And when Octavian becomes "Mariandel," the ghost arrives in the twentieth century. In the opera's final act, the hero sets out to destroy the reputation of Baron Ochs, his brutish rival for the hand of Sophie, by inviting him to an assignation in a local inn. There, resuming his disguise as the Marschallin's chambermaid, he entertains the duplicitous suitor, while secretly contriving to reveal his character to Sophie's father. To do so, Octavian fills the inn with a troupe of ghostly figures enacted by hired confederates. When the Baron remarks on Mariandel's uncanny resemblance to our hero ("That face! Accursed boy! Haunts me waking and sleeping!") the first of these specters rises, literalizing the apparitional identity of the serving girl. As the terrified Ochs points to the spot where the ghost has loomed and vanished, Mariandel insists that "There's nothing there." "There's nothing?" the

Baron asks, and running his hand over his/her face, repeats "And nothing there either?"

Eventually Ochs steadies himself for another pass at Mariandel, but when their eyes meet he is again startled by her resemblance to his rival. At a signal from Octavian, the room fills with apparitions, and in the ensuing uproar, the confounded Baron is finally exposed and forced to withdraw from his engagement to Sophie. With performances as enthusiastic as Fassbaender's, the young couple's final union can be read as a triumphant assertion of lesbian love, but this is not achieved at the expense of spirit. The ersatz specters, and Ochs's belief in them, can be identified with the superstitions of a doomed aristocracy about to be succeeded by the rising bourgeoisie, but they are also representative of the sexual ambiguity that haunts this work.

As the scene indicates, the uncertain gender of Ochs's object of desire is directly related to the uncertain ontology of the ghost (indeed, a *simulated* ghost, an apparition of an apparition): something/nothing, flesh/phantasy. Perhaps the most obnoxious collation of these multiple ambiguities occurs in the turn-of the-century epithet "fairy," combining as it does the notion of male homosexual inversion, effeminacy, with the disdainful accusation of diminution and disembodiment ("flitty," "airy fairy," "a bit light on his feet").[34] Similarly, but characteristically more positively in female to male cross-dressing, Octavian's sexual identity is also represented as ontologically ambiguous, "angelic" in its indeterminacy. Dressed to present the ornamental rose in a silver suit of lights, this figure modeled on Mozart's cherubic page is immediately compared to an angel by Sophie's duenna. And in a pose reminiscent of Gabriel at the Annunciation,[35] the angelic emissary proffers a floral ensign—itself both phallic bough and feminine bloom—to the future bride.

Noble knight, female vocalist, angelic messenger: Octavian's triadic identity retraces the triangles that structure this opera's sexual contretemps: the Marschallin, her husband, and Octavian; Ochs, Sophie, and Mariandel;

Octavian, Sophie and the Marschallin; Mariandel, Octavian, and the woman who plays both. The refusal of the binary—of one sex, one status, or the other—is given form in the figure of the silver rose. A hybrid flower if ever there was one, its precious petals are compared by its recipient to "roses of holy paradise." "It's like a greeting from Heaven," Sophie sings. "There's Time and Eternity in this moment of bliss." Listening to her ecstatic exclamations, Wayne Koestenbaum has observed that Sophie's instant infatuation with another woman (male though she is in character) undoes the reality of time "to create pockets—momentary, unending—of sacred or divine duration": "Disturb gender, and you disturb temporality; accept the androgyne, and you accept the abyss."[36] Tracing this "torquing" of time to the canonical figures of modernism, he cites Marcel Proust, Albert Einstein, Henri Bergson (who comments on the theory of relativity in the second edition of his *Duration and Simultaneity*), and, most centrally, Sigmund Freud.

Sexuality, Freud argues, develops in two temporalities. Our social initiation, the ordinary erotogenic exchanges between children and their carers, inevitably occurs too early, while organic maturation happens too late. The result is trauma, but a trauma that is experienced retrospectively, when the pubescent subject finally has the affective means to make sense of infantile arousal. The sense of *déjà vu* that accompanies Sophie and Octavian's first encounter expresses something of this dual temporality—but in the register of erotic ecstasy rather than pain: "Where and when have I been so happy? I must return there, yes, even if I should die on the way." (Note, however, that even here the shadow of death, the depredation of time that so troubles Sophie's predecessor, darkens the present moment, which both lovers promise to remember "till I die.")

In Freud's account of *nachträglichkeit*, or "deferred action," the adolescent, newly aroused by some sexual stimulus, reacts with an intensity provoked by an unconscious memory of an unassimilated excitation in the past. As that past obtrudes into the present and the present into the past, the disturbing stimulus suddenly registers as trauma. In *Der Rosenkavalier*, temporality is even more convoluted. The young lovers identify their "moment of bliss" with some prior state of *jouissance*, to which Sophie vows to return in the future. Temporalization—past, present, future—is momentarily absorbed into timelessness, into Eternity's silver rose. Yet this message from heaven is also a message *of* heaven, of the end of bodily life that Sophie—in that ambiguous act of negation which Castle observes in lesbian ghost stories—both denies and declares: "I must return there, yes, even if I should die on the way. But I shall not die. That is far away." For this young lover, as for the older one who preceded her, death is on the horizon, and with it the ghost.

How can we reconcile this specter, anticipation of the body's end, with Castle's phantom, precursor of the embodied lesbian to come? One key point of convergence, as Act III so vividly represents, is the related indeterminacy of Mariandel's gender and the ghosts that finally unnerve Ochs. The spectral harbingers of the Baron's failure—to marry the heiress and revive his class's declining fortunes—are also the apparitions of his own exuberant eroticism, the polymorphous lusts he proudly proclaims to the Marschallin and her maid in Act I:

> *Would I were as old Jupiter with a thousand forms!*
> *I'd have a use for every one!*
>
>   . . .
>
> *I'd have a use for a thousand different shapes,*
> *to embrace a thousand girls.*
> *None would be too young, too sour,*
> *none too humble, none too rude!*
> *I'd be ashamed of nothing.*
> *If I see something I like, I must have it.*

But as the Marschallin reminds the Baron, the price of such multifarious passions is the dissolution of identity, the successive metamorphoses of the divine seducer:

> *What, even for the bull? Would you be so crude?*
> *Or would you rather play the clouds and come*

whispering along
as a whiff of damp air?

As the true homosexual of this drama, the one character who, however unwittingly, pursues another of the same sex, the bovine Baron himself becomes nothing other than vapor. Homoeroticism, this opera endlessly suggests, confounds coherent identity, unambiguous embodiment. And thus it serves to illustrate all eroticism, the pervasive threat that passion poses to any subject's sense of self and temporality. In this very contemporary sense, *Der Rosenkavalier* must be described as a queer work.

"Repossessed," Terry Castle argues, "the very trope that evaporates can also solidify." Her own account of the historical transformation of the apparitional lesbian testifies to the continual metamorphosis of sexual identities, a phenomenon that *Der Rosenkavalier* takes as a theme. For all the solidity of its silver rose—ecstasy eternalized—the spirit of this work is one of constant volatility. The rapid rise of the Faninals marks the accelerated accession of the bourgeois epoch, and with it the vaporization of all that is solid, "all fixed, fast-frozen relations,"[37] including those of love. At the opera's finale, when the young lovers are united at last, Sophie sings to Octavian:

It is a dream, cannot be really true
that we two are together,
together for all time
and for eternity!

Then, even as the couple conclude their duet with the words "I feel only you alone!" and fall into a final embrace, the brevity of passion is signaled one last time, as Sophie's handkerchief slips unnoticed from her grasp onto the stage.

"The history of the ghost," Derrida writes, can be read two ways, as a "history of the becoming-true of a fable" or "the reverse, a fabulation of truth, in any case a history of ghosts."[38] My argument here is that Castle's history of the becoming-true of the apparitional lesbian since the eighteenth century must also account for its fabulous resignifications in her own. Like the reconfigured conventions of eighteenth-century opera, spectrality survived into the twentieth century precisely to signify those states of being that are at once liminal *and* legible. Given the proliferation of these at the fag end of the century—which witnessed the rise of such chimerical figures as the drag king and the virtual lesbian, as well as the countless gliding specters of the graduate student imaginary—it seems unlikely that sexual identities will settle down, solidify, any time soon. Indeed, such might be a fate worse than death, the veritable petrification of the subject and its desires. In any case, not a history of ghosts.

FLESH

5 MacKinnon's Dog

Antiporn's Canine Conditioning

Is not the eternal sorrow of life the fact that in most cases human beings do not understand each other and cannot enter the inner state of the other?

—IVAN PAVLOV

Treat your man like a dog!
Reward him for good behavior and he'll come when you whistle.

—*Cosmopolitan*

The following remarks deal with dogs, men, and the continuing debate on pornography. In declaring their relevance to women's lives, I am mindful of Tania Modleski's skepticism about the move in the late 1980s from women's studies to a "gender criticism" also engaged by considerations of masculinity: "What's in these new developments *for feminism* and for women?"[1] If (as would seem irrefutable) the central issue in the feminist debate on pornography is how that medium affects women, why bother about men?

My reply begins with the latest antipornography tract by the celebrated feminist legal theorist Catharine MacKinnon. In the ironically titled *Only Words*, she argues that pornography is not speech but sex, not "an 'idea' worthy of First Amendment protection" but a stimulus to male masturbation employing representations of female subordination: "The women are in two dimensions, but the men have sex with them in their own three-dimensional bodies, not in their minds alone. Men come doing this." The pleasures of these autoerotic practices, MacKinnon argues, compel men to subsequent misogynist acts—whether rape, murder, harassment, or simple sexism.

"Sooner or later, in one way or another, the consumers want to live out the pornography further in three dimensions. Sooner or later, in one way or another, they do. *It* makes them want to; when they believe they can, when they feel they can get away with it, *they* do."[2]

As I prepared this article for its original publication in 1996, *Only Words* was greeted in Britain with the extensive publicity refused opposing feminist views. In part, this may be attributed to the British fascination with a "feminism" understood more than ever as the polemical excesses of eccentric colonials, whatever their actual politics (Greer, Hite, Dworkin, Wolf, Paglia, and now MacKinnon). In part, it may reflect the book's apparent compatibility with the then Conservative government's increasing regulation of representation—as if to compensate for its deregulation of virtually everything else (wage minima, rail systems, banking practices, you name it).

This process reached its nadir when the murder of a Liverpool toddler by two ten-year-old boys, children of impoverished and violent families, resulted in an amendment to the Criminal Justice Bill further restricting the distribution of films on videotape. (This in a country where *The Exorcist* was banned on video until 1999 and where the photographic representation of sexual intercourse had by that date only become legal under severe restrictions.) The attempts to win feminist support for such measures, attempts that have been successful in many quarters, make the analysis of MacKinnon's assertion that certain forms of representation are central to women's oppression all the more urgent.

If the clamor over *Only Words* yielded any benefits in Britain, it was to take such analyses beyond the meeting hall and the classroom and into the usually unreflective realms of the press. There, quite predictably, reviewers complained about the book's "breathtaking" and "lurid" rhetoric.[3] Typically, these observations were then set aside (rhetoric being seen as an unworthy, and certainly un-British, form of demagoguery) in favor of whatever was discerned to be MacKinnon's "central argument."[4] Here the reviewers may have been too hasty. Elsewhere other commentators (notably the American literary critic Stanley Fish and the political theorist Wendy Brown) have made

MacKinnon's "supremely rhetorical" strategy the object of their inquiries, bearing down on "the logical and narrative structures of her prose" to analyze its potency as well as its political problems.[5] Encouraged by their example, I want to examine a recurring rhetorical figure in MacKinnon's writing on pornography, one that imbricates masculinity with bestiality in the discourses of behavioral psychology.

To begin, then, with a definition of pornography by Catharine MacKinnon. "Pornography," she has written, "works as a behavioral conditioner, reinforcer and stimulus, not as ideas or advocacy. It is more like saying 'kill' to a trained guard dog—and also like the training process itself."[6] The figure of the dog occurs frequently in MacKinnon's arguments, appearing whenever the subject turns to legal distinctions between words and deeds: "First Amendment logic, like nearly all legal reasoning, has difficulty grasping harm that is not linearly caused in the 'John hit Mary' sense. The idea is that words or pictures can be harmful only if they produce harm in a form that is considered an action. Words work in the province of attitudes, actions in the realm of behavior. . . . But which is saying 'kill' to a trained guard dog, a word or an act? Which is its training?"[7]

That passage is from a speech collected in MacKinnon's 1987 *Feminism Unmodified*. Two years later, it was reprised virtually verbatim in *Toward a Feminist Theory of the State*.[8] And most recently, in *Only Words*, the published collection of MacKinnon's 1992 Gauss Lectures at Princeton, it is reworked under the heading of "a theory of protected speech":

Social life is full of words that are legally treated as the acts they constitute without so much as a whimper from the First Amendment. What becomes interesting is when the First Amendment frame is invoked and when it is not. Saying "kill" to a trained attack dog is only words. Yet it is not seen as expressing the viewpoint "I want you dead"—which it usually does, in fact, express. It is seen as performing an act tantamount to someone's destruction, like saying, "ready, aim, fire" to a firing squad.[9]

MacKinnon's argument is part of a much-debated campaign to divest pornography of any legal protection as speech or expression. Her close collaborator, the writer Andrea Dworkin, has maintained that pornography not only *represents* sexual violence against women, it actually *is* that violence. The equation is not only one of words with deeds, but of resemblance with identity. As Dworkin argued in her 1979 polemic, *Pornography: Men Possessing Women*, "The valuation of women's sexuality in pornography is objective and real because women are so regarded and so valued. The force depicted in pornography is objective and real because force is so used against women."[10] Thus, if porn is real and so is the low status of women, and if the former depicts or narrates the latter, they therefore participate in the same, single reality, in which the relationship of image and act is not solely one of correspondence, or even causality. Instead, this "synecdochal"[11] logic awards pornography a significant (often commanding) share in the ontology of gender itself. MacKinnon puts it more eloquently: "Gender is sexual. Pornography constitutes the meaning of that sexuality. Men treat women as who they see women as being. Pornography constructs who that is."[12]

In offering these definitions, Dworkin and MacKinnon refuse the distinction between representation and action that animates much of the juridical discussion of permissible and impermissible expression under the First Amendment: "Congress shall make no law . . . abridging the freedom of speech, or of the press." Until the 1960s, this amendment was interpreted to protect only the "expression of ideas" in the narrowest sense. But with the dissenting movements of the 1960s came the modern doctrine of speech and its enlarged protection for unpopular, offensive, or sexually explicit expression, unless such expression is deemed to incite immediate lawlessness (racist speech is only proscribed when it is judged to cause imminent and significant harm); to offend community standards (the broader test for obscenity); or to be harmful in ways recognized elsewhere in the law—blackmail, bribery, libel with "actual malice," conspiracy to commit crimes, discriminatory housing ads, yelling "fire" in the proverbial crowded theater. One of the most significant additions to this list of exemptions was formulated in the early 1980s, when workplace remarks to female employees such as "Did you get any over the weekend?" or epithets such as "cunt" or "tits" was ruled sexual harassment in a number of U.S. courts.[13]

It was the judicial success in this arena—the establishment of sexual harassment (including verbal harassment) in the workplace as discrimination in employment—that led MacKinnon and Dworkin to their next legal move, the 1983 attempt to classify pornography as sex discrimination under the civil rights ordinances of the city of Minneapolis, Minnesota. "Pornography," the new ordinance read, "is central in creating and maintaining the civil inequality of the sexes." It went on to describe it as a "systematic practice of exploitation and subordination based on sex which differentially harms women," promoting "bigotry and contempt," fostering "aggression," and thereby reducing women's equality of rights to employment, education, public services, and the "full exercise of citizenship" itself.[14]

The upshot of this initiative was several years of judicial battles between the Minneapolis city council, which had passed it, and the city's mayor and civil rights officers, who opposed it; between the mayor of Indianapolis, Indiana, who passed a subsequent version, and the American Booksellers Association, which took the mayor to court; between antifeminist Christians who supported the initiative and antifeminist porn publishers who did not. Finally, the initiative divided feminists themselves, with a large group of writers, academics, and campaigners (ranging from Kate Millett and Adrienne Rich to Ann Snitow and Carol Vance) signing a Feminists Against Censorship Taskforce (FACT) brief opposing the ordinance's use of legally ambiguous terms like "degrading" and "objectification"; its neglect of other possible factors in women's subordination; and its apparent distinction between asexual women and sexually predatory men. In reply to the argument of the city of Indianapolis that pornography conditions the male orgasm to female subordination, making such subordination a stimulus to a "natural physiological response" and thus leaving "no more room for further debate than does shouting 'kill' at an attack dog," the FACT brief declared: "Men are not attack dogs, but morally responsible human beings. The ordinance reinforces a destructive sexist stereotype of men as irresponsible beasts."[15]

There have been several juridical consequences of this canine controversy thus far: The U.S. Supreme Court upheld a Federal Court judgment against the Indianapolis ordinance by refusing to hear the city's appeal (1986); the Canadian Supreme Court found for MacKinnon's argument in the landmark decision *Regina v. Butler* (1992); a British bill (which failed in 1989 and again in 1990) employed the ordinance's definition of pornography in order to restrict the sale of soft-core publications like *Playboy*; and Senate Bill 1521, better known as the "Bundy Bill" (which failed in 1992) would have made producers and distributors of "obscene material" liable for damages resulting from sexual offenses "foreseeably caused" by exposure to their wares. Although most of these initiatives have not been successful, their recurrence, as well as MacKinnon's newfound celebrity in the aftermath of Anita Hill's allegations against Clarence Thomas (allegations that notoriously included his workplace discussions of pornography), suggest that the "porn wars" are not over. To determine why, I suggest we turn from the regulation of pornography to a problematic that both antedates and animates it—the question of men and dogs.

My first observation is prompted by the FACT brief's ironic resort to the term "reinforces" in its critique of MacKinnon's use of conditioning theory. The discourses of behaviorism inform the terms of this debate, and feminist common sense in general, far more than we care to admit. And if FACT appropriated the very conditioning model it sought to challenge, this is not the only instance of the double talk, or ambivalence, or even disavowal, in which the pornography debate, and certainly its canine tropology, has been articulated. Indeed, behaviorism itself, as conceived by Ivan Pavlov and John Watson, is only one attempt to resolve the old dualities of human and animal, culture and nature, choice and compulsion, which find new expression in MacKinnon's dog. That dog descends from what Mark Seltzer has described as "the double discourse" that "insists at once on the artificial and on the natural character of the individual."[16] Following his influential reconfiguration of such apparent antitheses in his study of naturalist literature, *Bodies and Machines*, I'll begin with no less an authority on the canine condition than Seltzer's expert (and Pavlov's contemporary), Jack London.

London's Klondike tales are dog stories—stories whose central characters are not the prospectors of the Gold Rush or the MacKenzie River Indians, but Buck, White Fang, Brown Wolf, and Spot. The transpositions that turn sled dogs into psychologically elaborated protagonists and their drivers into mere "specks and motes"[17] in the Arctic wastes are part of a series of exchanges (between civilization and the wild, master and slave, California and Canada) in which men become bestialized, animals humanized, and everybody—as Seltzer points out—wears fur. In arguing that the violent pursuit of riches in the wilderness makes men no better (and quite possibly worse) than beasts, London could count on established connotations for the word "dog," which had long carried the meaning of a low or contemptible person. It also meant "male," both in canine terms (where "dog" is opposed to "bitch") and in human (where it is directed at men in sexual reproach or congratulation—"You dog, you").

And except for the odd mate or mother, London's dogs are a conspicuously male cast, matching the bachelor company of their frontier masters. If the latter should conventionally command the former, this opposition is also reorganized, with each species revealed as both compelling and compelled. The canine version of this double positioning is most simply rendered as "dog eat dog," a frequent occurrence in London's stories and a useful figure for his allegories of social Darwinism. Meanwhile, the masters are themselves mastered by greed, by their rivals for riches, and by "the great blind elements and forces."[18] But if the lesson is that humans, like animals, dwell in a state of nature where only the strong survive, the nature of that nature remains uncertain (or, in Seltzer's description, "unnatural").[19] The very anthropomorphism that makes London's dogs into heroes undoes the bestial metaphor. What are men who are like dogs *like*, if dogs are like men?

In 1904, the year after London published *The Call of the Wild*, the Russian physiologist Ivan Pavlov was awarded the Nobel Prize for his work on digestion—specifically, the discovery that the secretion of digestive fluids is controlled by the nervous system. To observe such functions Pavlov used dogs—because they could be trained to lie still or stand in a harness for long periods of time, during which their gastric or salivary juices could be collected in surgically externalized pouches drained to the outside of the body. (Both the dog and digestion were merely convenient, if retrospectively striking, choices for neurological research: The longevity of the animals offered a way to do comparative studies of the same subject, while the secretions of digestion provided a medium for precise measurement—the volume of fluid produced in each procedure.)

In the course of this research, Pavlov discovered that the nervous system initiates the flow of gastric juices in reaction to the taste of food, not its arrival in the stomach. The name he gave this phenomenon—"psychic secretion"—was itself a challenge to the prevailing division between physiological and psychological inquiry. Among the conventions still governing psychological investigation was the principle that research on animal behavior should be aimed at an understanding of the subject's conscious processes. Thus, to proceed with the question of psychic secretion, Pavlov's team was divided between observational physiologists and a colleague who undertook to analyze the "internal world" of the dog, assuming that the animal's "thoughts, feelings and desires," as Pavlov later wrote, were "analogous to ours."[20] The eventual impossibility of reconciling this subjectivism with the experimental data of the laboratory led not only to the project's abandonment, but the breakup of the team itself. As Pavlov ruefully reflected, "Where is there even the slightest indisputable criterion that our conjectures are correct, that we can, for the sake of a better understanding of the matter, compare the inner state of even such a developed animal as the dog with our own? . . . And then, where is the knowledge, where is the power of knowledge that might enable us correctly to comprehend the state of another human being?"[21] In response, Pavlov discarded any pretensions to introspection for an objectivism that concentrated "on studying the correlation between the external phenomena and the reaction of the organism,"[22] effectively incorporating the psychical into his "physiology of the higher nervous activity."[23]

But of course Pavlov's research did not escape psychology (of which he is now deemed a founder) any more than it eluded anthropomorphism. (His dogs, mongrels raised outside the laboratory rather than bred for it, continued to be granted both names and "personalities," and variations in response among individual subjects were analyzed rather than aggregated. Moreover, Pavlov often diagnosed them with psychological disorders such as hysteria and catatonia.) One could say, however, that Pavlov "caninized" experimental psychology by directing its attention toward forms of behavior easily observed in dogs. Among these was the secretion of liquids.

After "psychic secretion" came the famous discovery that an autonomic or involuntary reflex (salivation at the taste of food) could be paired with a learned or "conditioned" one (salivation at the ringing of a bell). The result was a liquid measure of association, a quantifiable materialization of an ostensibly psychical process. "Here are facts," Pavlov declared, "which show that our psychical material may also be included in a definite scheme and that it is subject to certain laws."[24]

But if the dog's digestive system was the original medium for psychological positivism, it wasn't long before its other bodily functions were also investigated. Among Pavlov's researchers in the 1920s was an American, W. Horsley Gantt, who later became his translator and academic advocate. Gantt opens a 1949 paper with references to the giant woodcock of the Russian forests and the earthworm of the Baltimore suburbs. His interest is their sexual excitement and the way it inhibits other sensory functions, including those that would signal hunger or danger. The Russian woodcock is said to be tragically oblivious to the approach of hunters when it sings its "love song"; while the worms disport themselves all over the Baltimore golf course each spring without regard to predators or passing foursomes. After a catalog of heroic male mating attempts (prefaced by an unapologetic citation of the masculine bias in the first Kinsey report), Gantt moves on to his central subject, the dog.

The *male* dog, I should say, since Gantt's subjects included Fritz the Alsatian, Peter the beagle, a male poodle known as "V3," and especially the mongrel Nick, subject of "the most meticulous and complete case history of a single animal to be found in the conditioned reflex literature."[25] These animals and others like them were subjected to a barrage of procedures to study conflicts of the drives between, for example, experimentally induced anxiety states and sexual excitement. As Gantt had observed on the golf course, sexual arousal can inhibit or block other sensations. Nick, in particular, exhibited symptomatic erections and ejaculations whenever he encountered stimuli associated with previous situations of anxiety. Years after one such experiment, in which anxious reactions were elicited by requiring dogs to make a difficult distinction between two tones of similar pitch (a distinction that determined whether the dog was fed), Nick would develop a "prominent erection . . . within a few seconds after the onset of the tone," Gantt enthused. "We could always count on Nick for a demonstration."[26]

As for the inhibiting effects of female arousal, Gantt notes in passing that bitches—like female cats—will accept food even during copulation. "A hint for Dr. Kinsey," he writes, "when he extends his study to the female."[27] Gantt himself had no inhibitions about extending his study to humans: He insists that "it is entirely within our right to believe that in man the sexual function may often assume the same dominant role, both excitatory and inhibitory, as we can show experimentally it does in the earthworm, the bird, the cat and the dog."[28]

The ascending scale on which Gantt concludes his report beckons us one step farther up the food chain, to the British behaviorists H. J. Eysenck and P. K. Nias and their influential 1978 study *Sex, Violence, and the Media.* Here, with fulsome acknowledgment of the dog and the dinner bell, behavioral psychology moves to the human male, who proves remarkably like his canine predecessors. Not only does he sit still—on successive occasions—in an experimental apparatus described as a penis plethysmograph, but he exhibits an objectively measurable hydraulic reaction to certain stimuli, in this case films portraying "*fellatio, cunnilingus,* intercourse from behind, *soixante-*

neuf, etc."[29] As for his female counterpart, despite admitted evidence of "considerable overlap" in reported rates of male and female arousal, Eysenck and Nias are at great pains to remind the adherents of "women's lib" that "high libido" and an enthusiasm for "pornography, permissiveness and impersonal sex" are correlated with masculinity—a proposition they support by questioning the "typicality" of women who volunteer for such studies, as well as adducing every conceivable hypothesis (anatomical, hormonal, evolutionary) for what they call the "biological basis of maleness and femaleness."[30] Another influential team of porn researchers, Donnerstein, Linz, and Penrod, are equally unrepentant about the male bias in their studies (whose typical subjects are college students), arguing that the highest incidence of rape, and indeed of all forms of violent crime, occurs in males between eighteen and twenty years of age.[31] But it took a contributor to the famed Meese Report on pornography to admit that the advantage of male subjects is the "independent and objective" evidence offered by "penile measures of arousal."[32]

The insistence of this penile positivism did not go unremarked by Andrea Dworkin. In a 1985 essay wonderfully titled after Virginia Woolf's phrase in *A Room of One's Own*, "Against the Male Flood," she argues that obscenity law has historically treated the erection as a form of proof: "Empirically, *prurient* means *causes erection*." With the advent of a female judiciary and juries, however, both the test and the crime become obsolete: "In order for obscenity law to have retained social and legal coherence, it would have had to recognize as part of its standard women's sexual arousal, a more subjective standard than erection."[33]

But why should female arousal be deemed "a more subjective standard"? In a rare discussion of women's relation to pornography in *Toward a Feminist Theory of the State*, MacKinnon briefly reviews three such experiments. In all three, the female subjects reported less arousal than their physical reactions—notably vaginal lubrication—seemed to suggest. But where, in the case of men, the physical and psychical are read as indivisible, here they are detached. In a sudden rejection of the Pavlovian ontology she has so carelessly espoused, MacKinnon challenges the body's claim to truth: "It seems at least as likely," she writes, "that women disidentify with their bodies' conditioned responses." Where male tumescence and ejaculation proved the measure of an ideological effect, vaginal fluids are now described as "so-called objective indices of arousal." "Not to be overly behavioral," she continues, "but does anyone think Pavlov's dogs were really hungry every time they salivated at the sound of the bell?"[34]

Like MacKinnon, and despite her own protests to the contrary, Andrea Dworkin must also foreclose the question of women's sexual arousal to pursue her figure of a male flood. The legal strategy she proposes returns to the penis, whose erection and ejaculation become the index not simply of arousal (as in the obscenity test), but arousal by gender subordination. For, unlike obscenity, pornography is defined in this essay as "the conditioning of erection and orgasm in men to the powerlessness of women." It is also defined as "a woman being fucked by dogs, horses, snakes."[35] Here the canine saliva to which human sexual responses have been compared in the conditioning model is transformed into the fluids of orgasm—both human and animal—a lethal ejaculate that flows through this essay to become, in Dworkin's comments on Sade, an ocean. The pornographic writings and sexual crimes of the marquis are described as "waves on the same sea: that sea, becoming for its victims, however it reached them, a tidal wave of destruction."[36] (In her own comments on Dworkin's essay in *Only Words*, MacKinnon complains of "a society saturated with pornography, not to mention an academy saturated with deconstruction.")[37] As for bestiality, it is revealed to be pornography's primal scene ("a woman being fucked by dogs, horses, snakes")—the originary moment of a natural catastrophe ("a tidal wave") that liquidates both the proper relations of the sexes and the species. In what is paradoxically called the copycat effect, the dog in the pornographic scene (let's call him Dworkin's dog) transforms the spectator into another dog, MacKinnon's dog. Both the subject and the stimulus have been *caninized*.

Here the history of behaviorism offers us one final illustration. In an early attempt to extend Pavlov's principles to human behavior, the American psychologist John Watson also used a dog. This time, however, the animal was not the subject of the experiment but a potential stimulus. To demonstrate that phobias could be conditioned, Watson exposed a nine-month-old boy to a number of potentially frightening sights: rats, burning newspapers, and dogs. But the infant, "Albert B.," described as "just about the most famous child in the whole of psychology," exhibited no fear.[38] Watson then established that Albert *could* be scared, by the sound of a steel bar struck loudly with a hammer right behind his head. An experiment was devised in which a dog was brought to little Albert, and just as he began to reach for it, the steel bar was hit with the hammer. With three or four repetitions, Watson reported, "A new and important change is apparent. The animal now calls out the same response as the steel bar, namely a fear response." According to Watson, this result rendered the origins of animal phobias totally transparent, "without lugging in consciousness or any so-called mental process. A dog comes toward the child rapidly, jumps upon him, pushes him down and at the same time barks loudly. Oftentimes one such combined stimulation is all that is necessary to make the baby run away from the dog the moment it comes within his range of vision."[39]

In fact, this much-cited experiment in inducing phobia is one of the great fakes of scientific history. As the British psychologist Dennis Howitt relates, Watson never succeeded in conditioning the fear caused by the clang of metal to the sight of the dog. When he brought the two stimuli together, the loud banging made the dog bark, and the ensuing cacophony terrified the unfortunate infant (who was then sent home in a state, and as a likely model for the child tormented by his psychologist father in the 1960 film *Peeping Tom*).

What we find in the case of Albert B. is the other side of the canine coin that circulates in the behaviorist narrative—the dog who attacks. The docile subject of Pavlov's research becomes the phobic object of Watson's. And if pornography can accomplish this double metamorphosis, if it can turn men—if not into Circe's swine, then into MacKinnon's dogs—what does that make male sexuality? On the one hand, it becomes the experimental subject par excellence, a ready reflex that can be stimulated, trained, observed, and hydraulically measured. On the other hand, this creature of the laboratory may suddenly jump up, bark loudly, and wreck your experiment—unless your experiment was designed, like Watson's, to induce phobia in the first place. (This is not idle speculation in the case of Andrea Dworkin, who punctuates her study *Intercourse*—intercourse as male dominance—with the question "Are you afraid now?")[40]

But what should we fear most? The danger of a male sexuality trained in sexism or the danger of it wild? The unconditioned reflex or the conditioned one? Bred in the biomechanics of late-nineteenth-century thought, MacKinnon's dog collapses these oppositions to figure a bestial man most natural when most patriarchally cultured, most mechanically manipulable when most physically aroused. Despite both Dworkin and MacKinnon's reiterated description of male sexuality as a social, political (and thus potentially changeable) phenomenon, they simultaneously stress the unvarying domination on which it is said to be predicated. The effect is to represent male sexuality as dangerous by nurture *and* nature, because they've become the same thing.[41]

By 1916, Jack London's dog stories had made him a millionaire. In his reflections on the writer's relationship with his reader, the determinism that had crushed his characters "with the weight of unending vastness and unalterable decree" reemerged in his aesthetics.[42] In "Eight Great Factors of Literary Success," the best-selling author listed his ability "to select the symbols that would compel [the reader's] brain to realize my thoughts, or vision, or emotion."[43] Among the hazards of a certain anthropomorphism, we might list a strong theory of performativity. The allegorical dog seems to come with a master, someone or something that issues those unalterable decrees. In London's fiction this is not, as we first expect, man but "the marvelous power and influence of the environment."[44] In behavioral psychology, it is the efficacy of conditioning. In MacKinnon's writings, it is pornography.

In *Only Words* the author of the slogan "Porn is the image that acts" discovers speech act theory. Arguing that pornography is "constructing and performative rather than . . . merely referential or connotative," MacKinnon footnotes J. L. Austin's famous formula, "The issuing of the utterance is the performing of an action—it is not normally thought of as just saying something."[45] Such a theory requires at least an implicit utterance, and she reads one: "The message of these materials, and there is one, as there is to all conscious activity, is 'get her,' pointing at all women, to the perpetrators' benefit of ten billion dollars a year and counting."[46]

To get technical, as MacKinnon might say, such a command would not be, in Austin's terms, an *illocutionary* speech act but a *perlocution*—an utterance that *causes* an effect rather than one that *is* an effect.[47] The difference, to cite the philosopher's own examples, is between pronouncing the marriage vows (the illocution "I do") and successfully persuading somebody to fire a gun (the perlocution "shoot her"). (The resemblance of the second example to MacKinnon's firing squad analogy in *Only Words* is probably not coincidental.) This difference matters because, whatever the consequences, a command is not identical to its effect in the same way that a vow is. Giving a pledge is not the same as giving an order. Not even the most persuasive utterance can be rendered as—to paraphrase Austin— "I convince you to get her."

To solve this problem, to establish that the pornographic message exercises the binding power attributed to the performative, MacKinnon might have moved beyond Austin to broader accounts of the "reiterative power of discourse to produce the phenomenon that it regulates and constrains"[48]— the definition of performativity favored by one of her most outspoken critics, Judith Butler, and, in *Toward a Feminist Theory of the State*, by MacKinnon herself. (There she propounds this Butleresque formulation: "Gender is what gender means. It has no basis in anything other than the social reality its hegemony constructs.")[49] But as MacKinnon admits in *Only Words*, such approaches "generalize the performative to all speech" (and thereby impugn the uniqueness that she now attributes to pornography in order to exempt it from constitutional protection).[50]

So *Only Words* takes the opposite tack, arguing that porn effects a particular performativity through its direction at an involuntary reflex. It isn't its content—"get her"—that distinguishes it from other sexist discourses, but its address: "directly to the penis, delivered through an erection."[51] MacKinnon concludes this description with the phrase "and taken out on women in the real world," but *Only Words* scarcely mentions the research on the social effects of pornography cited in her previous writings.[52] Instead (in a significant reversion to traditional definitions of obscenity), the erection is offered as the effect. (One can imagine Austin revising *How To Do Things with Words* to replace "I now pronounce you man and wife" with the bailiff's command in court, "All rise.") [53]

Such an argument deduces a performative from a performance, and not the performance of rape, or gender subordination more broadly, but the performance of sexual arousal. So potent is the erection's status as proof—of an imputed command at one end of the sequence and an imputed abuse at the other—that the alleged causal links between them are all but ignored in favor of the mere reiteration of the phenomenon itself. "In human society where no one does not live, the physical response to pornography is nearly a universal conditioned male reaction, whether they like or agree with what the materials say or not. There is a lot wider variation in men's conscious attitudes toward pornography than there is in their sexual responses to it."[54]

But suppose we agree, if not to this particular estimate, then to the likelihood that pornography will stimulate sexual arousal. Let's say that this likelihood constitutes not only its use-value as a commodity but its presumptive definition—what the 1979 Williams Report on Obscenity to the British Home Office described as a "certain function or intention; to arouse its audience sexually."[55] We might take this argument a step further and also agree that porn is "a real practice of sex using representations."[56] Or, as MacKinnon puts it, "Pornography is masturbation material. It is used as sex. It therefore is sex."[57]

But all sexual practices are not the same. Acknowledging porn's "excitatory" possibilities may raise moral questions about masturbation, but it says nothing about the abuse of women. If porn can "perform" erections (in the sense of stimulating them automatically or involuntarily), it does not follow that it performs harm to women "in the real world." The erection, most importantly, cannot "get her" without the cooperation of a man. Despite the "nearly universal" ascription of the conditioned condition to men, *Only Words* also posits man as master—in his "conscious attitudes"—whose dog is all too recognizable as that particularly animate entity, at once ungovernable and yet highly manipulable, the penis.

The familiar dualisms in which this opposition is articulated in the above-quoted passage from *Only Words* (the individual/society; conscious attitudes/conditioned reactions; reason/sensation) have most recently focused critical discussion of an even hotter topic than pornography—addiction. Following Eve Sedgwick's description of our culture's current addiction to addiction as its all-purpose alibi of compulsion and free will (in which our behavior is seen to be at once pathologically determined and voluntarily transformable),[58] Mark Seltzer has identified the principle's equally paradoxical prefiguration in the late-nineteenth-century plasma addict, the "living dead."[59]

Both the addict and the vampire also haunt the antiporn account, with MacKinnon seizing upon the first to characterize the porn-using rapist ("sexually habituated to its kick")[60] while Dworkin assimilates Bram Stoker's 1897 *Dracula* directly into the pornographic canon. Indeed, she describes the novel, with its climactic scene of Lucy Westenra's impalement by her fiancé in the sight of three male witnesses, as *the* founding spectacle of twentieth-century voyeurism: "an oncoming century filled with sexual horror; the throat as a female genital; sex and death as synonyms; killing as a sex act; slow dying as sensuality; men watching the slow dying, and the watching is sexual."[61]

The vampire Lucy is herself an example of this novel's "pathologies of agency," for she is both active and passive, Dracula's prey and an accomplished predator.[62] Seltzer pursues this ambiguity in the cybernetic figure of the dead steersman who, lashed to his wheel, pilots Dracula's ship ashore. But there is also the question of his passenger, the "immense dog" whose first

105

act on landing (to tear out the throat of another large dog) reveals that it *is* its master.[63] If the bloodthirsty Count is the modern addict par excellence, as well as the chief prick of the new pornography, he is also a decidedly behaviorist character, with a canine condition to match: an obedient dog that moves to the (internalized) master's command and a wild dog that attacks.

Given the irrepressible binarism of the behaviorist problematic (mind/body, choice/compulsion, human/animal), the doubling that implicitly matches every dog with a master would seem inevitable. But even if it weren't, it would still be crucial to MacKinnon's project. Despite the bravado of her "nearly universal" model of male reactions to pornography, her moral appeal—the appeal that rallied men like the critical race theorist Charles Lawrence and the philosopher Richard Rorty to endorse her book—requires that conscious attitude of male condemnation about which she professes such skepticism. For all her denunciations of psychoanalysis, MacKinnon is as reliant on a notion of a divided male subjectivity as any of her opponents.

And this, I suspect, is what makes the pornography debate, and its behaviorist rhetoric, so . . . undead. Not too much disagreement between the warring parties, but too little. Not only is feminism's popular theory of gender socialization a polite form of behaviorism, complete with "the patterning of reward, nonreward and punishment . . . and the principles of direct and vicarious conditioning,"[64] but even the supposed complexities of social constructionism are caught in the old tourniquet of agency and determination, as others have argued.[65] If our recent efforts to untie it have only twisted it tighter (in the agonistics of "ideology" or "the unconscious"), this may be, as Eve Sedgwick argues with a certain degree of exasperation, because they've originated in models, Marxist or Freudian, that depend on the very dualisms in question. MacKinnon's dog may have been bred in the "heroics of compulsion/voluntarity,"[66] but so have we all. And, most ironically perhaps, this model of the subject makes man—that exemplary human subject—bestial *in* his humanity rather than in spite of it.

Here I want to close with one final evocation of that canine figure. This is a scene that mingles the most desperate claims to humanity with sex, spectatorship, and slavery. In it, five men sit watching an act of intercourse in a stream of fluids. They are described "as dogs." They are also described as "erect." But this is not a passage from the porn wars. It is a story of slaves on a Kentucky farm whose master calls them "men" but treats them mostly like animals. And so, of course, he will not let them marry. Nevertheless, for a year, all five of these men court a young slave woman. When a different man is finally chosen, he seeks some place apart for their first union:

And taking her in the corn rather than in her quarters, a yard away from the cabins of the others who had lost out, was a gesture of tenderness. Halle wanted privacy for her and got public display. Who could miss a ripple in a cornfield on a quiet, cloudless day? He, Sixo, and both of the Pauls, sat under Brother pouring water from a gourd over their heads, and through eyes streaming with well water, they watched the confusion of tassles in the field below. It had been hard, hard, hard sitting there erect as dogs, watching corn stalks dance at noon. The water running over their heads made it worse."[67]

This extraordinary passage, from Toni Morrison's *Beloved*, also seems to be a gesture of tenderness to these men rather than any indictment of their terribly concentrated gaze. It *is* undoubtedly an indictment of a regime that compels both voyeurism and public sex, that treats people "like animals." But somehow the simile slips, and these men seem to be mastered not by their owner, nor by the awful heat, nor by an implacably cruel mode of production, but by their own sexual desires (desires, we have already learned, that have led them to intercourse with cattle). Instead of evoking an enslaved sexuality, these lines could be taken to suggest masculine sexuality *as* slavery. It says something about the obduracy of such ideas that even Morrison's men can become MacKinnon's dogs.

6 "Not in a Public Lavatory but on a Public Stage"

The Prosecution of *The Romans in Britain*

Even before it opened, Howard Brenton's new play for the National Theatre was in trouble.[1] Three days before its official first night (16 October 1980), the theater's board met to discuss part I, scene 3, in which a Roman soldier attempts the anal rape of a Druid priest. Advised by board member and barrister John Mortimer, QC, that the play was not prosecutable, they voted to continue it, but in the absence of one key member. The missing man was Sir Horace Cutler, Conservative leader of the Greater London Council, then the city's governing body and a funder of the National Theatre. Two nights later, Cutler emerged from a preview of the play to send a telegram threatening a reconsideration of the council's grant to the National's director, Peter Hall, away in New York. Hall, who had commissioned this and other plays by Brenton, replied in vigorous defense of the production. By 17 October, the day after the opening, the London *Evening Standard* ran his praise of "an ambitious and remarkable piece of dramatic writing" against Cutler's denunciation of "a disgrace to the National Theatre." "My wife," Cutler told the *Standard*, "covered her head during the sodomy scene."

The London critics were no more taken with the play than Lady Cutler was. Within days it had accumulated an unenviable collection of notices, including these from Fleet Street's more liberal papers: "so many misjudgments in the writing and the production that it is difficult to determine where things really went wrong" (Ned Chaillet, *Times*, 17 October 1980); "a vast disproportion between the extravagances of the form and the banality of the thesis" (Michael Billington, *Guardian*, 17 October 1980); "three hours . . . devoid of wit, beauty or drama" (B. A. Young, *Financial Times*, 18 October 1980); "a nauseating load of rubbish from beginning to end" (James Fenton, *Sunday Times*, 19 October 1980). One rare exception to this critical condemnation was provided by a reviewer who had already retired, Sir Harold Hobson, who entered into the vast newspaper correspondence debating the drama in the days after its opening to argue, "*The Romans in Britain* is a deeply serious play which reveals the conviction of its author, Howard Brenton, that the heart of man is desperately wicked, a conviction that has been held by many great and religious writers in the past, and the climax of its first act is as fine and thunderstriking as anything seen or heard on the London stage for a very long time" (letter to the *Times*, 29 October 1980).

But the most important comment on Brenton's play came from a woman who had not seen it—indeed, who never saw it—the then sixty-six-year-old moral campaigner Mary Whitehouse. On 17 October, the *Times* reported that, after reading newspaper accounts of the play, she had made a complaint to Chief Inspector Robert Shepherd of the Obscene Publications Squad. A day later, the *Guardian* quoted her concern about protecting "young people. I'm talking about men being so stimulated by the play that they will commit attacks on young boys." Whitehouse's horror at the homosexual aspect of the play's representation of violence—a play that also featured, in the description of critic John Lahr, "death by spear, sword and stone," "heterosexual rape," and "blood guzzling"[2]—was not unprecedented. As founder of the conservative pressure group the National Viewers and Listeners Association, Whitehouse was a prominent opponent of explicit sexual representation in the media, particularly representations of homosexuality. The latter orientation, she had claimed in her polemic *Whatever Happened to Sex*, could be "precipitated by the abnormal (in terms of moral as well as physical norms) sexual behaviour of parents during pregnancy."[3]

Two years earlier, Whitehouse had succeeded in a private prosecution against the editor and publishers of *Gay News* for printing a poem depicting sexual acts between the crucified Christ and the centurion guarding his cross. Despite author James Kirkup's intention to produce a devotional work in the religio-erotic tradition of the metaphysical poets, with Christ's homosexuality a metaphor for his love of all mankind, the newspaper and its Anglican editor were convicted of blasphemous libel, a common law offense not tried previously since 1922. Accepting the prosecution's arguments that the sole criterion for the crime was the offensive treatment of Christianity (and only Anglican Christianity; no other faith is protected by English law), the presiding judge, and the House of Lords on appeal, refused to hear evidence about literary precedents or religious intent. Attributing homosexual practices to Christ was held to be a criminal defamation of both his reputation and the beliefs of his followers. The consequences were fines and financial crisis for the newspaper and a still unresolved controversy about whether such protection should be extended to all religions, a controversy that intensified with the publication of Salman Rushdie's *Satanic Verses* in 1988.

But these were not the only consequences of the conviction of *Gay News*. Whitehouse's success in the prosecution of a literary work was, by 1978, in many ways a remarkable event. Since passage of the Obscene Publications Act of 1959, with its stipulations that, taken as whole, the obscene item must "deprave and corrupt" those likely to encounter it while offering no literary, artistic, or scientific compensation for the "public good," the law, in the description of the 1979 Home Office Committee on Obscenity and Film Censorship, had retreated from the written word. To the Metropolitan Police, the failure of the prosecution of *Inside Linda Lovelace* three years earlier marked a watershed: "Their view (which appeared from his summing-up to have been shared by the trial judge) was that it was difficult to imagine what written material would be regarded as obscene if that was not."[4] With juries unwilling to convict nonpictorial material for obscenity and prosecuting authorities becoming correspondingly cautious, opponents of sexually explicit writing were forced to amend the obscenity laws or resort to other ones. That Whitehouse's motive in using the blasphemy laws against *Gay News* was not wholly religious may be inferred by her reticence in regard to a far more prominent work of 1970s sacrilege. No action was taken against *Monty Python's Life of Brian* (1979), a popular film comedy whose enthusiastic ridicule of Christ and his disciples contrasted markedly with a poem in a low-circulation gay weekly celebrating his carnal love for men.

The same wave of liberalization that stymied the prosecution of sexually explicit publications also affected British drama, eventually abolishing the lord chamberlain's power to license stage plays in 1968. The Theatres Act of that year applied the "deprave and corrupt" test to plays, as well as permitting the submission of expert evidence to justify performances "in the interests of drama, opera, ballet or any other art, or of literature or learning." A final safeguard was offered in the stipulation that a prosecution of a play could only be instigated with the consent of the attorney general.

When, twelve years later, Mary Whitehouse complained to the Obscene Publications Squad about *The Romans in Britain*, the police referred the matter to the director of public prosecutions who, having sent representatives from his office to see the play, advised that a prosecution under the Theatres Act was unlikely to succeed. After a barrister representing the National Viewers and Listeners Association attended a performance and came to the opposite conclusion, Whitehouse asked the attorney general to take action or to grant her association leave for a private prosecution. But at the end of November, the attorney general refused to sanction either form of proceedings. Thwarted in its attempt to prosecute under the Theatres Act, the NVLA tried another law. On 19 December, Whitehouse's solicitor, Graham Ross-Cornes, attended the play and questioned its director, Michael Bogdanov. He then sought permission from a magistrate to instigate a private prosecution under section 13 of the 1956 Sexual Offences Act. In the following month, Bogdanov was issued a summons for procuring an act of gross indecency between two men, actors Peter Sproule and Greg Hicks, on the stage of the National's Olivier Theatre.

Such an attempt to apply the criminal law to a stage play was not wholly unanticipated by those who had drafted the Theatres Act. As Geoffrey Robertson and Andrew Nicol point out, the act is not intended to "protect persons connected with a play from prosecution for actual criminal offenses, simply because they happen to be committed on stage."[5] What Parliament sought to prevent was the moral and political censorship of the theater that the Victorians had deemed necessary "for the preservation of good manners, decorum or the public peace."[6] To protect dissident drama, the 1968 act had specifically abolished residual offenses such as conspiracy and, indeed, blasphemous libel in regard to staged performances. However, an error in the drafting of one of its sections left open the possibility of invoking other laws against a theatrical production.

In seizing upon sexual offenses, Whitehouse exploited a loophole that had recently been noted by a Home Office Committee. Chaired by the philosopher Bernard Williams, the Committee on Obscenity and Film Censorship published its thoughtful (and duly ignored) report in November 1979, one year before the opening of *The Romans in Britain*. Chapter 10 considers whether the depiction of illegal acts might be numbered among the possible harms involved in pornography. Noting in passing that the blanket proscription of all such depictions would outlaw "a photograph of someone driving across a double white line," the report turns to the more pertinent question of sexual offenses and the anomalies in their legal treatment. On the legality of group sex, it observes:

Heterosexual or lesbian behavior is subject to no sanction dependent upon the number of people involved. Homosexual activity between men, on the other hand, is legal only if it happens between two adults in private, and the presence of a third person creates the presumption that the activity was not in private. It seemed to us that the implied presence of a photographer might serve to make any photograph of a homo-

sexual act arguably one of an illegal act; but it would certainly show an illegal act if it depicted more than two persons.

As the report cautions, the discriminatory logic of the criminal law in sexual offenses would necessitate an "unsatisfactory" distinction between hetero-sexual and homosexual representations if "any prohibition on pornography . . . depended just on whether or not the act depicted was against the law."[7] But where the Williams Committee consequently advised against prohibit-ing representations of illegal acts per se, one of their chief witnesses con-cluded otherwise. Having herself provided written and oral evidence on be-half of the National Viewers and Listeners Association, Mary Whitehouse seized the opportunity offered by the criminal law. In prosecuting *The Romans in Britain*, she employed legislation that had no direct application to any form of representation nor to any heterosexual (or lesbian) practice—section 13 of the Sexual Offences Act.

The offense of procuring an act of gross indecency between men dates back to the infamous Labouchere amendment to the Criminal Law Amend-ment Act of 1885:

Any male person who, in public or private, commits, or is a party to the commission of, or procures or attempts to procure the commission by any male person of, any act of gross indecency with another male person, shall be guilty of a misdemeanor, and being convicted thereof shall be liable at the discretion of the court to be imprisoned for any term not exceeding two years, with or without hard labour.[8]

Historians disagree about the import of this offense, as well as how it came to be included in legislation originating in a moral panic over the alleged prostitution of young girls. As a proscription of unspecified sexual conduct between members of the same gender, as opposed to a practice understood in terms of acts (the crime of sodomy, which in 1885 was also heterosexually applicable and punishable by sentences of between ten years and life impris-onment), the Labouchere amendment has been hailed as the moment in which (male) homosexuality was first recognized in English law. However, most historians echo John Marshall's argument that, although the amendment "did seem to contain a tacit view of the homosexually inclined man," it was consistent with the 1885 act's overall "emphasis upon sexual decadence, public decency and the protection of youth."[9] The point of convergence, in Jeffrey Weeks's influential account, was the period's concern about the "continuum of undifferentiated male lust, products of men's sexual selfishness."[10] In Judith Walkowitz's interpretation, it was the unfettered libertinage of the male aristocracy, "as homosexuality was associated with the corruption of working-class youth by the same upper-class profligates, who on other occasions, were thought to buy the services of young girls."[11] Conversely, others have argued that Henry Labouchere's late-night amendment, the eleventh clause in the act, was a cynical attempt by a heterosexual roué to ridicule a social purity initiative by extending it to all practices of procurement.[12] But if his amendment was a ploy to wreck the bill by forcing it into committee, it failed. The Speaker refused to rule the bill out of order and Britain became the only European country to outlaw potentially any sexual contact between men.

Ten years after the Criminal Law Amendment Act, its most celebrated victim was convicted of seven counts of "gross indecency with another male person." That the accused was a playwright alleged, in the libel suit that led to his trial, to have solicited other men to commit sodomy and other acts of gross indecency, and that his writings were cited as proof of this allegation, as well as that of subverting public morality and encouraging "unnatural vice," makes the prosecution of Oscar Wilde an inverted precedent for that of *The Romans in Britain*. Where the later action founded its prosecution of representations on sexual acts, the earlier one founded its prosecution of sexual acts on representations.

As Ed Cohen maintains, the Marquis of Queensberry's defense in the original libel action brought by Wilde initially relied on literary evidence (notably *The Picture of Dorian Gray*) to demonstrate that the writer, in describing "the relations, intimacies, and passions of certain persons of sodomitical and unnatural habits, tastes, and practices," was himself "posing as a sodomite."[13] It was not until Queensberry's lawyer had extensively questioned Wilde about his own identification with the "vicious views" put forward in his novel, and the effect of those views on public conduct, that—in the wonderful description of the London *Evening News*—"the cross-examination left the literary plane and penetrated the dim-lit, perfumed rooms where the poet of the beautiful joined with valets and grooms in the bond of silver cigarette cases."[14] Forced to abandon his suit against Queensberry, Wilde was arrested for acts of gross indecency on the following day.

Sixty-one years later, the offense under which Wilde was indicted, convicted, and sentenced to two years' hard labor was incorporated within a massive new statute on "sexual crimes," the Sexual Offences Act of 1956. Section 13 of that act retains Labouchere's 1885 wording and with it the offense's unique combination of specified genders and unspecified acts. Although the 1967 Sexual Offences Act amended the law to permit homosexual acts between two male adults in private, those involving more than two or otherwise than in private continue to be crimes. In regard to the latter, the courts traditionally have been expansive in their interpretation. In a 1976 judgment on a case involving two men masturbating in adjacent toilet cubicles, gross indecency was deemed to include "the mere participation and cooperation of two or more men in an indecent exhibition."[15] Given this precedent, the magistrate's agreement to a private prosecution of the director of Brenton's play for a breach of section 13 was not quite as unlikely as it seemed.

Opening "north of the River Thames on 27th August, 54 BC,"[16] Brenton's drama of the first Roman invasion of Britain and its aftermath has been described as an anti-imperialist epic.[17] Both the play and subsequent remarks by the playwright draw explicit comparisons between the events portrayed and "the 1980s with another army, the British, blundering around in a foreign country, Ireland."[18] In the introduction to a 1989 collection of his work, Brenton maintains that "the subject of the play is really 'culture shock.' . . . It is a small war on the edge of the known world that gets bogged down, a wretched summer of little achievement and to Julius Caesar of little interest. . . . But for the Celts the appearance of the Roman army is the end of their culture, its touch is death." Of the scene that caused so much controversy, he writes:

I tried to imagine what it must have been like for three young Celts, seeing Roman soldiers for the first time. I titled the scene "Two Worlds Touch." The Celts had been swimming on a fine summer's day. On the river bank they fool about, brag and laugh, then stretch out in the sun. From out of the trees come three Roman soldiers. They have had a bad day, losing touch with their platoon in a confused skirmish in the trees, and want a swim. The Celts are between them and the river. To the Romans it's nothing, there are three natives, three "wogs," between them and a much needed swim. The Romans kill two of the Celts and grossly abuse the third, who runs off. To the soldiers it is nothing, nothing at all. To the Celts it is worse than death, it is the end of their world.[19]

Brenton was never able to make this statement in court. The trial of Michael Bogdanov began on 15 March 1982, with the prosecution's admission that "the case is not usual; for this type of case the act of gross indecency that you are going to hear about took place not, as is more usual, in a public lavatory but on a public stage in a London theatre and the two men were actors."[20] The jurors were then given a summary of the play up to the rape scene and an explanation of why its director was the person charged: "The case against the defendant is that he directed the play and caused the play to be played on stage in full light on centre stage. . . . [I]n taking the decisions in the way he did, he was himself a party to that act because the law does not look merely at those who perform an act, but in this case . . . at anyone who stands behind and says, 'Go on.'"[21] Dismissing potential arguments about artistic merit or motive, the prosecution insisted that the question was whether an act of gross indecency had occurred. To establish this, Graham Ross-Cornes was questioned at length about his night at the National's Olivier Theatre. In the first day's cross-examination, the defense established that Ross-Cornes had sat in the balcony, ninety feet from the stage, and that the rape attempt had taken thirty seconds in a running time of almost three hours.

On the second day of the trial, Ross-Cornes's cross-examination continued with a discussion of the difference between reality and simulation. In reply to a question about actual and simulated urination onstage, the solicitor declared, "No doubt there is a difference between the reality and the simulation but I would still say that they are both indecent."[22] Following this, the defense read from the material included in the program notes which set the rape scene in its historical context. This sequence of events encapsulated the overall strategy of the defense: (1) to challenge the accuracy of Ross-Cornes's description of the rape scene; (2) to distinguish between reality and pretense; and (3) to defend, if permitted, the artistic logic of the play. However, in the hope that such a lengthy submission would be unnecessary, Bogdanov's lawyer ended day two with a preemptive strike, arguing that the case against his client contradicted the legal intention behind both the Theatres Act and the Sexual Offences Act, and should be dismissed.

On the following day, the judge replied with a multiple ruling that (1) "conduct in theatres" need not be exempted from the Sexual Offences Act; (2) the Theatres Act did not preclude prosecution for such conduct under the Sexual Offences Act; (3) simulated conduct could be an offense under the Sexual Offences Act; and (4) prosecution of the director—as opposed to any other National Theatre employee—for being party to such conduct was not necessarily "ill-founded." Having gained judicial recognition of all these points, the prosecution then took an exceptional decision. Justifying their move in the interests of the taxpayer and Bogdanov's personal and professional reputation, they withdrew their case. Although she was assigned the prosecution's costs, Whitehouse could claim an important precedent, one that the *Guardian* (19 March 1982) described as an "alarming . . . refusal to distinguish precisely between the simulated and the real."

As for Bogdanov, Brenton, and the defense, they were left without a legal platform from which to argue for the play or against the prosecution's application of the Sexual Offences Act to the stage. Nor were they able to exploit an interesting admission in Ross-Cornes's testimony—that sitting "appropriately enough, in the Gods"[23] he might have mistaken the thumb of one actor holding his genitals next to the buttocks of the other for the tip of his penis.

Whether the "thumbs-up" defense would have succeeded we shall never know. As earlier judgments on gross indecency suggest, genital contact per se is not required for conviction. Nor, had they been admitted, would Brenton's claims for the gravity of the rape scene necessarily have aided his cause. Played downstage in nearly full light to emphasize its cruelty, "the scene," in Peter Hall's defense of its staging, "is meant to horrify in what is a highly moral play."[24] This may explain why, unlike a heterosexual rape, which occurs offstage, and sundry other assaults, which are enacted more rapidly, the abuse of the young Celt is "sadistic, protracted and presented in detail."[25] The complaint is from Robert F. Gross, who argues that homosexual rape is the play's central figure for imperial conquest. Although that violence briefly mutates into tenderness when another of the soldiers caresses the wounded victim, it quickly changes back when the Celt regains consciousness and curses the soldier in Latin: "Fucking Latin talking nig nog!" The soldier exclaims in surprise, "Suck me off!"[26] As Gross points out, the shame of this effective "feminization" is further represented in the statuette of Venus that Caesar ties around the captive Celt's neck, an affront both to his manhood and to the Druid priesthood for which he is preparing. "Defiled" (in his own words) twice over, the young man abandons all resistance and commits suicide.

To these examples could be added the suggestions by one of the soldiers that the empire's eastern reaches are a hotbed of perversion, that colonial contact involves the risk of a certain re-orientation, as it were: "My friend has been to the Orient. Persia? Funny little ways he's picked up, in his career. But what the fuck do you expect, from a man who's been in Persia?"[27] Such an association of homosexuality with imperial conquest makes consensual anal sex between males virtually unintelligible, as it effectively has been in Eng-

curious confession that the anal rape scene would be read as an irresistible command to commit similar acts seems more telling in itself than in its warning of copycat assaults on young boys.[37] Despite the best efforts of liberal jurisprudence to separate sex from its simulation, the representation of forbidden pleasures seems, for Whitehouse and her supporters, to have been disturbingly sexy, procuring, perhaps, an effect of arousal as well as dramatizing one. To deny this possibility seems as self-defeating as the defense's neglect of the legal discrimination against male homosexuality that permitted the indictment in the first place. In the case of *The Romans in Britain*, the intensely eroticizing taboo that has made the representation of male homosexuality so vulnerable to prosecution could not be kept offstage.

In 1996, a Dino de Laurentiis feature about a gangster's moll and lesbian ex-con who fall in love and steal $2 million from the mob was submitted to the U.S. ratings board. To the consternation of the film's fledgling directors, the Motion Picture Association of America demanded cuts in the sex scenes. "In the end," co-director Larry Wachowski later recalled, "they came up with this concept of 'hand sex.' They said that 'hand sex' is too graphic."[1] The MPAA were not the only ones to object to *Bound* (directed by Andy and Larry Wachowski, 1996). Duly censored to secure its U.S. "R" and U.K. "18" ratings, the film opened to verdicts of "trendy trash," "fast-diminishing returns," "a stultifying lack of creativity and a pervasive juvenility."[2] Particular opprobrium was reserved for *Bound*'s allusions to film noir and, more specifically, to the auteurial style of another fraternal production team, the Coen brothers, as well as for a broader reflexivity condemned as "self-conscious," "meretricious," "showing off," and—ubiquitously—"flashy." Nor did the film's lesbian thematics escape rebuke. "Kinky chic for guys," jeered the *Village Voice*. "Deliberate marketing to both icon-starved lesbian audiences and the dirty mac brigade," chorused *Time Out*.

But if the latter constituted a provocation to lesbian critics to distinguish their spectatorial pleasures from those of the male voyeur, it signally failed to come off. "It would be easy to dismiss this film by saying that this is merely straight men's view of what lesbians are and do and is for their titillation," replied the U.K. lesbian monthly *Diva*. "But why should they have all the fun? The lead actresses are to die for. The outfits are drool-inducing. The sex scene is divine."[3] Icon-starved or not, lesbians liked *Bound*. Moreover, they liked it for precisely the reasons the straight press abhorred it. The allusions to the Coens' 1984 *Blood Simple* and 1990 *Miller's Crossing* were noted and approved (not least as a step up from "'lesbian film' á la *Desert Hearts*").[4] The noir narrative was praised as camp parody, the monochrome mise-en-scene, conspicuous camera angles, and extreme close-ups celebrated as an unusually successful redeployment of "a style that hasn't worked since the 40s."[5] Finally, and notwithstanding all this artifice, the manual seduction scene was saluted as "one of the most sexy—and surprisingly authentic—lesbian love scenes on celluloid."[6]

In the most sustained appreciation of the film I've encountered, Jean Noble singles out its success in updating film noir's engagement with the construction and interpretation of sexual identities. In her reading, *Bound* restages the genre's traditional crisis of masculinity, this time beset by a very "femme" fatale whose legibility as a lesbian becomes the central conundrum for both the male mobsters and the butch ex-con who desire her. The lipsticked and lacquered Violet may be Caesar's mistress of five years standing and his audibly active bed partner, but her name connotes a lavender menace that ultimately proves violent. Other critics have also praised *Bound*'s resignification of film noir's characteristically enigmatic woman ("at issue is the ambiguity of sexuality . . . rather than the otherness of woman")[7] as well as its manifest interest in the question of "femme invisibility,"[8] but Noble elucidates Violet's passage through an elaborate geometry of sexual triangles to emerge—indeed, to come out—as the publicly intelligible product of an innovative partnership of mass and subcultural ethnography. The lesbian sexologist Susie Bright, credited in the production as "technical consultant" and actress (in the role of another femme), is argued to serve as native informant and guarantor of the film's verisimilitude. The resulting production both privileges and publicizes the lesbian audience's "'in the know' viewing position, simultaneously weaving both the content of the production and the context of its consumption into the narrative itself."[9]

There are many merits in Noble's ethnographic reading, notably the explanation it offers for the film's air of knowingness (the arch self-consciousness which irritated so many critics) as well as its occasional descent into didacticism (notably the labored reference to the lesbian significance of the labrys, much derided by British reviewers). Even more compelling is her detailed description of the symbolic and narrative triads that figure in Violet's move from the homosocial triangle of Caesar's sexual rivalry with a succession of colleagues, to the homosexual passion that enables her to leave him, to the final triangulation, which counterposes both butch and femme to the naturalized third term, female. But, despite the care with which this scheme is laid out, its apparently seamless progression toward the knowledge with which the lesbian audience is invested, together with the "realness" attributed to Bright's participation in the production, tends to emphasize the film's ostensible authenticity at the expense of its artifice. And although Violet's "I want out!" takes epigraphic primacy in Noble's reading, it is less than clear that her final departure from Caesar's shadowy domain represents coming out of the closet as much as getting out of town.

What I'm gesturing at here are the other conventions at work in *Bound* that complicate Noble's interpretation, notably the secrecy of the robbery plot, which requires that Violet must not disclose her lesbian passion at the film's end but instead leave the mob believing that she is departing Chicago devastated at Caesar's disappearance with the money. Similarly, *Bound* counters the punitive protocols of the film noir—which typically renews masculine authority by taking revenge on the seductive woman—with the broadest conventions of a notoriously conventional

genre, pornography. Finally, it deploys these conventions via a set of characters and situations so hyperstylized as to make the Commedia dell'Arte
look like Chekhov. How does this artifice come to figure authenticity? The
answer, I will argue, is at hand.

The lesbian hand has a cultural history in which it figures both as an instrument of sexual contact and as a marker of gender transitivity. In Radclyffe Hall's 1928 apologia for the invert, *The Well of Loneliness*, Stephen
Gordon's hands are a conspicuous feature of one of the most indiscreet
anatomies in literature. The little girl born with broad shoulders and an in-
cipiently cleft chin quickly exhibits the masterful grip of the congenital
equestrienne, a "queer, vital strength of [the] hand" which will later attract
her county neighbor Angela Crossby. When Stephen is ultimately rejected,
the same hands will mournfully stroke her own boyish body as she contemplates it in the mirror. Exiled to bohemia, she smokes incessantly and
acquires indicative nicotine stains on the fingers of "her bony masculine
hands"—hands that are expressly contrasted with those of her Noel Cow-
ardesque colleague (and mirror invert) Jonathan Brockett, "as white and
soft as a woman's." When her second novel fails, a critic notes its "lack of
grip." Subsequently Brockett encourages Stephen to Paris and the lesbian
milieu of Valerie Seymour with the injunction to "just plunge in your fist
and see what happens." And later in Paris she renews the erotic use of the
hand prefigured in her impassioned grasp of Angela's jeweled fingers. Returning to the city after the war with Mary Llewellyn, the young woman
she has met in the ambulance corps, Stephen proposes a recuperative jour-
ney to Tenerife. As the undeclared lovers discuss their travel plans, Mary
lays her hand on Stephen's knee. The latter, convinced of the younger
woman's innocence of all things inverted, pretends not to notice until,
suddenly moved beyond caution, she places her hand on Mary's. The incident, which anticipates the notoriously elliptical evening in Tenerife in
which the two women are finally "not divided," is a key scene in this romance, and Hall takes care to underline its significance:

The strange sympathy which sometimes exists between two human bodies, so that a touch will stir many secret and perilous emotions, closed down on them both at that moment of contact, and they sat unnaturally still by the fire, feeling that in their stillness lay safety.[10]

My second example of the literary lesbian hand predates *The Well of Loneliness* and may have influenced its articulation of what Joanne Winning describes as "an as yet untheorised system of lesbian erotics."[11] In the 1916 novel *Backwater*, the second in Dorothy Richardson's *Pilgrimage* sequence, Miriam Henderson is given a moment of self-contemplation similar to Stephen's at the mirror. And like its successor, the scene centers on the hand.

It was not perhaps a "good" self, but it was herself, her own familiar secretly happy and rejoicing self—not dead. Her hands lying on the coverlet knew it. They were again at these moments her own old hands, holding very firmly to things no one might touch or even approach too nearly, things, everything, the great thing that would some day communicate itself to someone through those secret hands with the strangely thrilling finger-tips.[12]

Unlike the hands of other women in the sequence—the consumptive Miss Dear's "slender . . . hands,"[13] or "Eve's plump, white, inflexible little palms"[14]—Miriam has masculine hands. "[Hands] like umbrellas,"[15] her piano teacher observes, with long fingers, "the tips squarish and firmly padded, the palm square and bony and supple, and the large thumb-joint stood away from the rest of the hand like the thumb-joint of a man."[16] The capacity of such hands for sexual contact is emblematized in their autoerotic embrace:

When the two were firmly interlocked they made a pleasant curious whole, the right clasping more firmly, its thumb always uppermost, its fingers separated firmly over the back of the left palm, the left hand clinging, its fingers close together against the hard knuckles of the right.[17]

The gendering of the hands in this description, while suggesting something of Miriam's almost hermaphroditic self-sufficiency, also evokes sexual possibilities, possibilities that are further multiplied by our individual endowment with two such instruments. But despite its extensive eroticization in novels like those in the *Pilgrimage* sequence and *The Well of Loneliness*, the hand has scarcely received its due in contemporary lesbian culture.

If, as Jean Noble complains in her comments on *Bound*, butch-femme relations were widely condemned by lesbians in the 1970s for mimicking "the worst heterosexual coupling,"[18] "hand sex" has become an object of disdain in more recent lesbian discourse. Thus, *Making Out*, a British publication billed as "the definitive guide to lesbian sexual experience in the 1990s," consigns "finger-fucking" to the "increasingly disparaged" category of vanilla sex.[19] Only in the guide's entry on fisting does the hand come into its own as "arguably the most sensitive and therefore intimate part of the body, having a sensory capacity even greater than that of the genitals—more nerves run from the hand to the brain than from any other part of the body."[20]

This reluctant acknowledgment of the hand's erotic function by lesbian sexology is duplicated in lesbian criticism. In her study of cover images of American paperback editions of *The Well of Loneliness*, Michèle Aine Barale selects four jacket designs, published between 1951 and 1981, each of which prominently displays a hand or hands. But, in arguing that such texts have been marketed to engage and reassure the presumptively straight consumer, she reads these manual images as allegories of genital difference. The inscription of such a difference, Barale maintains, convinces the buyer that "the secrets of lesbian sexuality"[21] are both knowable and subsumable to heterosexual enjoyment, since they effectively become its projection.

Surveying a 1951 cover, which features a drawing of two women sitting close together in front of a blazing fireplace, she notes that one figure's converging hands form an indicative V which extends back along her arms to frame the pubic mound beneath her dress. Conversely, the figure she gazes at, depicted in truncated profile with lowered eyelids, is exempted from any such genital figuration and thus said to assume a position of (masculine)

129

dominance. In another analysis, a 1964 cover illustration of a green hand reaching up to clasp a descending blue one is interpreted in both racial and sexual terms: the upper blue hand, with its V-shaped opening between the index and third finger, is taken to signify vaginal receptivity as well as racial superiority (the white femme), while the extended index finger of the green hand thrusting from below is argued to represent the enlarged and penetrating clitoris ascribed by nineteenth-century colonial and medical discourses to both black women and lesbians.

Despite the remarkable abundance of hands in Barale's examples, she excludes the possibility of their self-referentiality in all but one overwhelming instance. The cover image of a 1974 edition of Hall's novel is a photograph of two women in a paperback porn pastiche of Victorian costume. The foregrounded blonde, in curls and lacey decolletage, carries a bouquet of roses. The taller brunette behind her sports a tailored jacket and sharply parted hair. With her left index finger she touches the blossom closest to the blonde's parted lips. Barale takes the figures' differing endowments ("one has the finger and the other has a rose") as evidence of the genital difference she reads in all these illustrations. But the emphatically centered hands of both women cannot be ignored. In this example, she concedes, the dark woman's "finger is still a finger in a lesbian reading of the cover." Moving, at last, from the clitoral to the literal, Barale acknowledges the image's suggestion that a woman's "hand can function as a means of sexual pleasure for another woman," whether or not this is communicated to the mainstream book browser.[22]

In a similar analysis of two 1980s films with lesbian themes, Judith Roof claims that, like Barale's jacket designs, *Lianna* (1983) and *Desert Hearts* (1985) offer "an illusory sexual knowledge for the [films'] spectators, producing a superficial pretense for a curious scopophila—'what do they do in bed?'"[23] Seeking to allay castration anxiety by affirming a phantasmatic sexual difference, they feature in their initial kissing scenes fetishistic images of the hand "standing in for the phallus literally absent between women"[24] and once again resolve the enigma of lesbian pleasure as heterosexuality by other means. Recall that in both films the pursuing woman first kisses the pursued, an initiation in which the hand plays a controlling role. In *Lianna*, Ruth strokes Lianna's face with her hand as a preface to kissing her, while in *Desert Hearts* Kay holds the back of Vivian's head. Moreover, in the latter film Kay's hand acquires its visual centrality at the moment in which the spectator's view of the kiss itself is obscured. In alleviating this frustration of the gaze, as well as the broader threat of male exclusion from the erotic scene, the hand, Roof argues, assumes its fetishistic function.

While I share Roof's disdain for the egregious invitations to male enjoyment extended by these films (notably *Desert Heart's* inclusion of a double nude bathing scene intruded upon enthusiastically by a male character who remarks, all too aptly, that the foam-covered women look "like two desserts"),[25] I want to question her phallic interpretation of these hands. Rereading it one decade—and many attempts to extend the remit of the fetish—after its original formulation, I am struck by her acknowledgment of the literalness of the fetishism operating in these films. Unlike the metaphorical fetishism that Mulvey ascribes to screen images of women and Metz to cinematic technology, these lesbian fetishes approximate the actual function of the penis for which Freud declared the fetish to be a substitute. Thus, the hand's suitability for its symbolic role is based on its capacity to be an "instrument of vaginal penetration"[26] and therefore to threaten the exclusion of the male organ, an exclusion that its fetishization disavows. Yet Freud points out that the fetish object is not necessarily chosen for any such homology. Indeed, he remarks that the fetishist characteristically fixes upon "the last impression before the uncanny and traumatic" vision of the female genitals—the woman's shoe, female underclothing, etc.—in a far more circumstantial substitution.[27]

Conversely, in Roof's reading of *Lianna* and *Desert Hearts*, the castration anxiety produced by the erotic conjunction of two women's bodies forces the fetish back to its anatomical prototype in what might be understood as defensive self-display. But if this anxiety is so extreme, perhaps we should give it its due. Might the hand in these scenes be self-referential, representing the erotic potential that it threatens rather than the phallic endowment with which that threat is said to be averted? Suppose the woman's controlling hand is just a hand—and all the more menacing to the male spectator for being so. The severity of this anxiety, if unallayed, might explain the subsequent repression of manual stimulation in these films' artfully incoherent scenes of love-making—notably in *Desert Heart*'s notorious staging of Vivian's "mystery orgasm."

But if the lesbian hand might present the male spectator with the daunting prospect of erotic rivalry or phallic obsolescence, what is its function for the lesbian spectator? Replying to Roof, Teresa de Lauretis considers whether the clitoris, with its own capacity for erection and orgasm, functions as a lesbian fetish. She agrees that it may, but only insofar as it comes to signify lesbian desire, a signification that does not rely upon any anatomical characteristic, let alone resemblance to the male appendage whose claims to represent desire are so disputable. In de Lauretis's analysis, fetishism requires fantasy and lack. For the lesbian, that lack is the primordial loss of the beloved female body—the other's and her own—exemplified in the abandoned Stephen Gordon's anguished contemplation of her masculine appearance in the mirror. The fantasy is the disavowal of that loss which informs Stephen's compensatory investment in a brocade dressing gown, silk pajamas, and other elements of *haute bourgeois* male display. Invoking Judith Butler's argument for the transferability of phallic attributes, de Lauretis interprets this regalia as signifiers of a masculine-coded desire for the female body and dubs them fetishes. But although both fetish and phallus derive, as she admits, from the same anatomical prototype, there are significant differences between Butler's lesbian phallus and de Lauretis's lesbian fetish.

Where de Lauretis emphasizes "not the loss of the penis in women but the loss of the female body itself"[28] as the impetus for lesbian fetishism, and therefore its detachment from any necessary phallic reference, Butler stresses the transferability of the phallus as signifier of desire, and anatomy "as a site of proliferative resignifications."[29] Instead of the metonymical masculinity of Stephen Gordon's pajamas, she proclaims the metaphorical capacity of "an array of purposefully instrumentalized body-like things" to symbolize lesbian possession of the phallus: "an arm, a tongue, a hand (or two), a knee, a thigh, a pelvic bone." Instrumentalized indeed, for unlike Stephen's tailored nightwear, however alluring, Butler's symbolic inventory has been carefully composed to include only anatomical entries, and only those parts of the woman's body that can readily stimulate another woman to orgasm. (Thus, no clitoris, despite its penile isomorphism, nor any of the more traditionally eroticized zones of the female anatomy.) Although she maintains that certain "discursive performances" and "alternative fetishes" may also acquire phallic significance, it is clearly the physical capacity to make women come which qualifies particular body parts for inclusion in Butler's list.[30] But so functional a selection of physical features runs counter to her definition of the phallus as an idealization, a phantasm. If for this reason the phallus can never be equated with the penis, neither can it be equated with any female attribute. The physical specificity of Butler's catalogue renders it neither phallic nor even genital, but sexually significant nonetheless.

In an argument posed at both Butler's phallus and de Lauretis's fetish, Louise Allen discusses lesbian fans' descriptions of Martina Navratilova's athletic arms and hands:

Her hands are muscular and veined—my favourite type of hands. They look so strong and capable, she seems someone I could depend on because of her hands, if we were lovers.

Her muscles are outrageously gorgeous, her physique is so beautiful, her legs are so sexy and strong and her arms and hands are just so muscular and gorgeous.[31]

In these accounts the displacement of interest from the traditional foci of pin-ups directed at straight men is unmistakable, with the attention on those parts of the female body that can be instrumental in sex between women, as well as other sports. But while acknowledging the connotation of "the male attributes of action, prowess, strength, triumph, dedication and, importantly, *agency*" suggested by particular photographs of "these famous lesbian hands"[32] and their legibility in terms of traditional definitions of fetish and phallus, Allen refuses any such assignment. Despite her concern that "lesbian chic" has been appropriated to mainstream commodity fetishism, she reads these fans' celebrations of such fashionable figures as kd lang and Navratilova as evidence of an identification with, as well as desire for, these stars which precludes the consumption of their images as mere objects of exchange value or erotic instrumentality.

In resisting the subsumption of lesbian sexuality in "the language of the dominant,"[33] Allen has an ally in Eve Sedgwick, whose reading of eroticism in Henry James challenges "the unswervingly phallic way that sexual acts are envisioned throughout psychoanalysis":

Notoriously, if sex means penetration, and penetration means penis, then there's no sex in the absence of a penis or penis prosthesis, and no sex between or among women except insofar as we may simulate having the phallus.[34]

Declaring that she can take or leave the phallus, Sedgwick takes leave of it in a reading of the relationship of Kate Croy and Milly Theale in *The Wings of the Dove* which stresses both its homoerotic intensity and its complex dynamics. In pursuing the thematics of the hand throughout the novel, she lays emphasis on Kate's "'high' 'handsomeness' (you don't lose points for registering that subliminally as high-handedness)" and its encounter with Milly's self-avowedly "huge" hands. Emboldened by her account of a manual eroticism which might elude "the polarities that a phallic economy defines as active or passive,"[35] I return to the lesbian hand—or two— elsewhere.

Reviewed from the perspective of *Bound*, the cinema's lesbian sex scenes take on a decidedly manual character. The first of these to be considered *as* a sex scene, in *The Killing of Sister George* (1968), was hailed by *Variety* on the film's release as "unnecessary, gratuitous, offensive and crude."[36] And certainly the seduction of George's lover Childie by the sinister Mercy Croft is a grotesque scene in director Robert Aldrich's very dark adaptation of Frank

FIGURE 7.1. *The Killing of Sister George:* Mercy Croft (Coral Browne) manually seduces Childie (Susannah York). BFI Films: Stills, Posters and Designs. Reprinted by permission.

Marcus's stage comedy. As the predatory Croft urges the tipsy Childie to pack her things and leave George, the younger woman lies on her bed and dreamily caresses her dolls. Eventually Croft picks up another doll and sits at her side (figure 7.1). After hypnotically bidding the doll to sleep, she caresses Childie's breast and, it is suggested, brings her to orgasm with her hand. Vito Russo's comment on this scene is instructive:

When she reviewed The Children's Hour *in 1962, Pauline Kael noted that audiences felt sorry for poor Martha Dobie because she and Karen "don't really* do *anything, after all," and Kael added parenthentically, "I always thought that was why lesbians needed sympathy—because there isn't much they* can *do." Six years later, when Aldrich released* The Killing of Sister George *with 119 seconds of footage showing exactly what lesbians could do, Kael's review of the film was titled "Frightening the Horses."* [37]

If the perennial question "What do lesbians do?" was answered by demonstration in *The Killing of Sister George*, the reply was subsequently given verbal expression in a Hungarian feature set in the dark days following the failed anti-Soviet uprising of 1956. The central character of *Another Way* (1982) is Eva, a journalist who opposes state censorship. Her political dissidence is pointedly paralleled with her sexual nonconformity, for Eva is an unapologetic lesbian engaged in an affair with a married female colleague. When the jealous husband retaliates by shooting his wife, Eva is questioned by the Chief of Police. After inquiring about her relationship with the wounded woman, the colonel gets to the point. "How" he asks "do you do it?" Raising her right hand the distraught lover indignantly replies, "With our fingers!" and sequentially extends her index, second and third fingers in a disdainful salute to the despised regime.[38]

By 1995, cinematic references to the lesbian hand were iconized in the gigantic thumbs of Sissy Hankshaw (again the manual homonym), hitchhiking heroine of *Even Cowgirls Get the Blues* (figure 7.2). In the film's pretitle sequence, young Sissy's mother seeks reassurance from a palm reader as to her deformed daughter's marriageability. "I see men in your life," Madame Zoe tells Sissy. "I also see women. Lots and lots and *lots* of women." Yet if, as she declares, "there's nothing about your past, present or future that your hands do not know," that knowledge is not easy to interpret, particularly in the case of a girl who is "all thumbs" but therefore endowed with the freedom of movement that the thumb's opposition to

FIGURE 7.2. *Even Cowgirls Get the Blues:* Sissy Hankshaw (Uma Thurman) thumbs a ride. Courtesy of PolyGram/Rank. BFI Films: Stills, Posters and Designs.

the other digits offers the human hand—a freedom realized in Sissy's sexual as well as geographical mobility.

The symbolic potency of Sissy's hands may depend, like those of Stephen Gordon and Miriam Henderson, on size, but one recent film stages a lesbian seduction in which the fingers are deliberately shorn in order to be

FIGURE 7.3. *Go Fish:* Max (Guinevere Turner) manicures Ely (V. S. Brodie). Courtesy of Mainline Pictures. BFI Films: Stills, Posters and Designs.

made sexually functional. Consider the scene in *Go Fish* (1994) in which Ely arrives for her first date with Max. Almost immediately Max announces that her embarrassed suitor's nails need clipping and sets to it herself (figure 7.3). Far from figuring castration, this manicure is an unambiguous sexual invitation. In getting trimmed, Ely is being groomed to penetrate Max. In doing the trimming, Max is declaring her own receptivity to that penetration. The fact that both these women, though styled respectively butch and femme, have masculine names seems entirely to Sedgwick's point about the confusion of gendered polarities wrought by manual eroticism. In *Bound* these erotics, and their consequent complication of identities and expectations, expand beyond the scenes that caught the censors' attention to structure the entire film.

Bound begins in the closet, a woman's wardrobe whose contents (shelves, hatboxes, hangers, dresses, high heels) are extensively surveyed by the film's incessantly moving camera until it discovers a female body— trussed and gagged (figure 7.4). The contrast between the lesbian signifiers on this body (boots, trousers, tattoos) and the hyper-feminine apparatus that surrounds it, together with a series of voiced-over declarations climaxing in "I want out," lead Jean Noble to conclude that this scene "establishes the desire to come out as *Bound*'s subtextual femme quest narrative."[39] But, as the film subsequently reveals (and as we might readily surmise from her appearance), the woman who lies unconscious—knocked out—in the closet already is out in the sexual sense. Moreover, she could easily have eluded capture. How she comes to be "bound" seems at least

FIGURE 7.4. *Bound:* Corky (Gina Gershon) captive in the closet. Courtesy of Guild Pathe Cinema.

as compelling a narrative enigma as the coming out plot examined by Noble.

As we soon discover in the flashback that ensues, the captive in the closet has been imprisoned before. Corky (Gina Gershon) has just emerged from a five-year term for robbery to more legitimate employment renovating apartments. In the film's second scene she encounters Violet (Jennifer Tilly), who has also served five years as the mistress of a minor mobster. A sound match linking the "I want out" voice to Violet's thanks for holding the elevator as she enters its closet-sized confines suggest her as the wardrobe's owner and symbolic occupant (a match underlined by both women's black leather jackets) while re-establishing the spatial constraints that figure so powerfully in this film. And yet, as Violet will complain seductively to Corky in the next scene, the walls of this building are "so terribly thin"—thin enough to allow Corky to hear the sounds of her love-making while she works in the adjacent apartment. Violet's visit to apologize for this acoustic anomaly enables her to signal sexual attraction even more obviously than her stare of appreciation suggested in the elevator. After offering Corky coffee, she surveys the scene of her labors and declares her "awe of people who can fix things" like her father. "His hands were magic," she breathes, over a close-up of Corky's own.

Two scenes later, Corky is summoned to Violet's flat by the building manager to retrieve an earring from the kitchen drain. The sexual entendre already signaled by a scene in which Corky operates a mechanical probe whose instructions read "Don't force snake. Slow and easy does it" is intensified still further as she crouches to unscrew the U-bend in a low-angled shot that frames her head next to Violet's thighs. A close-up displays her hand loosening the pipe as water begins to flow down her fingers and the errant earring descends. The sex scene that follows plays out this manual conceit for all it's worth. Protesting her desire to the skeptical Corky—"You can't believe what you see, but you can believe what you feel"—Violet wets the handywoman's fingers with her mouth, guides them up her skirt, and begs her not to take them away. A few scenes later we see Violet using her own hand to orgasmic effect on Corky as she caresses her mouth with the other one—marked emphatically by its violet nail polish.[40]

This is, in every detail except its exclusion of genital nudity, pornography. Not only have the two principals met and mated within minutes of the film's opening, they are classic porn characters down to their deeply implausible names: Violet and Corky, the bored housewife and the virile laborer. Here the characterization of the ex-con as a handywoman comes into focus, for pornography—straight and gay—relies on the laboring body both to signify and to provide the occasion for sex. Thus, the cowboy and the pool boy and, indeed, the plumber in gay men's porn, and in its lesbian counterpart the postal delivery woman, the camp counselor and—my own favorite—the landlady who unblocks her female tenant's chimney in a forgotten film called *Where There's Smoke*. The ridiculous speed with which these characters get off together is more than equaled in *Bound*, which contradicts the traditional lesbian romance by starting with the sex, in scenes whose ludicrously suggestive dialogue and cheap background music—the tinny marimba tune on Corky's radio—*sound* pornographic. Then there is Corky's retrieval of a jewel from the sink in a metaphor straight out of Diderot's *Les bijoux indiscrets*, the eighteenth-century erotic fable that compares the female genitals to jewels, jewels that can be made to speak the secrets of women's sexual pleasure by means of a sultan's magic ring.[41]

How could so comically conventional a coupling be celebrated by a queer critic like Judith Halberstam as "one of the most sexy—and surprisingly authentic—lesbian love scenes on celluloid"? One explanation is that pornographic realism is conveyed, not by narrative plausibility or psychological depth (two of the missing traits lamented in less intelligent reviews of *Bound*), but by the promise that the actors really have sex—or, in this case, have been coached by a real lesbian pornographer, Susie Bright, to simulate it convincingly. The genre's traditional neglect of other signifiers of realism in favor of the indexical guarantees of sexual authenticity—nudity, genital conjunction and, conventionally in men's porn, the "come shot"—often exposes the conditions of its making. Paradoxically, the consequent lack of verisimilitude perceived in pornography operates to secure its reality effect. Moreover, *Bound*'s reordering of the standard romance plot spares lesbian sexuality the epistemological objectification that Roof complains of in *Lianna* and *Desert Hearts*. By the time Caesar asks Violet what Corky *did* to her (and not what she did to Corky) the spectator has long known. Whatever the narrative enigma of this film, it isn't what lesbians do in bed. The very assignment of the question to the frustrated fall guy underlines its inanity.

Nonetheless, pornography is only one genre at work in *Bound*. In addition to the lesbian characters in the women's prison film suggested by Corky and her confinement, there is its obvious debt to the gangster film and its noir subgenre. Here the issue of masculine propriety becomes paramount. By name, Caesar (Joe Pantoliano) should rule and his wife (or, in this case, mistress) be above suspicion, but from the moment he enters the elevator with Violet, she is flirting with Corky behind his back. Moreover, he is "little" Caesar, shorter than Violet in her stilettos and a mere money launderer. In a sexualized mafia hierarchy where "fuck" means "double-cross," pistols are called "peckers," and gunmen aim for the groin, Caesar is feminized by his middling status, which in one scene requires him to wash, dry, and iron a suitcase full of bloodied bills. Conventionally, film noir would correct these gender transgressions by punishing the faithless woman. But equally conventionally, pornography would pursue her sexual pleasure. When the conventions collide to fracture generic expectations, their existence as conventions is all the more evident.

Bound revels in this exposure and not just at the level of narrative. Critic after critic complained of its "look-at-me style (ultra close-ups of objects, flashy transitions, and annoyingly arch overheads)."[42] "Here's the camera pulling out of the barrel of a gun. Here it is following the path of a telephone cord, right down to imitating the kinks and curls in the wire."[43] But as analysis of the telephone motif will show, this reflexivity is a thematically motivated attempt to foreground the film's own status as an artifact. In the scene in question, the anxious Violet—fearful that the scam to steal the $2 million

Caesar has laundered is going wrong—enters her bedroom and dials the telephone. The camera tracks along its twisting cord to the plug in the wall and then (in an invisible edit) along the cord of the phone in the next apartment, which rings and is answered by Corky. The scene confirms what the film's soundtrack has already indicated—that the room in which Violet has sex is only a wall away from the one where Corky works. A few scenes later, Violet returns to the room, terrified that her accomplice has taken the money and abandoned her. This time the camera remains at her back as she dials the phone and pleads, as she did in the first sex scene, "Please, Corky, please." When Corky answers and Violet confesses her fears, she reassures her by promising "You don't quit on me, Violet, I don't quit on you." In the ensuing moment of romantic declaration, first one and then the other punctuate their terse endearments by placing their hands against the wall. Meanwhile the camera arcs above them to reveal that the two are touching the same spot.

Here the logic of the film's manual eroticism becomes clear, for the hand, instrument of love and labor, is also the historic agent of binding agreements. "By our hands we promise," writes the renaissance anatomist Andreas Laurentius. Laurentius' treatise is a summary of the characteristics that have since classical culture been attributed to the limb: the most noble and perfect organ of the body, proof of God's design, implement of reason, servant of the will, builder of temples, writer of laws, painter, drawer, carver, and communicator. "By our hands we promise, we call, we dismisse, we threaten, we intreate, we abhorre, we feare, yea and by our hands we can aske a question."[44] In the anatomical works of the renaissance, the hand is represented as the pre-eminent object of that science, displayed in dissection by Vesalius, Rembrandt's Dr. Tulp and—on the title page of a 1600 textbook—Anatomia herself.[45] There she grasps with her own hand one of the flexor muscles whose intricate connection with the tendons and bones of the forefingers enables the hand's unique prehension. Such illustrations identified the hand, as subject and object of scientific inquiry, with reason (apprehension as intellectual grasp), creativity, and the will. Proposed as proof of the

143

divinity in humanity, the creator in the creature, these attributes inevitably provoked questions of origins.

From the pre-Socratics onward, philosophers have debated which came first, the human hand or humanity itself? Where Anaxagoras argues that the hand's capacities stimulated the development of human intelligence, Aristotle replies that nature gave the "instrument for [using] instruments" to the species most rationally able to do so: "it is not that man is the most intelligent animal because he has hands, but rather that he has hands because he is most intelligent."[46] The difficulty of resolving this dispute is demonstrated by another remark of Aristotle's, in which he apparently contradicts himself in attributing human intelligence to the species' superior sense of touch. Similarly, the ancient anatomist Galen claims to agree with Aristotle, yet effectively concurs with Anaxagoras in beginning his treatise *On the Usefulness of the Parts of the Body* with the hand on the grounds that it is characteristic of humanity.

Seventeen centuries after Galen, Friedrich Engels was still pondering the question. In an explanation indebted to Darwin, he traces a dialectical relation between the biological and the technical development of the species. From the adoption of an erect gait and the freeing of hands for making tools, to the consequent increase in social cooperation and eventually speech, "the brain of the ape gradually changed into that of a man."[47] And if the hand is the instrument of labor, and labor created humanity, then the human hand effectively fashioned itself: "the hand is not only the organ of labour, *it is also the product of labour.*"[48]

Returning to *Bound*, we can see this dialectic of the hand in the film's representation of lesbian sexuality. Where Corky's strong hands could be said to represent the process of labor, coded masculine, and Violet's manicured fingers its feminized product, the commoditized body she accuses Caesar of renting, both characters are lesbians, women who actively fuck women with, it is shown, their hands. Moreover, as Violet insists to Corky, she too is a laborer, whose sexual servicing of Caesar and other mobsters is her work. Finally, Violet must become the prime mover in the plot when Corky is kicked unconscious by Caesar and tied up. In keeping with manual eroticism's confusion of the presumptive polarities of activity and passivity, Corky ends up "bound" through an act of her own volition, her refusal to quit on Violet. Like the embezzler Shelly (Barry Kivel), whose desire for Violet fatally delays his escape with the $2 million, she "could have run at any time but . . . didn't want to go." This theme of voluntary suffering for the sake of eros, also suggested in Violet's story of the painful tattooing of her breast, is hyperstylized in the sadomasochistic pose with which the film opens and to which it returns—Corky tied and gagged. But contrary to the critics who interpreted this as an image of lesbian impotence, Corky's bonds are an emblem of her erotic commitment.

Historically, the touching of hands has been a powerful performative, binding the parties to vows, contracts, and wagers. "What we put our hand unto we are infallibly understood to will and intend," declares the Renaissance physician John Bulwer.[49] The voluntary nature of these undertakings is guaranteed by the anatomical epitome of elaborate sensory capacity, complex coordination, and rational control. Caesar may not grasp the advantages of such a limb for love-making, yet he can refer to pistols as "peckers" because both are explosive, erratic, and subject to external control. ("Women," another mobster complains, "make us do stupid things.") And when Caesar wants to overcome Violet's willful opposition, it is her hand he attacks, threatening the same digital amputation that made Shelly squeal.

But if, as an instrument of such stubborn intent, the hand can represent binding commitment, it also does so as an instrument of production, the process that materializes representations of sexuality and sexualities as representations. In *Bound*, this process is illustrated before the film opens, in an anticipatory sequence in which the camera tracks along what looks like a shadowed interior wall intersected by a series of lighted corridors and then tilts and angles to reveal this noir setting as three-dimensional letters spelling out the title. In what follows, the mise-en-scene of an apartment undergoing renovation functions as a reminder of the constructed origins of the film itself, climaxing in the shot that reveals the two lovers touching from opposite sides of the wall and in the process discloses that it is not a wall but a flat, a false wall erected in a set. Like a number of other shots that incensed the critics, this one is conspicuous for its lack of subjective motivation and impossible placement in the diegetic space of the two apartments. The point of view, if anyone's, is that of the film, seeing past the walls of its own construction and, by implication, the normative boundaries of its generic predecessors. And what it beholds are two women touching hands, bound to each other in a gesture both promissory and erotic.

Perhaps the most famous celebration of making love to a woman with one's hands dates from the era of the renaissance anatomists. Yet Donne's Nineteenth Elegy, "To His Mistris Going to Bed," is also one of English poetry's most imperiously phallic productions. Unremittingly colonialist in its elaboration of the trope of the woman's body as the treasure of the Indies, it rides the conceit right through to a punning comparison of sexual license with the royal license awarded to explorers seeking to seize territories for the crown and riches for themselves:

> License my roaving hands, and let them go,
> Before, behind, between, above, below.
> O my America! My new-found-land,
> My kingdome, safeliest when with one man man'd,
> My Myne of precious stones, My Emperie,
> How blest am I in this discovering thee!

At the end of this stanza, the poem predictably moves from manual foreplay to penile penetration—where the lover's hands explore, his "flesh upright" shall enter. Here the penis is figured as a seal, emphasizing its power to penetrate a softer substance while sustaining the image of a royal patent signed by the licensee:

> To enter in these bonds, is to be free;
> Then where my hand is set, my seal shall be.[50]

Setting hand and seal to such a document would confer certain bonds on the signer, but as the responsibilities of the colonial master to his subjects, they are more liberating than onerous. After all, license to enter the woman's body is worth the wealth of the Americas to her conquistador, who instructs his lover to cast off her actual jewels so that he might take possession of his "Myne of precious stones." This image returns me one last time to *Bound*, and its bejewelled figure of the female genitals, the sex that can be made to speak its pleasure in Diderot's fable and that Donne's lover will demand to see that he "may [carnally] know." *Bound* is part of a long tradition that equates women with wealth and their desire with an enigma whose solution is the phallus, but it has a better idea. In this film women get away with the money *and* the jewel of female desire. And they do so not by erotic conquest, but by a freely given love that binds each to the other—and that is made *by hand*.

8 Savage Nights

In 1987, an unusual essay appeared in what was perhaps an even more unusual edition of an academic journal. Under the editorship of Douglas Crimp, *October* 43 devoted 271 pages to the "critical, theoretical, activist alternative to the personal, elegiac expressions that appeared to dominate the art-world response to AIDS."[1] The contributors to this issue included two video producers, an attorney, a community activist, a medical editor, a former executive director of the New York City Minority Task Force on AIDS, and a performance artist campaigning for the rights of prostitutes. Its contents ranged from a critical glossary of the epidemic's "keywords" ("In discussions of AIDS, because of distinctions *not* made—between syndrome and disease, between infectious and contagious—there is often a casual slippage from *communicable* to *contagious*")[2] to a manifesto for New York City policy in regard to the medical, housing, and educational needs of women and children devastated by HIV infection.[3]

Introducing this issue, its editor notes several cultural projects that stimulated its production. The first to be listed is Simon Watney's study of

"Pornography, AIDS and the Media," *Policing Desire*, published in the same year. Watney's book is a pioneering investigation of the popular representations of male homosexuality in the first decade of the epidemic, among them that cluster of morbid figurations that renders the two terms of the expression "gay plague" effective equivalents:

as if the syndrome were a direct function of a particular sexual act—sodomy—and, by extension, of homosexual desire in all its forms.[4]

AIDS offers a new sign for the symbolic machinery of repression, making the rectum a grave.[5]

Describing the norms that pathologize homosexuality, he maintains that the practice

as it is currently construed, contravenes both limited codes concerning the depiction of specific acts such as sodomy between men, as well as much larger, regulative dichotomies which are derived from the anatomical distinction male/female, the attributes of which inform the entire taxonomic field of Western logic. Above all, homosexuality problematizes the casual identification of primary power with the figure of the biological male as masterful penetrator. It equally problematizes the parallel identification of powerlessness and passivity with the figure of the biological female as submissive and penetrated.[6]

Given the influence of Watney's study (in the United States—it has been almost wholly ignored in his native Britain) and the stress it lays on (male) homosexuality as a contravention of gender dichotomies, it is not surprising to find a lengthy meditation on its premises in the same edition of *October*. But Leo Bersani's questioning reply to *Policing Desire*, "Is The Rectum a Grave?" sounds a darker note. Together with other lesbian and gay polemics for the radical subversiveness of sadomasochism, the democratic *camaraderie* of the bathhouse, and the parodic performativity of the lesbian butch-femme couple, Watney's attempt to separate the significations of anal sex from those of sickness and death is subjected to severe critique. "[W]e

149

have been telling a few lies," Bersani announces, "lies whose strategic value I fully understand, but which the AIDS crisis has rendered obsolescent."[7]

Chief among these lies is any attempt to distinguish the fantasies of homosexuality from the dichotomous imaginary Watney ascribes to heterosexuality. In Bersani's view, the leather queen desires, rather than discomfits, masculinity, just as the butch-femme couple submits to, rather than subverts, sexual difference. And to those who would contest the condemnation of sodomy as a lethal violation of that difference's fateful protocols, he replies with a celebration of its murderous power—to slay the imperial ego, "the masculine ideal . . . of proud subjectivity," in the very act of gay sex. "Male homosexuality," his essay concludes, "advertises the risk of the sexual itself as the risk of self-dismissal, of *losing sight* of the self, and in so doing it proposes and dangerously represents *jouissance* as a mode of ascesis."[8]

The argument here derives in part from a more extended meditation on sexuality, *The Freudian Body*, which Bersani published the previous year. There, in a reconsideration of Freud's writings on sex and metapsychology indebted to Jean Laplanche's *Life and Death in Psychoanalysis*, Bersani reads "beyond" *Beyond the Pleasure Principle* to a general definition of sexuality as pleasurable unpleasure. To this end, he adopts Laplanche's elaboration of Freud's argument for "the marginal genesis of sexuality and the genesis of sexuality in a moment of turning round upon the self."[9] According to this account, "sexuality" emerges as a drive through the detachment of an instinctual function (such as infantile sucking) from its natural object (nurturance) and the reflexive redirection of that function at an object reflected within the subject (the breast as fantasized source of pleasure). *Life and Death in Psychoanalysis* links this reflexivity to Freud's description of how the subject's primary aggressiveness spirals into a sexualized sadism via a masochism which ultimately displaces its apparent primacy. (As Freud maintains in "Instincts and Their Vicissitudes," it is only in the turning back of the subject's aggression upon himself that the resulting pain can be transformed through fantasy into sexual excitation.) Combining these observations, Laplanche concludes that (1) all nascent sexuality involves the conversion of a nonsexual activity into sexual excitation via fantasy; and that (2) such excitation involves a necessary breach of the subject's defenses, causing its "first psychical pain and is thus intimately related, in its origin, to the emergence of the masochistic sex drive."[10]

The logic is difficult to evade: All sexuality must be founded on masochism, Bersani argues, finding support in the contradictions of Freud's successive discussions of sex and death in his metapsychological speculations. Rejecting the various hierarchies of libidinal and death instincts that Freud erected and inverted across these writings, he discerns "a collapse of Freud's dualisms and a reconsideration of sex as death, or, more exactly, the hypothesis of an identity between a sexualized consciousness and a destabilized, potentially shattered consciousness."[11] *The Freudian Body* assigns this masochism to human sexuality in general, forced from birth to find pleasure in sensations that overwhelm its infantile capacities for psychic organization. Indeed, it proposes masochism as an inherited survival mechanism for a species whose lengthy sexual maturation would otherwise ill-adapt it to reproduction.

One year—and the acknowledgment of a new, sexually transmitted epidemic—separate this hypothesis from Bersani's *October* article. The latter recapitulates his general observations on "sex as self-abolition," this time alluding to Georges Bataille's contention that eroticism signifies "a violation of the very being of its practitioners," "a violation bordering on death, bordering on murder."[12] (This resort to *Erotism*, it should be noted, appears somewhat selective. Where Bataille describes stripping naked as a quest for bodily "communication" in the face of our "discontinuous existence,"[13] Bersani cautions that he nevertheless "seems to be describing an experience in which the very terms of communication are abolished.")[14] Whether this violent sexuality constitutes a threat to the solipsism of the contemporary subject (as Bataille seems to be arguing) or its intensification ("the irremediable privacy of a masochistic *jouissance*" as Bersani puts it in *The Freudian Body*),[15] both commentators perceive a political dimension to its transgressions: "Eroticism," Bataille insists, "always entails a breaking down of established patterns, the patterns . . . of the regulated so-cial order."[16]

If this is the macro version of a potentially politicizable account of eroticism, Foucault provides Bersani with the micro version, in the second volume of his *History of Sexuality. The Use of Pleasure*, on sexual protocols in ancient Greece, underwrites what might be the motto for the *October* arti-cle, and its final phrase: *"jouissance* as a mode of ascesis." The provenance for this usage of "ascesis" ("training" or "exercise" in the Greek) is Socratic, specifically, the physical and mental preparation enjoined for the ethical exercise of power.[17] But, in his later interviews, Foucault employed the term to describe a method by which the contemporary subject might ex-ceed his own limits—go beyond himself. To this purpose he stressed the self-transformative potential of using one's sexuality to invent new forms of "pleasure . . . relationships, co-existences, attachments, loves, intensi-ties."[18] The most notorious of these, particularly since James Miller's biog-raphy,[19] is homosexual sadomasochism, a practice Foucault regarded, not as a reversion to an aggression and submission latent in the culture or the unconscious, but as a means to different indices and temporalities of pleas-ure than those that "climax" with ejaculation. Such innovations he praised for assuaging men's shame at sexual passivity, a shame that *The Use of Pleasure* considers at some length.

There Foucault argues that, despite the ancient Greek idealization of love between men and boys, an adult male's sexual submission to another could disqualify him from public esteem and political position. For this ar-gument, he is indebted to K. J. Dover's pioneering study of the moral and legal regulation of homosexuality in antiquity. These regulations included an Athenian edict that debarred a citizen who sold sexual favors to an-other male from a range of civic rights (on the grounds that "one who had been a vendor of his own body for others to treat as they pleased would have no hesitation in selling the interests of the community as a whole")[20] as well as moral strictures on the correct conduct of erotic relations be-tween men. As Dover demonstrates, in a society that proscribed nonmari-

tal contact with citizen women, the Athenians sanctioned, indeed celebrated, sexual relations between an active adult male lover (*erastes*) and a
younger male beloved (*eromenos*), but only if each observed the requirements of roles carefully calibrated to maintain the masculinity of both
partners. Thus, the importunate *erastes* was encouraged to be loving, gen-
erous, and gallant, while the object of his affections was enjoined to be
modest, reticent, and—even if he eventually conceded sexual favors—
wholly without sensual pleasure.

In these circumstances, the approved method of intercourse involved a
decorous upright embrace in which the active partner was allowed to place
his penis between the thighs of the passive youth (a practice known to this
day as "Greek sex"). Protocols such as these not only precluded the youth's
acceptance of payment for sex, but any "readiness—even appetite—for homosexual submission, adoption of a bent or lowered position, reception of
another man's penis in the anus or mouth."[21] Citing a ribald pastoral by Theocritus, as well as a vase that pictures a defeated Persian bending over for a
Greek with his erect penis in hand, Dover observes that in classical Greek culture "homosexual anal penetration is treated neither as an expression of love
nor as a response to the stimulus of beauty, but as an aggressive act demon-
strating the superiority of the active to the passive partner." "To choose to be
treated as an object at the disposal of another citizen," he concludes, "was to
resign one's own standing as a citizen."[22]

In the third chapter of *The Use of Pleasure*, Foucault describes this ancient attitude as a "principle of isomorphism between sexual relations and
social relations"[23] in which both spheres are analogously divided between
oppositions of activity and passivity, command and compliance, victory and
defeat. This structural connection of sexual and social relations is the central
theme of "Is the Rectum a Grave?" enabling Bersani to turn from *The
Freudian Body*'s account of human sexuality in general to the disparaged
sexualities of two subordinated populations, gays and women. Taking its
cue from Watney's comparison of Victorian representations of female prostitutes as "contaminated vessels" of syphilitic contagion with AIDS-related

characterizations of gay men, the *October* article relates the promiscuity attributed to both groups to their popularly imagined lust for annihilation:

The realities of syphilis in the nineteenth century and of AIDS today "legitimate" a fantasy of female sexuality as intrinsically diseased; and promiscuity in this fantasy, far from merely increasing the risk of infection, is the sign of infection. *Women and gay men spread their legs with an unquenchable appetite for destruction.*[24]

A footnote to this rather extravagant description underscores the homology it proposes between the vagina and the rectum as "privileged loci" of HIV infection as well as widely fantasized counterparts. Not noted is the homology of sexual position that secures the comparison. It recurs on the next page in Bersani's evocation of the "seductive and intolerable image of a grown man, legs high in the air, unable to refuse the suicidal ecstasy of being a woman."[25]

Seductive, intolerable, and, most of all, uncomfortable. While not uncommon for anal sex, the supine position so vividly evoked in this account is, I suspect, a contrivance, enforcing the identification of the penetrated gay man with the woman embracing her male lover, embracing—in effect—the fatality of sex. Unlike the more conventional *coitus a tergo* Bersani makes so much of in his later *Homos*, precisely for the way "the configuration of the front of one man's body against the back of the other most closely respects, so to speak, the way the anus (*as distinct from the vagina*) presents itself for penetration,"[26] or the intercrural intercourse permitted the Athenian *erastes* and his *eromenos*, the image here of the man on his back ecstatically raising his legs to facilitate penetration combines a literally inferior position with intense volition. If the Greeks never expressed it quite so graphically,[27] this rendition of abandoned anality certainly can be taken to represent the lustful self-subordination which Foucault tells us they condemned as a culpable yielding to the appetites.

I dwell on this, as Bersani does, and for the same reasons. The combination of prostration and desire (of desired prostration) imputed to this particular practice of intercourse opens the way for the principle of sexual and social isomorphism identified by Foucault. Politically (the argument goes), gay men and straight women are *fucked*[28]—because they want to be. In their lustful receptivity to the phallus, they submit to the penetrator's superiority as a topographical and social fact, as well as to a narcissistic wound of potentially fatal proportions. Enter Andrea Dworkin and Catharine MacKinnon, admittedly "unlikely bedfellows" for a gay sadomasochist like Foucault, but as convinced as any ancient Greek of what Bersani describes as "the distribution of power both signified and constituted by men's insistence on being on top."[29] Indeed, Bersani reads MacKinnon's description of the "male suprematist definition of female sexuality as lust for self-annihilation" as a rhetorically enhanced version of Foucault's account of gender in antiquity, the social-sexual isomorphism on which her condemnation of pornography's fusion of "the eroticization of dominance and submission with the social construction of male and female"[30] is also based. Not only does Bersani endorse her consequent claim that legal pornography is legalized violence against women, he congratulates both MacKinnon and Dworkin for condemning the practice as well as the representation of intercourse: "[They] have at least had the courage to be explicit about the profound *moral revulsion* with sex."[31]

In this salute to their unflinching recognition of the awful truth about sex, feminism's greatest mistresses of hyperbole finally meet their match. For the joke, of course, is on Dworkin and MacKinnon, since Bersani will fan the flames of their philippic, endorse their critique of intercourse, in order to praise precisely what they regard as intolerable about it: "Their indictment of sex—their refusal to prettify it, to romanticize it, to maintain that fucking has anything to do with community or love—has had the immensely desirable effect of publicizing, of lucidly laying out for us, the inestimable value of sex as—at least in certain of its ineradicable aspects—anticommunal, antiegalitarian, antinurturing, antiloving."[32] Where sexual reformers lament the solipsism of sex without relation, a selfishness sorely emblematized for Dworkin and MacKinnon in men's masturbation to images of female submission, Bersani—via a glancing citation of Foucault's argument for the immanence of power in social relations—condemns the relational itself as the occasion of those narcissistic investments that lead to the desire for mastery. Moreover, he goes on to mock the two women (and, albeit with slightly less derision, contemporary apologists for homosexuality like Weeks and Watney) for their "pastoralizing, redemptive" attempts to clean up sex, to purge it of its power.

This argument anticipates its fuller development in Bersani's 1990 *Culture of Redemption*, with its Nietzschean dismissal of the corrective power of thought, specifically those critical projects that could be said to elevate exegesis to a form of textual sublimation. Here Joyce's *Ulysses* comes in for a particularly pointed reproach, as a text that "substitutes for the interpretative ordeals posed by such writers as Lawrence, Mallarmé, and Bataille a kind of affectless busyness, the comfortable if heavy work of finding all the connections in the light of which the novel can be made intelligible but not interpreted":

The intertextual criticism invited by Ulysses *is the domestication of literature, a technique for making familiar the potentially traumatic seductions of reading.*[33]

This opposition of "domestication" to trauma, both textual and sexual, structures Bersani's criticism. Thus, the *October* article rebukes Watney's call for the recognition of sexual diversity as "unnecessarily and even dangerously tame . . . disingenuous about the relation between homosexual behavior and the revulsion it inspires."[34] Moreover, Bersani suggests that machismo itself may simply represent the denial of "the seductiveness of an image of sexual powerlessness," the same "domesticating, even sanitizing" impetus that animates its feminist opponents.[35]

Counterposed to "the domestic," "the redemptive," "the pastoral," "the tame," we find—in a subsequent meditation on "Sex and Death" much influenced by Bersani—"the wild": "the wild space of the promiscuous encounter," "the wildness of a once vaguely defined illicit sexuality became in a sense even wilder."[36] Jonathan Dollimore's subsequent discussion of these oppositions returns to the *October* article to quote its accusation against the "normalizing vision of gay desire": "unnecessarily and even dangerously tame." His "wilding"[37] of Bersani's already fierce denigration of any attempt to "tame" the trauma of seduction brings the logic of both their arguments into relief. Not for the first time is "our savage sexuality," as Bersani repeatedly describes it in *The Freudian Body*,[38] made to play nature to a culture variously associated with domesticity and dishonesty, religion and repression. In particular, sex is counterposed to "homework" (as Bersani describes the endless exegetical exercises which Joyce sets the reader of *Ulysses*) and to housework, whether it be the anal character's "compulsively renewed emptying of ashtrays"[39] or that of those feminists and queers obsessed with "sanitizing aggression."

With these distinctions before us, it is tempting to invoke Biddy Martin's observations on "femininity's traditional association with attachment, enmeshment and home"[40] and read this opposition of wild and tame as one of gender, in which the libido is reconfirmed in its masculine character and femininity effectively set against sex itself. This is, in part, my complaint, but it must be qualified with the observation that, in his comparisons of heterosexual women and homosexual men, Bersani seems at times to be describing two different "femininities."[41] A cursory reading of his rendition of rectal sex reveals a heroic rhetoric of "demolition," "danger," and "sacrifice" (all terms from his essay's final page) that is nowhere attributed to vaginal penetration. Might it be Bersani's view that male "femininity" is butcher than its female equivalent, precisely because the subject's masculinity is at stake? The idea that subordination to another male can "make a man of you," however alien to the Athenians, would be all too familiar to the Greeks on America's campuses, as well as to numerous other men subjected to sexual hazing by their male superiors in ritual inductions ranging from boot camp to stag night. While neither of these is legally available to Anglo-American gays at present, some homosexual equivalent (Bersani mentions a "tough and brutal" evening of rejection at a bathhouse) might save them from what he portrays as a fate far worse than any shattering of the self—being taken home by a swaggering leatherman who turns out to talk like a "pansy," reads Jane Austen, "gets you into bed, and—well—you know the rest."[42] Again, going home *tames* gay sex, transforming the phallic cruiser into the pansy, whose sexuality is as domesticated as (shades *of The Culture of Redemption*) his reading. His fate—and his sort of femininity—await gay men who accept recruitment into the relational. Only in the wrong place, in the "wild," can femininity attain to the condition of its opposite, allowing the gay subject both his *horror feminae* and his de-gendering adoration of the phallus.

Jonathan Dollimore's discussion of the "wild space of the promiscuous encounter" is part of a larger project on what he describes as "the perverse dynamic in western culture which binds together desire, death and loss (mutability), and especially the belief that desire is in a sense impossible."[43] Although his general remarks on that dynamic adduce literary examples from Plato to Montaigne, those on the homosexual death-drive concentrate on gay men's writings since the 1970s, particularly contemporary works that take AIDS as their context, if not their subject. This focus on the epidemic is understandable, since Dollimore follows Watney in observing that the responses to it have construed homosexuality as "death-driven, death-desiring and death-dealing."[44] But, like Bersani, whose work is discussed at some length, Dollimore is profoundly ambivalent about this claim, arguing that "it's one thing to disarticulate the lethal connections between death and homosexuality made by, say, the moral right, quite another to censor or disavow insightful gay writing about the death/desire paradox."[45] Against the former's crude association of gay sex with morbidity, he counterposes the latter's exploration of a fundamental contradiction in subjectivity: "the self riven by, constituted by, loss."[46] Yet the very generality that Dollimore attributes to this paradox is immediately circumscribed by both its homosexualization and masculinization in his account. The fatality that culture assigns to homosexuality is matched by the male homosexual's own fatalism, an "AIDS-related fatalism" evidenced in the fiction of Oscar Moore and the journalism of Rupert Haselden, "both of whom . . . share an acute sense that desire is driven by a lack inherently incapable of satisfaction."[47] In Moore's 1991 novel, *A Matter of Life and Sex*,[48] this conviction is represented in the unsatisfiable yearnings of the central character, a promiscuous youth whose intimations of mortality come true in the epidemic. Haselden's *Guardian* article of the same year argued that London's cruise bars were again busy because "biologically maladaptive" gay men, unable to reproduce, continued to abandon themselves to a perpetual round of self-destructive pleasure, "living for today because we have no tomorrow."[49]

This is not, as Dollimore carefully points out, the only possible understanding of gay male sexuality and its relation to fatality. A footnote from Douglas Crimp[50] argues that it is precisely the plurality of homosexual practices that has enabled the invention of safer pleasures, while a flashback to the seventies fiction of John Rechy and Michael Rumaker reminds us that the promiscuous gay "outlaws" of the decade, however much they were figured as the street-fighting revolutionaries of the period, still stood for "satisfied bodies instead of dead ones."[51] Nevertheless, both Rechy and Rumaker's acknowledgments of their own suicidal impulses, as a result of frustrated or condemned desire, are taken by Dollimore to support "the death-sex connection" in what is an undeniably teleological argument. Just as the insatiability of the seventies cruiser is read to anticipate the unsatisfiability of desire registered in the AIDS writings of the nineties, so his suicidal longings come to fruition with actual death in the epidemic.

All of which makes me wonder if it is the case, as Bersani claims in his *October* article, that AIDS has merely "literalized" the fantasmatic connection between sex and self-destruction, or whether it has played a more constitutive role in the new gay literature of the death drive. Although Dollimore can point to this theme in the pre-AIDS writings of Wilde, Baldwin, and Holleran, his contention that the "sexually dissident have always tended to know more about . . . the strange dynamic which, in western culture, binds death into desire"[52] consigns those activists with whom he disagrees to a sexual conformity even less radical than the redemptive project savaged by Bersani. Among those who would dissent from Dollimore's dissidence is Jeff Nunokawa, whose attempt to historicize the "lethal characterization"[53] of homosexuality in both gay and straight culture is bizarrely appropriated in "Sex and Death" to the opposite purpose. Where Nunokawa grounds his discussion of *Dorian Gray* and his Karposi's-scarred successors in a nine-teenth-century hellenism preoccupied with beauty's brevity, Dollimore discards the genealogy from the gayness to claim his essay as yet more evidence that homosexuals have themselves regarded their sexuality "fatalistically, morbidly, and as somehow doomed of its very nature."[54]

If true sexual dissidents, in Dollimore's account, avidly await their rendezvous with death, the gay who associates homosexuality with healing and nurturance—to cite his sole example, the narrator of Michael Rumaker's 1977 novel *A Day and Night at the Baths*—is a big sissy, keen on moisturizer and personal hygiene, hilariously polite in pick-ups, his lunch packed all-too-literally with health food. "[C]autious, domesticated, and very much on the side of ordinary life," Rumaker's hero (whom Dollimore renders as a sort of gay lib Candide) wanders naively through an increasingly dangerous milieu, whose "wildness" becomes "even wilder" as bathhouse sex gets "more transgressive"[55] in the sadomasochistic seventies and the epidemic looms ahead. When we learn that this exponent of "mutually consenting and courteous erotic play" identifies with women while being fucked, the feminization of his anodyne vision of an American utopia "where gay sex is free, benign and healing, and sufficiently sanitized to be reincorporated in civic society"[56] is contemptuously driven *home*.

So, "Sex and Death" . . . and wildness, transgression, and masculinity. My purpose in questioning these equivalences is not to deny the poignancy of Dollimore's account of lovers whose illness renders "desire itself as a kind of grieving,"[57] nor to refuse any notion of a sexual drive to an ecstatic self-shattering, nor to ignore the practice of homosexual sadomasochism. It is, however, to resist the conflation of these three instances, and their implicit gendering, in the "epidemic of signification"[58] which he and Bersani survey. To do so, I suggest that we heed the call of the wild and pursue the political consequences of its erotic narratives. My model for this inquiry is Cora Kaplan's pioneering essay on feminism and eroticism, "Wild Nights" (of which more below). My first object of investigation is a French novel whose author was described by *France-Soir* as "convinced like Bataille that eroticism and death are inextricably linked" and whose Paris setting, promiscuous hero, and references to AIDS lead Dollimore to compare it to Moore's *A Matter of Life and Sex*.

Cyril Collard's *Savage Nights* is better known in the 1992 film version in which its author starred. Seventy-two hours after his death from an AIDS-related illness on 5 March 1993, it was awarded four Cesars, the French equivalent of the Oscar. Collard's own appearance in a film about an HIV-positive film-maker, a film he himself wrote and directed, and his death at the very moment of its recognition, accomplished a publicity coup to, so to speak, die for. The enthusiastic responses to a film that belatedly provoked public discussion of an epidemic long (and lethally) ignored in France are themselves instructive. But to understand its title, to pursue the savagery in Collard's portrait of a sadomasochistic cameraman with a taste for "stiff cocks, degrading gestures, strong smells,"[59] and Arab youths, it is necessary to turn to the original novel, first published in 1989 under the title *Les nuits fauves*.

Like the film, the novel follows the 30-year-old bisexual narrator's tortured relationship with Laura, a seventeen-year-old aspirant actress, across two years. But unlike the film, it deals at equal length with his friendship with Omar—a director with whom he is making a film about young Algerians in the Nanterre slums and their encounter with a white French doctor "completely at the mercy of his desire for Arab bodies"[60]—as well as his sexual relationships with four young men: Kader, an eighteen-year-old whom he follows to Algeria; Sammy, who claims Spanish-Arab parentage, yet becomes a fascist; Olivier, a Burgundian of Arab extraction; and Jamal, a seventeen-year-old Islamic rapper. As one might expect, the hero of the novel is an aficionado of Arab culture, who travels to Morocco and Algeria, shoots a film about African musicians living in Paris and another about a gay white Frenchman who offers his services to the Fedayeen. Genet, as the narrator modestly observes, comes to mind. So do the French colorists who championed Islamic and African art and painted in the wild style that secured their nomination as "Fauves."

Here Collard exploits the multiple references of the French *fauve(s)*: "fawn-colored," "musky," "deer," "game," as well as the Neo-Impressionist school of Matisse, Derain, and Vlaminck, whose apparent recklessness with color and brushwork earned them the sobriquet "wild beasts." Laura is the first of the narrator's lovers to be described in these terms. The daughter of an Algerian mother, she has skin that glows with "a tawny color, a savage colour,"[61] and certainly the crazed intensity of her relation with the hero, and the risks they run in abjuring condoms, make their agonistic couplings as wild as any in the book:

She came with a scream, clawing at my back. I fucked her again, then came with a throaty yell, feeling I was coming as I'd never come before. . . . I was floating, knowing that I had shot her full of sperm that was infected with a deadly virus, but feeling that it was all right, that nothing would happen, because we were starting what could truly be called "a love story."[62]

But it is with the narrator's homosexuality that Fauvism is directly invoked, connecting the savagery of his masochistic encounters beneath the Seine bridges to the strange hues of their shadowy setting, and both with the tawny skin of his Arab amours.

When I leave, with the skeleton of a night with the savages behind me, the bony shell of the miracle, my back is streaked with red welts, my chest bruised by combat-boot soles, my tits burning, my pants soaked, dried spittle on my face and streaks of cold piss tickling my thighs.

The savages take on the colors of the Fauve painters of the past. Somber, evanescent pastels in the jackets brushing pillars; the washed-out grays of faces; blue fragments of jeans enveloping arses, cocks and balls. . . .

The black and white memory of the tangled bodies bear Fauve traces: Sammy and his fellows' golden color, which the darkness can't extinguish.[63]

Collard's description evokes only a little of the Fauve style—the purity of color, flattened perspective, and arbitrary accents—but it is redolent of its ethos, the cultivated primitivism with which Matisse painted, among many subjects, his Moroccan series of 1912. Such primitivism, with its associations of impetuosity, irrationality, and intensity, is what Collard's narrator seeks, a "savagery" predictably represented by race, but also by class, youth and an inclination to violence. This violence is meted out to him in scenes of gay sadomasochism, in which his body, unlike that of Bersani's subject, is not penetrated but beaten and dirtied. Nonetheless, the narrator's ecstatic response to this pain and humiliation, combined with the novel's knowing invocation of Bataille (to whose play *Le Mort* the narrator is "inexplicably" invited on page 112), seems intended to signal the self-annihilating *jouissance* identified by both Bersani and Dollimore with sexual radicalism. And yet, in the predictably perverse dialectics of sadomasochism, these scenes prove not to be ones of submission, no funerals for proud masculine subjectivity, but celebrations of mastery.

Some bodies hesitated, circled, spoke; for me, it had to be all or nothing. I announced my tastes; if the answer was no, I roughly shoved the man away; if yes, I'd follow him and scream out my pleasure on the steps of an iron staircase on the other side of the bridge.

Standing soiled and bruised at the river's edge after orgasm, I felt graceful and light. Transparent.[64]

Later, I went walking across the constantly erased footprints left by the passengers of sex. A half-moon shrouded by clouds shines on the roof of the barges. Dust and gravel mixed. For a few hundred yards, full of an immediate desire, I am free of restraints and powers. I feel I am lord and master.[65]

The narrator's tricks may beat him savagely, but they do it *to order*. Like his Arab boys with their fawn-colored skin and the attendant cervine connotations of man's favorite quarry, the Parisian rough trade is ultimately dominated by its submissive superior in class and race, who rises again from their ministrations to stand "graceful and light." Far from illustrating any isomorphism between male sexual passivity and a commensurate social subordination, *Savage Nights* insistently—one might say narcissistically, given its autobiographical tenor—reveals its bourgeois bottom to be a top, older, wealthier, and whiter than his sexual objects.[66] Indeed, the emphatic *non*abjection of the hero may explain its crossover success in France.

If this upends the social-sexual topography claimed by Bersani to subordinate gay men, via the heterosexual association of their sexual receptivity with a self-annihilating propensity to pleasure originally identified with female concupiscence, what of women themselves? Here it is important to remember the political responses to the ancient isomorphic principle relayed by Foucault and summarized by Bersani as "the distribution of power both signified and constituted by men's insistence on being on top." Many feminists have recognized the *Weltanschauung* which informs this denigration of the supine position ("Dworkin takes a pornographic image as a kind of world view: the law on top, men in the middle, women at the bottom") and refused it: "I don't see an image of a woman being penetrated in the missionary position as symbolic of a woman as a *victim*."[67] And in a further questioning of MacKinnon's identification of sexual penetration with personal violation, they have noted how exquisitely *masculine* this terror is: "What is the worst imaginable disaster to the masculine self? To be fucked."[68] Reflecting ironically on the apocalyptic rhetoric so characteristic of this argument, Drucilla Cornell has asked, "But why is it the end of the world 'to be fucked'?" The answer, in her reading of *Feminism Unmodified*, is that MacKinnon unwittingly subscribes to the phallic imaginary she purports to oppose and its equation of masculinity with selfhood, a selfhood defined as assertion rather than reception:

Indeed, she cannot affirm carnality as long as she recasts the subject as seeking freedom, not intimacy, in sex. If it is accepted that to be masculine, to be a self, is not to "be fucked," then if women are "fucked," we cannot be individuals.[69]

Cornell reads this phallic identification in MacKinnon's diction as well as her logic, citing this exquisitely self-revealing salvo from *Feminism Unmodified*: "I am getting hard on this and am about to get harder on it."[70] And, in a related observation, Wendy Brown remarks on "the insistent and pounding quality" of MacKinnon's prose, its "stylistic mirroring" of the porno-graphic text's repetitive thrustings and rhythmic crescendos, "suspending us in a complex pornographic experience in which MacKinnon is both pur-veyor and object of desire and her analysis is proffered as substitute for the sex she abuses us for wanting."[71]

In comparison, Bersani's investments in the very phallic identifica-tion—"the masculine ideal . . . of proud subjectivity"—whose demise he cel-ebrates are both more overt and more oblique than MacKinnon's. The logic of the *October* article precludes the acknowledgment of the gay male top, as well as women's active eroticism, whether hetero- or homosexually directed. (The female superior position in straight sex is dismissed as a mere game compared to the powerful probing of the penis beneath, while lesbianism is wholly ignored.) Nonetheless, the gay man's desire for masculinity is distin-guished from the collaborative longings of other oppressed subjects (those of blacks for whites, Jews for Gentiles are instanced) by the possibility homo-sexuality offers for both appropriation *of* and identification *with* the erotic object. Bersani's 1995 *Homos* elaborates this point in a confession of gay men's misogyny and its "narcissistically gratifying reward of confirming our membership in (and not simply our erotic appetite for) the privileged male society."[72]

The related reversibility of the supine position in sex, if not in society—the possibility of a gay man experiencing what Bersani terms "sex as self-hy-perbole," "psychic tumescence"[73]—suggests another reading of "Is the Rec-tum a Grave?" not as the funeral of the phallus, but rather as its resurrection. The penis, like the prostrate male to which it is attached, will rise again. Nothing in the anal receptivity of the penetrated male precludes its posses-sion in actuality, let alone his identification with its potency. For what is all this talk of its "shattering" and "annihilating" powers but phallic narcissism by other means?[74] (And isn't this why both Bersani and MacKinnon, for all their ostensible interest in women's sexuality, so rarely address those women who fuck without the penis, the lesbians?)

This occlusion of the lesbian is not the sole liability of a sexual politics

that reassigns femininity to passivity and (however positively) erotic receptivity to self-destruction, although it is an undoubtedly related effect. There
are further drawbacks to Bersani's homology of the grave, the rectum and the
vagina. As that historic exponent of anality, Guy Hocquenghem, so memorably observed, "The anus is not a substitute for the vagina: women have one
as well as men."[75] Any equation of the rectum with the vagina effectively denies the very existence of the *woman's* anus and the possibility of its own
erotic deployment. Whatever "the widespread confusion in heterosexual *and*
homosexual men between fantasies of anal and vaginal sex"[76] on which
Bersani remarks, that sex endowed with both organs of pleasure may prefer
to keep all its options open.

Not that this has ever been a simple matter for feminism. If we turn
from Collard's *Savage Nights* to Kaplan's "Wild Nights," we are reminded that
the liberal humanism that begot feminism out of *The Rights of Man* also prop-
agated a modernized derogation of female sexuality. First published in 1983,
the era of the "sex wars" in which Dworkin and MacKinnon were such celebrated combatants, "Wild Nights" looks back to feminism's foundational
anxieties about women's sexual pleasure as the surrender of social power. Beneath three provocative epigraphs—from Dickinson's eponymous poem,
Dworkin's *Pornography*, and Wollstonecraft's 1792 *Vindication of the Rights of
Women*—the last, "the founding text of Anglo-American feminism,"[77] is
reread to remind us that it too identified female desire with a moral laxity
meriting civil subordination. In unhappy anticipation of her successors two
centuries later, Mary Wollstonecraft dedicated the *Vindication* to persuading
women "to become more masculine and respectable."[78] Her argument—that
femininity, in its vanity, coquettishness and cultivated ignorance, is tailored
to the requirements of heterosexual attraction—established an uncanny
precedent for Dworkin and MacKinnon's description of the eroticized en-
gendering of female subordination.[79]

Writing at a time when a new perception of pleasure as danger meant
that "eros rampant [was] more likely to conjure up a snuff movie than multiple orgasm,"[80] when pornography, rape, and child abuse became central, if

highly contested, issues in feminist politics, Kaplan opens her remarks by singling out sexuality as "the wild card whose suit and value shifts provocatively with history. As dream or nightmare, or both at once, it reigns in our lives as an anarchic force, refusing to be chastened and tamed by sense or conscience to a sentence in a revolutionary manifesto."[81] But if so exuberantly romantic a formulation threatens to put sex back into Bersani and Dollimore's wilderness—amoral, irrational, anarchic—Kaplan's own sense of how this spectacularly shifting signifier changes with history refuses it that naturalization. Indeed, what makes her essay so exemplary is its historicization of both feminisms and femininities, and their complex relation to each other,[82] as well as to other conditions of existence. Sex is a wild card, she tells us, because its value is contextual rather than inherent. Reflecting, at her essay's conclusion, on the ironic similarities between Wollstonecraft the liberal feminist and her radical feminist successor Adrienne Rich, who respectively condemn and celebrate lesbianism for virtually identical reasons, she resists their appeals against a corrupting (Wollstonecraft) and compulsory (Rich) heterosexuality to insist upon the contingency of our sexual practices and the values we assign them:

The identification of the sources of social good or evil in the sexual drive of either sex, or in any socially specific practice, is a way of foreclosing our still imperfect understanding of the histories of sexuality. The moralization of desire that inevitably follows from such an analysis colludes with those dominant practices which construct human sexuality through categories of class, race and gender in order to divide and rule.[83]

Surely it would be perverse to accuse a critic like Bersani, so resolutely opposed to all that is "redemptive," "pastoral," "salvational," of the moralization of desire? Better to take up Kaplan's opposition of a transcendent sexual ethics to specific sexual histories and describe his homology of sex and social standing as "ahistorical." This ahistoricism reappears conspicuously in his more recent attack on the *bien pensant* presumptions of queer theory, *Homos.* There, enlarging upon the *October* article's passing scorn for those who would redeem "fascistic" S/M as a parody of fascism, Bersani argues that sadomasochism does nothing to undermine actual social power. In what could be a comment on Collard's bourgeois masochist, he maintains that "the concession to a secret and potentially enervating need to shed the master's exhausting responsibilities and to enjoy briefly the irresponsibility of total powerlessness allows for a comfortable return to a position of mastery and oppression the morning after, when all that 'other side' has been, at least for a time, whipped out of the executive's system."[84] But, having conceded the nonequivalence of sexual practice and social power, Bersani moves from sadomasochism's failure to challenge actual authority to propose its *complicity with* that authority, as the necessary principle of the master-slave relation. Foucault's attempts to distinguish S/M from any structure of power are given short shrift. In Bersani's view, S/M's eroticization of dominance without the practical supports of racism or economic exploitation merely reveals its worship of unalloyed authority, a devotion that need not be confined to the sexual arena.

Curiously, Bersani offers these speculations on the nonideological appeal of dominance and the possible "intractability of extreme forms of oppression"[85] in the name of history. History is what S/M is said to deny in its attempt to separate sexual fantasy from social consequence: "[T]he polarized structure of master and slave, of dominance and submission, is the same in Nazism and S/M."[86] Why should the masochist, he asks, having discovered the irresistible pleasure of "bondage, discipline and pain," confine his submission to sex? To assume that he will not bring his erotic inclinations to his politics is to "remove fantasy from history."[87]

This raises the imminent prospect of a mass, indeed universal, move to fascism, since the argument for the masochism of all human sexuality is also reiterated in *Homos*. To this Bersani offers no solution except S/M's own (masochistic) flaunting of its social unacceptability, and thus the future possibility of its abolition in the name of anti-fascism. How seriously we are to entertain either of these possibilities is not revealed. Instead, in an attempt to retain the fantasy within history, Bersani returns to his *Ur*-history of ancient Greece and its isomorphism of gender roles and social status, this time quoting the Foucauldian classicist David Halperin's description of Athenian sexual norms:

"Active" and "passive" sexual roles are therefore necessarily isomorphic with superordinate and subordinate social status.[88]

Again, the classical convention is said to have feminized those men who accepted phallic penetration, and again, their position is compared to that of the bottom in the contemporary sadomasochistic scene. And if every (implicitly masochistic) gay man finds an erotic appeal in fascism, so must every (implicitly heterosexual) woman, since the two groups are yet again argued to be effectively identical.

In a sense, the Greeks were so open about their revulsion to what they understood as female sexuality, and so untroubled in their thinking about the relation between power and phallic penetration, that they didn't need to pretend, as nineteenth-century sexologists did, that men who went to bed with other men were all secretly women. Only half of them were women, and that judgment had enormous social implications; the adult male citizen who allowed himself to be penetrated, like inferior women and slaves, was politically disgraced. The persistence of this judgment throughout the centuries and in various cultures is well documented.[89]

Fortuitously, *Homos* presents this account of the transhistorical subordination of the sexually penetrated subject in a chapter titled "The Gay Daddy." I say fortuitously because its argument so insistently summons to mind Sylvia Plath's "Daddy" and its famous lines:

Every woman adores a fascist,
The boot in the face, the brute
Brute heart of a brute like you.

Are we returned to Bersani's wilderness, where women (and womanish men) repine in masochistic thrall to the brute beast of masculine sexuality? One reading of "Daddy," as a work that questions rather than produces identifications, argues otherwise. Reflecting on the vicissitudes of identification manifested in the analyses of Holocaust survivors, Jacqueline Rose cites numerous cases of patients "in fantasy occupying either side of the victim/aggressor divide,"[90] a fantasy which, she also argues, structures Plath's poem. To feminists, the masochism in that divided fantasy is bad enough. But "most awkward,"[91] writes Rose, is the poem's sadism, not the defensible revenge of Plath the spurned wife and abandoned daughter, but that of a possible identification with the fascist permitted by the unspecified agency putting the boot in. For if absolute authority can elicit desire, it can also, as we have seen, command identification—here, the identification of the fatherless daughter with the German Daddy she calls "bastard." The boot may be on the other's foot.

However we interpret Plath's poem, Rose's reading concludes with an argument that should be addressed to any isomorphic account of social and sexual subordination. As she observes, it is *in absentia* that the dead patriarch of "Daddy" rules most powerfully. The poem is therefore indeed a matter of fantasy, as well as the "concrete history" of Nazism. Those who collapse the two risk losing fantasy and history both, Rose warns, "for fascism must surely be distinguished from patriarchy, even if in some sense it can be seen as its effect." To refuse this distinction, to assimilate each to the other, effectively suspends patriarchy in an "eternal sameness"[92] of historical invariability.

I read this as a caveat against the identification of fascism with any erotic practice, as well as the hypostatized historiography which would explain contemporary homophobia in terms of a protocol some 2,500 years old. But although *Homos* restates the Foucauldian account, it seems less comfortable in its analytic straitjacket than the *October* article of eight years before. Bersani may retain his history of a prohibition that persists in feminizing gay men "throughout the centuries," but his discussion of what that femininity might consist of is now subject to question:

To be a woman in a man's body is certainly an imprisoning definition, but at least it leaves open the possibility to wonder, as Freud did, about the various desiring posi-

tions a woman might take. She might awaken in the male body the wish to be phal-
licly penetrated, but she might also lead him to love himself actively through a boy
(as, according to Freud, Leonardo sought to relive his mother's love for him as a child
by becoming attached to younger men); or she might awaken in him a complex sce-
nario of orality in which his homosexuality would, strangely enough, be best satisfied
with a lesbian.[93]

Strange indeed, to contemplate the eroticization of a lesbian in Bersani's writing. Or "lesbianism," I should say, since his subsequent citation of Proust makes it clear that this is the aestheticized appropriation of an elegant erotic *chiasma* rather than the awkward recognition of a subject who might confound his theory. Still, if male homosexuality continues to be conjugated in terms of the "desiring positions a woman might take," shouldn't this belated discovery of their variety feed back to the women who might take them?

This may be the logic of Bersani's evocation of the "hypothetically endless crisscross of sexual identities,"[94] but it is not one *Homos* pursues. Instead, the focus remains resolutely on the fellas, albeit now in a more open prison. Where "Is the Rectum a Grave?" offered only one possible position for their imputed femininity (the bottom), *Homos'* attempt to posit a gay identity without essence loosens this identification into "several positions" of desire. Insofar as they make a cross-sex identification, Bersani argues, gay men are spared the defensive adoption of a paternal ego ideal. Instead, they take up an "indeterminate identity,"[95] that of the self which desires its own sex through disidentification with that sex. Not only is the misogyny caused by equating femininity with castration thereby escaped, so is the antagonism to the father created by his identification with the Law.

This process is illustrated in a rereading of a famous account of an infant boy's identification with his mother's pleasure in penetration, and his erotic attitude toward his father. But unlike Freud, who argues that the boy's subsequent repression of that feminine passivity resulted in the replacement of his desire for his father with a fear of his castrating powers eventually manifested in an animal phobia, Bersani stresses the "compassion" in the Wolf Man's later recollection of the (real or imagined) event:

During the copulation in the primal scene he had observed the penis disappear . . . he had felt compassion for his father on that account, and had rejoiced in the reappearance of what he thought had been lost.[96]

As Bersani points out, this is not the only evidence of filial tenderness in this case. Not only does the patient remember his pity when visiting his sick father in a sanitorium at the age of six, he also recalls elaborate religious fantasies structured around the father-son relation. For the leading lover of *Homos*, latest in the works of the pre-eminent critic of the culture of redemption, is a little boy with a Christ complex.

Born on Christmas Day and instructed in the tenets of Russian Orthodoxy by his nurse, the Wolf Man recounts to Freud a childhood of obsessive religiosity and an eventual identification with the Redeemer himself. The identification is interpreted to provide the active masculinity necessary to repudiate the boy's passive homosexual attachment to his father. But Freud admits that this attempt to sever the attachment is a failure: "If he was Christ, then his father was God. But the God which religion forced upon him was not a true substitute for the father whom he loved and whom he did not want to have stolen from him."[97] To redeem humanity, God the Father must sacrifice his Son. To redeem his father, the pious son must sacrifice God. Rejecting the patriarchal cruelty of the Gospels, the boy turns against religion. In order to save his father from becoming the merciless executor of the Law, he forswears the sublimation of paternity into divinity, and his own identification with God's Son.

Bersani concludes the penultimate chapter to *Homos* with a celebration of that child's compassion, for the father almost lost to religion and the phallus (paternal, filial, both) almost lost to the analyst's insistence on the castrating bar between father and son. In his account, the case of the Wolf Man "unintentionally provides us with one genealogy of gay love." It does so, I would stipulate, not in spite of "the redemptive" and "the salvational," but precisely through those means. Not only is the Wolf Man the Redeemer re-deemed, the Christ whose compassion saves his would-be crucifier from his murderous destiny, but his mission is the resurrection of the body—in Bersani's terms, the restoration of the "oblated" (sacrificed) organ. His chapter on "The Gay Daddy" closes with a rewriting of the scene of homosexual penetration (now called "lovemaking"), one that awards the power of phal-lic representation to the bottom, whose visible penis makes good the tem-porary loss of his penetrator's:

We might imagine that a man being fucked is generously offering the sight of his own penis as a gift or even a replacement for what is temporarily being "lost" inside him— an offering not made in order to calm his partner's fears of castration but rather as the gratuitous and therefore even lovelier protectiveness that all human beings need when they take the risk of merging with another, of risking their own boundaries for the sake of self-dissolving extensions.[98]

Earlier in this chapter, I described this fantasy of recovered potency as one of narcissism. So does Freud, observing that his patient's youthful com-passion for others (beggars, cripples, the old, as well as his sick father) in-volved a large measure of uncomfortable identification, which he fended off by ritual exhalations echoing his father's heavy breathing during sex. At the end of the passage on the Wolf Man's anxiety at the disappearance of his fa-ther's penis in the primal scene, he notes: "The narcissistic origin of com-passion (which is confirmed by the word itself) is here quite unmistakably re-vealed." As in the English "compassion," the German *Mitleid* ("suffering with") associates pity with identification.

If we read this compassion back into an article whose point of depar-ture is a lethal epidemic devastating the author's own community, its sav-agery takes on a different hue. For surely the *October* essay's projection of redemption onto the feminine and the feminist belies its own rhetorical investments in precisely that process? "Gay men's 'obsession' with sex, far from being denied, should be celebrated," Bersani writes at its conclusion, "because it never stops re-presenting the internalized phallic male as an infinitely loved object of sacrifice."[99] Here sacrifice is commended and the denigrated language of redemption is itself redeemed. But if the phallic male is the object of the sacrifice, on whose behalf is it made? The answer, of course, is also the phallic male, who (Bersani tells us endlessly) the gay man is and is not. Without performing the same obeisance to that idol, I am moved to say that this narcissistic association of the phallus and the (gay) man[100] enables, if only by its gruff disguise, the author's expression of love for those he *suffers with*, the victims of the epidemic, the dead he would have rise again. Beyond the high-flown rhetoric of a fatal eros, one can discern another love and a wish (pastoral, redemptive, and selfish as it undoubtedly is): a wish for life.

How might the gendered opposition of wild and tame, savagery and domesticity, be thought otherwise? Three very different cultural initiatives offer a postscript to this problem. In 1989, the American artist Millie Wilson mounted a "retrospective" of an imaginary early twentieth-century painter entitled *Fauve Semblant: Peter (A Young English Girl)*.[101] Loosely based on the lesbian painters Gluck and Romaine Brooks, Wilson's artist is both an actual and aesthetic cross-dresser, who wears men's clothes and seeks recognition in an art world closed to women. Denied admission to the school of Matisse and Derain on grounds of sex, Peter is a triumph of imagination over interdiction, a defiant artist who is herself a work of art by the lesbian artist Wilson, who poses for a photograph of Peter in drag, bow-tied at her easel, a counterfeit of the already *faux* Fauve. And so *en abîme*. Wilson's participation in the retrospective recalls critical attention to the continued male domination of contemporary art, as well as the sexual apartheid of those celebrated French painters whose "wild" colorism was proclaimed as freedom.

My second example follows the original Fauves to North Africa, and a discussion of feminist politics and Francophone literature in postcolonial Algeria. In *Transfigurations of the Maghreb*, Winifred Woodhull examines the traditional figure of *la femme sauvage*, the ogress of folktale whose "wild femininity [is] by turns fertile and sterile, nourishing and devouring, domesti-

cated and untame, economically productive and ruinous."[102] Like the wild-
fire to which she is compared, this savage woman may rekindle the hearth or
burn down the house. In the literature of the Algerian War and its aftermath,
she becomes an agent of revolution, maker and unmaker of identities, an im-
placable force for cultural as well as political transformation. Rather than opposing them, Woodhull allies this wild femininity to the "wild masculinity"
of male homosexuality in the post-Liberation fiction of the Algerian novelist
Rachid Boudjedra. Both are argued to disclose "the instability of the sexual
binary and other social oppositions intersected by it," that of "colonizer and
colonized" as well as "men and boys, ruler and ruled, the sane and the in-
sane, and heterosexuality and homosexuality."[103]

"Domesticated and untame," the savage woman of the Maghreb beckons me finally to the poem whose title and first stanza preface Kaplan's meditations on Pleasure/ Sexuality/ Feminism:

Wild Nights—Wild Nights!
Were I with thee
Wild Nights should be
Our luxury!

It is interesting to note that nowhere in *Sea Changes*, the volume in which
Kaplan's essay is collected, does the author offer a reading of Dickinson's
poem, except to observe in passing the poet's preference for "overt statement, as in 'Wild Nights,'" to "project sensuous or lascivious images."[104] And
indeed, the poem's famous first quatrain—its staccato succession of mono-
syllables, the erect exclamation points, the repeated invocation of "Wild
Nights"—does seem "overt." But what is being stated so overtly? Only in the
quatrain's final multisyllabic "luxury" is a dissonant note sounded (a disso-
nance many readers ward off by recalling the final word as "liberty"). For although "luxury" is rooted in "lechery" (via the Latin *luxuria*: "rankness, ex-
cess") its contemporary connotations of opulence and indulgence jar with
those of the wild.

The second stanza offers a possible resolution to this contradiction by suggesting that the (wild) winds are precisely a luxury, in the sense of a "futile" or useless propulsion, to "a Heart in port":

> *Done with the Compass—*
> *Done with the Chart!*

Yet, as the third and final stanza makes clear, passion will not be excluded from the pastoral. The poem concludes with the narrator imagining not a turbulent evening on the high seas of a conventional coupling, but an ecstatic passage in paradise.

> *Rowing in Eden—*
> *Ah, the Sea!*
> *Might I but moor—Tonight—*
> *In Thee!*

Here I am reminded of Wollstonecraft's "wild wish" in the *Vindication* "to see the distinction of sex confounded in society, unless where love animates the behaviour."[105] But in "Wild Nights" it is love that confounds this distinction and all that it subtends, from the traditional sexing of the sailor and the harbor to the commensurate division of land and sea. The final stanza vindicates the poem's appropriation to Kaplan's defense of female desire by triumphantly defying the gendered division of civility and savagery that our sexual politics must continue to resist.

9 Fuckface

Desire and Disgust in High and Low Places

"Our topic deals with the giving and taking away of faces, with face and de-face, *figure*, figuration and disfiguration." Thus Paul de Man, in his famous examination of *prosopopeia*—a rhetorical figure that assigns speech, and thus a mouth, and therefore a face, to the entity represented.[1] But if prosopopeia is the figure of personification, that which creates the face (*prosopon*) in De Man's interpretive etymology, what of the reverse procedure, the taking away of faces? A long tradition maintains this deprivation as women's fate, the consequence of "the classic gender distinctions that have linked men to speech, power, identity, and the mind." So one critic describes the cultural motives for the veiling and silencing of women, at one extreme, and the eroticization of the female face and hair at the other. His resolution of this apparent contradiction is a now familiar one: The eroticization of these features is argued to be "another form of decapitation, turning the female head into a symbol of desire, rather than a symbol of identity and of the capacity for speech and language."[2] (Or as a commentator on the events under consideration here put it, "Honey, women talking is a waste of a perfectly good mouth.")[3]

To illustrate this argument, Howard Eilberg-Schwartz cites Rene Magritte's *Le viol* ("The Rape"), one of a series on this theme painted by the artist between 1934 and 1945. The rape in question is that of the woman's face, the eyes, nose, and mouth of which are cruelly parodied by the traditionally eroticized features of the female torso: breasts, navel, and vagina (figure 9.1). (To appropriate an influential commentary on de Man, her face is indeed figure.)[4] *This* giving of face is not read as an assertion of woman's identity but as its violation, in which she is personified by her private parts.

Magritte's dirty joke recalls the Medusa, another victim of decapitation with bad hair. Both the staring torso and the severed head are missing something, and this lack has been interpreted as a symbol of women's castration. But the vulnerability this interpretation might suggest is never unambiguous. Chosen by Andre Breton as the cover girl for his *Qu'est-ce que le surréalisme?*,[5] *Le viol* may emblematize the surrealists' notorious delight in cutting up women, but this eerie figure has also been seen as phallic—bearded and coiffed with those extravagant locks whose snakey abundance on the Medusa Freud described as "a classical multiplication of penis symbols." In his remarks on the classical myth, such symbols are said to be multiplied in "mitigation of the horror"[6] of female castration: the more horror, it seems, the more reptilian curls required to offset it. If so, Magritte's own multiplication of *Le viol*, his many renditions of the theme in various styles and media, might suggest a decade's worth of castration anxiety, projected onto a female figure whose repeated decapitation never quite assuages the apprehension it is designed to dispel.

Ambiguous as *Le viol* may seem, it has nevertheless been used to illustrate another defacement of woman, said to occur when her mouth takes the normatively designated place of the vagina in an act of sex. That act is, of course, fellatio.[7] In the 1970s, American culture would produce an even more emblematic figure for this practice, Linda Lovelace's fellatrix in the film that made "hard-core pornography . . . a household word."[8] In *Deep Throat* (1972) Lovelace plays Linda, a sexually active single woman who despairs of ever having an orgasm. On the advice of her older friend Ellen (a swinger

FIGURE 9.1. *Le viol*, Rene Magritte, 1934. Private Collection. The Bridgeman Art Library, London and New York. © ADACP, Paris and DACS, London 2000.

who pronounces the film's moral of "diff'rent strokes for diff'rent folks"), Linda consults Dr. Young, a sexologist. During an extensive examination, he discovers that her clitoris is located at the back of her throat. With Dr. Young's willing assistance, Linda learns to satisfy herself by performing "deep" fellatio and becomes a physiotherapist for his male patients. Among them she meets Wilbur, a sadistic voyeur in clinical role-play but a small and gentle man in real life. When she warns him that she needs a lover with a nine-inch cock in order to come, he summons Dr. Young. The punchline is that to suit Linda, Wilbur will consent to an operation—cutting his thirteen-inch penis down to nine.

Deep Throat became a huge hit in the American porn cinema, playing to record audiences on the strength of its unusually coherent narrative, Lovelace's oral expertise, and the well-timed prosecution of its New York theater's owner for obscenity. And when Lovelace, under her real name of Linda Marchiano, later claimed that she had been kidnapped, hypnotized, and beaten by her manager during the film's production, *Deep Throat* was discovered by a new constituency. In 1983, Marchiano appeared before the Minneapolis City Council to give evidence on behalf of the anti-pornography ordinance drafted for the city by Andrea Dworkin and Catharine MacKinnon. During those hearings, MacKinnon cited *Deep Throat* in support of the legal proscription of both coercion into pornographic performance and the representation of women as sexual objects "in postures of sexual submission or sexual servility."[9] Subsequently, on behalf of a related ordinance for the city of Indianapolis, she referred to the fellatio in the film as a subordinating practice, representing the film's female performers as "eager servicing receptacles for male genitalia and ejaculate."[10] As for the film's theme of female sexual exploration and pleasure, MacKinnon has frequently replied with Marchiano's account of being "hypnotized under threat of death to suppress the normal gag reflex."[11] Her introduction to *Feminism Unmodified* offers *Deep Throat* as evidence of the coercion claimed to be fundamental not only to fellatio, nor pornographic performance, but to heterosexuality itself: "Dominance, principally by men, and submission, principally by women, will be the ruling code through which sexual pleasure is experienced."[12]

In 1985, *Deep Throat*'s feminist critics went to Washington, where both Dworkin and Lovelace testified to the Commission on Pornography convened by the Reagan administration's Attorney General, Edwin Meese. The Commission's proceedings, which have themselves been marketed as pornography in the United States, include the testimony of a female witness who complains that her husband talked incessantly about *Deep Throat* and insisted that she imitate Lovelace. Lovelace repeats her account of how she was violently compelled to perform oral sex during the production of the film. By contrast, in a chapter entitled "The Imagery found among Magazines, Books and Films in 'Adults Only' Pornographic Outlets," a blow-by-blow synopsis of *Deep Throat* concludes: "Dr. Young is able to fix Wilbert's [sic] penis, and when Linda sees the new version, she immediately performs fellatio on Wilbert. When he ejaculates in her mouth and on her face, bells ring and fireworks go off. Linda smiles."[13]

But *Deep Throat* had played in the nation's capital before, becoming memorialized in its political history. When, in 1972, the *Washington Post* reporters Carl Bernstein and Bob Woodward began their investigations of a break-in to the Democratic Party headquarters in the Watergate complex, their research was crucially confirmed by a White House source known only to Woodward and still anonymous today. "Their discussions," the pair later wrote, "would be only to confirm information that had been obtained elsewhere and to add some perspective."

In newspaper terminology, this meant the discussions were on "deep background." Woodward explained the arrangement to managing editor Howard Simons one day. He had taken to calling the source "my friend," but Simons dubbed him "Deep Throat," the title of a celebrated pornographic movie. The name stuck.[14]

All the President's Men, and the 1976 film of the same name, dramatize the reporter's clandestine communications with his informant: signals from a plant on Woodward's balcony; coded marks on his daily copy of the *New York Times*; 2:00 A.M. trysts in an underground car park. Telephone conversations between the two were tappable and therefore rare, but Woodward recalls one in which his contact guardedly confirmed the involvement of key White House employees in Watergate: "He sounded resigned, dejected. . . . 'Let's just say I'll be willing to put the blossoming situation in perspective for you when the time comes.' But there was disgust in the way he said it."[15]

By February of the following year, the Nixon administration had begun to trace news leaks by bugging reporters' phones. Eventually, this led them to Woodward's partner Carl Bernstein. To elude an imminent subpoena and the search of his files, the reporter was ordered out of the *Post*'s offices for the day while his editor consulted lawyers. "'Get out of the building,' he said. 'Go to a movie and call me at five o'clock.'"[16] The movie Bernstein went to see was *Deep Throat.*

A great many pundits have pointed to the contrasts between Watergate and Zippergate, as the sexual scandals surrounding President Clinton were inevitably dubbed: an attempt to sabotage the opposition in a presidential election versus an adulterous affair; the subversion of the democratic process versus sexual dalliance; "All the President's Men" versus "All the President's Women." And yet, as Bernstein and Woodward's account reveals, sex, and particularly oral sex, was hardly absent from the political imaginary of the far-off seventies. But notwithstanding the crucial role of the *Post*'s owner Katherine Graham—without whose financial and social clout the paper would never have dared take on Nixon—*All the President's Men* is remarkably short of women. Indeed, rereading the book twenty years later, one wonders what to make of the relation between cub reporter Woodward and the man he meets at night in underground car parks, described in the telling passage below:

Aware of his own weaknesses, he readily conceded his flaws. He was, incongruously, an incurable gossip, careful to label rumor for what it was, but fascinated by it. He knew too much literature too well and let the allurements of the past turn him away from his instincts. He could be rowdy, drink too much, overreach. He was not good at concealing his feelings, hardly ideal for a man in his position. Of late, he had expressed fear for the future of the Executive Branch, which he was in a unique position to observe. Watergate had taken its toll. Even in the shadows of the garage, Woodward saw that he was thinner and, when he drew on his cigarette, that his eyes were bloodshot.[17]

If this portrait evokes the character of Brandon in Hitchcock's *Rope* (1948) or any number of other movie homosexuals—thin, cultured, voluble, and anxiously drawing on their cigarettes—the scene also calls to mind one sexual encounter not portrayed in *Deep Throat*, that in which a man meets another man late at night for a blowjob. To this day, the question that haunts *All the President's Men* is who exactly went down in history? The star of the porno film where Bernstein hid from the Feds, or the man in the garage where Woodward did? In either case, oral sex had come to stand for something in the chronicles of the American presidency long before Zippergate. "Inside the Beltway," as the federal capital has been designated, *Deep Throat* signified authority without accountability; the sexiness of secrecy; incurable gossip and deep disgust. The later claims that the film's star, smiling though she was, had been coerced into her spectacular acts of fellatio, hypnotized "to suppress the normal gag reflex," only intensified the ambiguities that would climax in the 1998 promise of presidential sex so "kinky" (in *Newsweek*'s quaint usage) that it would make us all "want to throw up."[18]

When, in late January 1998, it was reported that independent counsel Kenneth Starr was investigating whether President Clinton had tried to cover up an alleged affair with a White House intern in her early twenties, the American feminist response varied. Mindful of Clinton's support for reproductive rights, affirmative action, and family leave, commentators like Betty Friedan refused to condemn the president. Several, such as Susan Faludi, argued that a private relationship between two consenting adults was politically irrelevant. In a dissenting view, Naomi Woolf invoked the contemporary American objections to workplace relationships, particularly between bosses and employees, as a form of sexual favoritism. More frequently, however, this argument was inverted to represent the affair as one of sexual victimization, in which the Leader of the Free World so outclassed the young intern that any notion of her freedom became negligible. Since the allegations in this case had first surfaced in a lawsuit for sexual harassment brought against Clinton by a former Arkansas state government employee, Paula Jones, this line of interpretation already had considerable impetus. Claims that Monica Lewinsky had solicited the president's attentions, repeatedly introducing herself and engaging in intense flirting from the outset of her internship, were frequently met with some version of the argument first popularized in 1970 by—again—Catharine MacKinnon:

Since employed women are supposed to develop, and must demonstrate, regard for the man as part of their job, and since women are taught to identify with men's feelings, men's evaluations of them, and with their sexual attractiveness to men, as a major component of their own identities and sense of worth, it is often unclear and shifting whether the coercion or the caring is the weightier factor, or which "causes" which. . . . Plainly, the wooden dichotomy between "real love," which is supposed to be a matter of free choice, and coercion, which implies some form of the gun at the head, is revealed as inadequate to explain the social construction of women's sexuality and the conditions of its expression, including the economic ones.[19]

Twenty-eight years later, this analysis had become so commonplace that congressional Democrats faced with the Starr Report hired a Stanford law professor to advise them on sexual harassment. As one journalist noted, "A full impeachment hearing may well ripple with difficult gender issues. How much is Lewinsky herself responsible for her relationship with Clinton? Is an intern really capable of informed consent to a relationship with a President? When, if ever, are bosses and subordinates allowed to have sex with one another?"[20] Moreover, Lewinsky's allegations were not of unspecified sexual acts, nor of the only sexual practice legal in all fifty states—conventional coitus in the missionary position. Instead, she claimed that her physical contact with her employer consisted largely of the very activity whose consensual performance had become a related subject of debate. Within days of the initial report of her allegations, Germaine Greer announced plans for a sequel to *The Female Eunuch*, arguing that contemporary women "have a duty to say yes to whatever their partners may desire, no holds are barred. Women cannot admit to feeling disgust or to not enjoying the stuff that is going on—not if they want to seem cool, even if they have to take muscle relaxants to do it." As for the Starr investigation, Greer proclaimed, "I couldn't believe that Betty Friedan said that Clinton hasn't done anything wrong. Here he is fucking the faces of little girls and she says she doesn't care!"[21]

Civilization, Freud memorably declared, began when human beings stopped sniffing each other's genitals. Our rise to an erect posture led to the triumph of sight over smell as a sexual stimulant, and with it an end to intermittent coitus determined by the menstrual cycle. The consequences, in his view, were threefold: the formation of the family (bonded by the possibility of continuous sexual satisfaction); shame (at the newfound visibility of our genitals); and disgust (at those now obsolete olfactory stimuli generated by bodily wastes).[22] Burdensome as these developments proved to be, they signally failed to consign oral-genital conjunction to the primitive past. Writing in 1905 about the psychoanalysis of a young Viennese woman he called "Dora," Freud undertook the first sustained discussion of oral sex in psychoanalytic literature. Its relevance to contemporary affairs of state has not gone unremarked.

Freud first met his patient when her father insisted that the sixteen-year-old consult him about her attacks of nervous coughing and hoarseness. Since the symptoms abated, Freud's suggestions for psychological treatment were not pursued. But two years later, Dora was again brought to him after her parents discovered a suicide note from their despondent daughter. Dora's father offered an immediate explanation: Her depression had occurred after she had complained that a family friend, Herr K., had made a sexual advance to her on holiday. But when challenged, the man denied everything, attributing the episode to the fantasies of a girl obsessed with sex.

It was, in anticipation of later events, Herr K.'s word against Dora's, but Freud believed from the outset that she was telling the truth, about the holiday and also about an afternoon four years earlier, when Herr K. was said to have kissed the then fourteen-year-old on the mouth. Indeed, the earlier scene became the presentational moment in this case history of hysteria, a condition Freud defines in it as that in which "an occasion for sexual excitement elicited feelings that were preponderantly or exclusively unpleasurable."[23] Moreover, in his interpretation, this *reversal of affect* was accompanied by a *displacement of sensation*:

Instead of the genital sensation which would certainly have been felt by a healthy girl in such circumstances, Dora was overcome by the unpleasurable feeling which is proper to the tract of mucous membrane at the entrance to the alimentary canal—that is by disgust.[24]

This is a very literal definition of disgust, derived from the term's etymological root in the Middle French *desgouter*, distaste, with its location of repugnance in the mouth—at the back of the throat, in Freud's even more precise terms, at the entrance to the alimentary canal. But then Dora, in Freud's reconstruction of her psychical development, is an extremely oral girl, whose pleasure at her nurse's breast is retained in thumb-sucking until the age of four or five, and later in adolescent discussions of oral sex with Herr K.'s wife, culminating in an unconscious fantasy of oral gratification represented by that symptomatic tickle in the throat. "So we see," Freud concludes, "that this excessively repulsive and perverted phantasy of sucking at a penis has the most innocent origin."[25]

Here Freud's apparent disgust at fellatio seems—deliberately or inadvertently—ironic, not least because he has spent so much of this case study establishing that such an aversion is inevitably based on the libidinal inclination to the contrary. And if he too may have experienced some reversal of affect in this matter, one of his dreams provided a striking example of oral-genital displacement. Five years before he treated Dora, Freud dreamt of meeting "Irma," an actual patient whose case history he'd written up the night before. When, in the dream, she complains of stomach pains and a choking sensation, he discovers some infected structures resembling certain nasal bones inside her throat. Eventually, he concludes that his patient has contracted an illness from an injection of trimethylamin given by his colleague "Otto," possibly with a contaminated syringe.

In his analysis of this dream, Freud decided that the trimethylamin was a reference to his then closest friend Wilhelm Fliess, who believed that the substance was a by-product of the sexual metabolism.[26] (Lacan identifies it as "a decomposition product of sperm.")[27] Perceiving a connection between the turbinal bones in the nose and the female genitalia, Fliess was also an advocate of the nasal treatment of women's sexual disturbances. Indeed, he had nearly killed one of Freud's dysmenorrheal patients by a botched operation on her nose shortly before this dream,[28] which Freud duly interpreted as a wish to be innocent of any malpractice. Moreover, Freud's attachment to Fliess was then intensely passionate, a disturbingly homosexual bond which may explain the allusion to oral sexuality in this guilty dream, as well as the disgust he later professed for the "extremely repulsive and perverted phantasy of sucking at" an organ all too reminiscent of that infectious syringe.

The belief in oral-genital isomorphism is much older than Fliess's nasal reflex theory or Freud's own specification of the mucous membrane of the mouth as our first erotogenic zone. The seventeenth-century anatomist John Bulwer drew a vivid analogy between "the extension of the two unruly members"[29] of the body—the tongue and the penis—while his sixteenth-century predecessor Charles Estienne described the clitoris as resembling a "little tongue."[30] By the nineteenth century, such comparisons were literalized in the surgery of Marion Sims, the American physician credited with founding the modern profession of gynecology.

Sims was an unlikely candidate for his eventual accolade "architect of the vagina," since he began his career with a confessed loathing for "investigating the organs of the female pelvis." His first surgical breakthrough was at repairing the mouth of a woman suffering from a hare-lip. Only then did he go on to make his name, and the huge fortune he sought in medicine, by applying his technique at oral surgery to perforations of the vaginal wall caused in childbirth. Perhaps to overcome his aversion, Sims joined his medical contemporaries in characterizing the female genitalia in facial terms: the "lips" of the vagina, the "neck" of the womb, and so forth. It was Sims who named the genital contraction that prevents penetrative intercourse "vaginismus" after "laringismus," a nineteenth-century term for the spasmodic contraction of the vocal apparatus. Inventing the speculum enabled him to view the interior of "an immense number of vaginas," he later wrote, "and I never saw two that were in all particulars exactly alike. They are as different from each other as our faces and noses."[31]

If the giving of face to the female genitals was medicine's attempt to re-press its own misogyny—to make it possible perhaps, in Sim's case, to prac-tice gynecology at all—the genitalization of the female face predictably pro-duces the obverse effect. At the beginning of the twentieth century, the ex-pression "cunt face" entered English usage as an accusation of extreme ugliness. At its end, Monica Lewinsky's sexual use of her own face undoubt-edly contributed to her indictment for the same failing. As the American comic Scott Capurro brutally admitted: "I don't want to impeach Clinton for shagging women other than his wife. I want to impeach Clinton for shagging ugly women. Paula Jones? Maybe, if it's late and he's drunk. Other than that, he shouldn't have bothered. And Monica Moo-insky. She's as big as a house. She's a blow-up doll with a helmet."[32] Since Lewinsky came to public atten-tion through her allegations of oral sex with the president, she became im-mediately identified as a fellatrix, and her sexual tastes were deemed to be written all over her face.

Camille Paglia provides us with a prototype of this reading in her com-parison of Lewinsky's face with that of Paula Jones:

People keep saying, very ignorantly, "Oh, she's not very attractive—what would he have seen in her?" Well, I can see very clearly that she has this big wide mouth and a lot of teeth, and there's a sort of slackness about her jaw—which is what women porn stars develop when they learn how to relax their jaw muscles to perform great oral sex. I think Paula Jones was at every stage a walking, talking advertisement for oral sex! So I was stunned when I first saw the pictures of Monica Lewinsky on TV—the big wide smile, the nicely relaxed lips with all those teeth—and I thought, Oh my God, here we go again![33]

Paglia's account purports to be anatomical—coolly detailing the physi-ological characteristics necessary to give good head—but her *blazons* of Paula and Monica are allegorical and traditional. The correlation of full lips and a

large mouth with sensuality is an ancient trope derived not from pornography but from physiognomy, the interpretive system that claims to discern
character from facial features. Grounded in critical traditions that extend
from classical Greece and Rome to Confucian China, first codified in a treatise on *Physiognomics* attributed in the Middle Ages to Aristotle, "the science
or knowledge of the correspondence between the external and the internal
man"[34] was expounded at length in the late-eighteenth-century study of the
Swiss moralist, Johann Caspar Lavater, *Essai sur la physionomie destiné à faire
connaître l'homme et à le faire aimer*. Translated into English as *Essays on Physiognomy: Designed to Promote the Knowledge and Love of Mankind*, the work
gained huge popularity and was published in a succession of editions—expensive and pocket-sized—for 168 years. Where late-seventeenth and earlier
eighteenth-century textbooks by Charles Le Brun and William Hogarth had
sought to systematize the representation of temperament in painting,
Lavater's study instructed its readers in the reverse procedure, the decoding
of character from countenance:

*The moral life of man, particularly, reveals itself in the lines, marks and transitions
of the countenance. His moral powers and desires, his irritability, sympathy, and an-
tipathy; his facilities of attracting or repelling the objects that surround him; these are
all summed up in, and painted upon, his countenance when at rest.*[35]

The advantages of such discernment, Lavater declares, include those
required by the painter "who, if he be not a physiognomist, is nothing."
But the "greatest is that of forming, conducting, and improving the
human heart."[36] As a guide to self-improvement, an eighteenth-century
conduct book, Lavater's *Essays on Physiognomy* offers its science for economic, as well as moral, gain. The book's first examples of the human
propensity to judge things by their "physiognomy, their exterior temporary superficies," are commercial matters—the merchant scrutinizing
wares to be purchased, the salesman who proffers them, the stranger entering his shop. Indeed, one of the first countenances under consideration in
this massive tome is the face on the coin: "Does he not judge money by its

physiognomy? Why does he take one guinea and reject another? Why weigh a third in his hand? Does he not determine according to its colour, or impression; its outside, its physiognomy?"[37] It is not surprising then, to learn that in the nineteenth century Lavater's *Essays* became a *vade mecum* for the bourgeois gentleman, "to be consulted when hiring staff, making friends and establishing business relations."[38]

Both the belief that there are facial guides to moral disposition, and their particular application to the workplace, persist to this day. *Reading Faces*, a 1997 social psychology treatise by the Brandeis University Professor of Social Relations Leslie A. Zebrowitz, endorses Lavater's analysis in its opening pages, and goes on to recount an exercise in workplace physiognomy with remarkable pertinence to Camille Paglia's characterization of Monica Lewinsky:

A secretary has just been assigned for the first time to the vice president of the company, who is a young, dynamic, fast-rising married man. He has just thanked her for taking dictation. The woman, standing at the door, asks "Is there anything else you would like?"

"When people are shown a photograph of the secretary and asked what she really means by this question," *Reading Faces* continues, "their perception of her intentions depends on her face. Some faces are likely to be perceived as suggesting the woman's availability for a more personal and intimate relationship."[39]

Which faces? The studies cited in this survey conclude that "soft facial lineaments"[40] can indicate agreeableness, the "greater submissiveness" that Lavater and Zebrowitz attribute to "thick-lipped adults."[41] The accuracy of such judgments is deemed proven first by their extension across diverse cultures and second by the genetic advantages that they are claimed to confer. Thus, a cross-cultural preference for lighter skinned women is said merely to register the sex difference in pigmentation that occurs in a variety of ethnic groups at adolescence to signal the onset of female fertility. But the racial and colonial ideologies that Zebrowitz's sociobiology discounts cannot be repressed. While citing medieval French and Spanish poetry, with its anti-Moorish celebrations of golden hair and lily-white skin, in support of the transhistorical, and therefore nonideological, character of such valuations, Zebrowitz admits "there is a relationship between ethnicity and facial appearance, although the correlation is not perfect. . . . People with broad noses and thick lips tend to be categorized as members of the Negroid race."[42] And when we turn back to Lavater, we are further told that "very large, though well-proportioned lips, always denote a gross, sensual, indelicate; - and sometimes a stupid or wicked man."[43]

This association of sexual receptivity with ethnic stereotypes clearly survives in the contemporary epithet "trailer park trash" and the cluster of sexual and class slurs that lead one exasperated journalist to write in defense of Gennifer Flowers:

And then there was her appearance: the gale-force Lily Savage backcomb, the sink-plunger mouth. White House aides could say that Gennifer looked like the kind of gal who would make stuff up for money. If that didn't work, they could say that she looked like the kind of gal who was asking for it anyway.[44]

The physiognomy that this writer parodies reads the mouths of Gennifer, Paula, and Monica as signals of sexual availability, wordless invitations. And, in keeping with its ancient equation of fleshy faces and sensual indulgence, Monica's weight problems, like those of Clinton, were taken as additional evidence of concupiscence, a passion for junk food consummated in the ingestion of the presidential weenie (figure 9.2). The specifically oral nature of the pleasure promised *per os*, the blowjob, was endlessly caricatured in representations of Lewinsky as the pneumatic fellatrix of the sex shop. But unlike her conveniently deflatable counterpart, "Monica the Mouth Organ"[45] proved, in the words of one columnist, a "walking, talking . . . blow-up doll."[46] To the consternation of those who would oppose women's speech to their sexuality, the young intern was not only adept at the one practice which requires both, telephone sex, she also apparently spent a considerable amount of time just talking to the president in what has inevitably become known as the Oral

FIGURE 9.2. **Monica Lewinsky caricatured in** *George,* **April 1998, by Adrian Tomine.**

Office.[47] And if his impeachment originated in an oral act, it was speech, not sex, that did him in.

Captured on Linda Tripp's hidden wire, recorded from her phone calls, confided to friends, family, and two psychotherapists, confessed to Kenneth Starr, Monica's talk was the whole case. Without it, the stain would have stayed in the closet and the Special Investigator eventually retired. With it, a pronounced displacement occurred, and the President of the United States became, in the terms of an e-mail from Lewinsky to Linda Tripp later bowdlerized by *Newsweek*, "F——face." As in, "F——face should (if Betty is nice) get my tie today. I sure hope he likes it."[48] Long

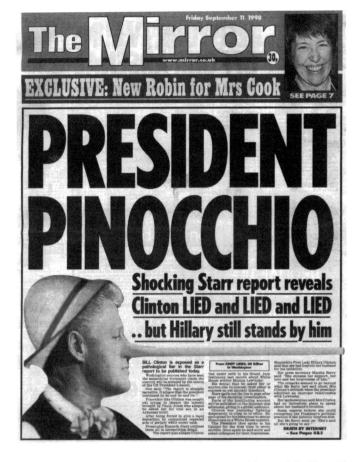

FIGURE 9.3. "President Pinocchio" on the front page of the UK daily *Mirror*, 11 September 1998.

caricatured as a porcine hick with a bulbous snout, the physiognomy of Clinton's alleged inclinations became as clear as the nose on his face. Accused of lying about his extramarital amours, "President Pinocchio,"[49] in the British daily *Mirror*'s banner headline, was repeatedly pictured with the extended proboscis of the wayward puppet, perhaps the most celebrated phallic symbol in children's literature (figure 9.3). (And here the phallic imposture of the high office was unmasked, since this presidential erection was precisely the result of deception: The more he lied, the longer it became.) Meanwhile, in the more literal world of Internet porn, the symbolic yielded to the iconic, as the presidential protuberance morphed into a penis (figure 9.4) in recapitulation of the British artists Jake and Dinos Chapman's infamous mutant mannequin sequence, also entitled *Fuck Face*[50] (figure 9.5).

Unveiled for all to see, the presidential phallus was revealed to be—as the American columnist Barbara Ehrenreich pointed out citing Lacan—no more than a "prick, a ding-a-ling."[51] Its bearer, forced to wear his badge of authority on his face, became—in the words of Marina Warner—a "dickhead."[52] But this was not disgusting enough. The Chapman brothers' 1994 staging of the polymorphous perversions of childhood also included boys

FIGURE 9.4. The president grows a penile nose on *www.netwebsites.com/impeach/* 6 October 1998.

FIGURE 9.5. *Fuck Face,* Jake and Dinos Chapman, 1994. Courtesy Jay Jopling (London).

with mouths puckered for sexual reception. In a similar strategy, the cartoonists deprived Clinton of the limited powers of a face that fucks, representing him instead as the face that is fucked, the face that sucks. Thus, *Time*'s "Whitechocolate" cartoon portrays the president denying oral indulgence with his mouth full. (The same issue captions a photograph of Clinton, "tight-lipped on TV," offering "unconvincing, legalistic denials" to Lewinsky's allegations.)[53] Often, in a reversal of the upward direction of hysterical displacement (from the unspeakable site of genital excitation to the inexplicable tickle in the throat), Clinton's face descended to crotch level, from whence, in a *Guardian* cartoon, it addresses the nation at the presidential podium (figure 9.6). With the president's mouth rivaling Monica's as the

FIGURE 9.6. Cartoon by Steve Bell for the *Guardian* newspaper, 27 January 1998.

site of transgression, the *Mirror* asked the inevitable question—"Is Clinton Going Down?"[54] But this was not disgusting enough. There was still the cigar.

When, in August 1998, details of Monica Lewinsky's testimony to Kenneth Starr began to circulate, allegation of a "bizarre sex act" with a cigar convulsed the columnists. Amidst many delighted "Did *what?*'s" and "you-know-where's," the pundits invoked Kennedy, Castro, Churchill, Kipling ("A woman is only a woman but a good cigar is inappropriate")[55] and—of course—Freud. Sometimes, the man is supposed to have said, a cigar is just a cigar, but that was not his interpretation of a recurrent dream of Dora's: "A house was on fire," she told him. "My father was standing beside my bed and woke me up. I dressed quickly. Mother wanted to stop and save her jewel-case; but Father said: 'I refuse to let myself and my two children be burnt for the sake of your jewel-case.' We hurried downstairs, and as soon as I was outside I woke up."[56] On the next day of her treatment, Freud tells us, Dora added that each time after waking up she smelled smoke. Convinced of his patient's erotic engagement with her father, Herr K., and, not least, himself—all "passionate smokers"—Freud crows, "no smoke without fire."[57] But as his own analysis of the dream goes on to show, there *can* be smoke without fire. As was the notorious case in the Oral Office.

Much of Freud's commentary on Dora's dream is taken up by the figure of the jewel-case, in German *schmuck-kastchen*, a common expression for the female genitals. Herr K. had actually given the girl an expensive jewel-case just before it began to appear so regularly in her dreams, and Freud argues that Dora burns with an unconscious desire to make him a "return-present" of her own. But he also sees a connection between nocturnal accidents like the fire and her childhood propensity to wet the bed. In the latter case, paternal awakening would prevent the genital area from becoming wet, but what if the child had—as Freud argues of Dora—a passionate attachment to the rescuing parent? "[F]or love," Freud points out, "also makes things wet."[58]

And if the apparent antithesis of fire and water proves false in Dora's dream, how much more so in the White House, where a president who loved cigars could not escape his own allergies and his wife's ban on smoking. The answer, according to one aide, was to ingest rather than inhale. For the man who literally chews up his cigars to avoid smoking them, eating ain't cheating. It may, however, complicate the erotic significance of the stogie, which has recently experienced a yuppie revival. In its current resignification, argues one journalist, "the cigar is phallic and exotic and conflates the need to display, just occasionally, naughty-but-nice sexual raunchiness coupled with way-cool political incorrectness."[59] This is especially so for female stars like Madonna and Demi Moore, who have at times affected the flaming protuberance along with shaven heads and pinstripes. But their naughtiness is nothing in comparison to Monica and Bill's erotic application of the aphrodisiac cylinder.

In a spectacular feat of double displacement, the oral adornment affected to advertise a similar endowment elsewhere was appropriated to the latter's literal function, and then returned to the original owner's mouth. "It tastes good," the president is reported to have said,[60] sucking on his unusually humidified Corona. And "sucking" is the operative term, since here Clinton was clearly going down, and what a descent it was. For was he not savoring both oral conjunction with the female genitals and with those of the male—by tasting the very tube whose phallic properties had just been so graphically demonstrated? (It was rumored that when Lewinsky was asked if Clinton went down on her, she failed to recognize the term cunnilingus.[61] Perhaps this was because the more appropriate word for the oral sex he performed was fellatio.) Such polymorphous practices may have inflamed the Republican Congress as well as the presidential passions, but Bill's cigar remained unlit—dampened more likely by contact with two bodily orifices. "I'll smoke that later,"[62] Clinton was said to have joked, in a gag that closes the scene so confidently predicted to nauseate the nation.

But did it? Despite the many declarations of revulsion that greeted the Starr Report upon its publication, the vast numbers who chose to access it on the Internet in the first hours of its release,[63] combined with the many who purchased it in printed form, seem to bear out Freud's claim for a direct relation between the rising of the gorge and the engorgement of the genitals, between the physical reactions of disgust and those of desire. If a large section of the public was sickened by sex in the Oral Office, they may also have been, in that useful English phrase for the overwhelming desire to smoke, *gagging for it*. Having accused those multitudes—as well as Sigmund Freud and the President of the United States—of entertaining "the most excessively repulsive and perverted phantasy of sucking at a penis," what more can I say?

One obvious recommendation would be the rejection of the hierarchy of sexual acts which led to both the shaming (and the pitying) of Monica Lewinsky for performing fellatio, and to the president's denial that what they did was sex at all. If, as Freud observed of kissing, the most esteemed form of oral eroticism is the perverse conjunction of body parts that "do not form any part of the sexual apparatus but constitute the entrance to the digestive tract,"[64] no erotic use of the mouth is entirely natural. Nor is, in Paul de Man's discussion of poetic language, the face itself. Writing in *The Rhetoric of Romanticism*, he avers,

Man can address and face other men, within life or beyond the grave, because he has a face, but he has a face only because he partakes of a mode of discourse that is neither entirely natural nor entirely human.[65]

As these portraits from the files of Zippergate suggest, the meanings of the face do not inhere in the flesh or its putative functions—they are *rhetorical*. And so, de Man argues, is the face itself—a figure, an entity whose coherence as an entity is created by representation, and not by its expressive relation to speech, power, identity, or the mind. In which case, I will conclude, giving head should never have to mean losing face.

Postscript

As this book was going to press, it was reported that Bernard Lewinsky, Monica's father, was demanding an apology from the producers of NBC's *Law and Order: Special Victims Unit* for screening an episode in which a detective describes oral sex as "getting a Lewinsky." Lewinsky *père*'s indignation at the intended insult to his daughter was understandable. More intriguing, in light of the sexual displacements that structured Zippergate, was his anger at the use of Monica's patronym to represent a blowjob. "There is a family behind this name," he protested, "and I think it's disgusting that they would even consider saying something like that." Yet again, disgust signified a notable displacement of sexual sensitivity, in this case from the mouth of the daughter to that of her dad. For the family name is, of course, the father's, and the libel he perceived was on himself. "They can't use my name and assume it's OK with me," he declared. "I deserve an apology and so does Monica." Speculating on the response of the Beverly Hills oncologist to the discovery of his newfound nomination as a slang term for fellatio, a British journalist predictably observed, "One imagines Dr. Bernard Lewinsky nearly choked into his TV dinner while watching the offending episode."[66] Meanwhile, the running gag on oral sex showed no sign of termination. Instead, Monica's father proposed a further displacement, the one anticipated by the press throughout the scandal: "Why don't they say he got a Clinton job," he asked of the series' writers, "and see how the White House responds to that?"

Notes

Notes to the Introduction

1. Brian Sewall, "We Don't Care a Fig Anymore," *Evening Standard* (6 October 1998): 13.

2. Lee Siegel, "The Gay Science," *New Republic* (9 November 1998): 30.

3. Ibid., 39.

4. Ibid., 42.

5. Deborah Orr, "Sex! Sex! Sex! And Sex!" *Independent* (27 January 1999): 5.

6. Henry Abelove, Michèle Aina Barale, and David M. Halperin eds., *The Lesbian and Gay Studies Reader* (New York: Routledge, 1993), xv.

7. Judith Butler, "Against Proper Objects," *differences* 6.2–3 (Summer–Fall 1994): 2.

8. Jacques Derrida, *Specters of Marx: The State of the Debt, the Work of Mourning, and the New International* (New York: Routledge, 1994), 10.

9. See Sue-Ellen Case, "Tracking the Vampire," *differences* 3.2 (1991): 1–20.

10. Richard Burt, *Unspeakable ShaXXXspeares: Queer Theory and American Kiddie Culture* (London: Macmillan, 1998), 37.

11. Susan Stryker, "The Transgender Issue: An Introduction," *GLQ* 4:2 (1998): 153.

12. Biddy Martin, "Introduction," *Femininity Played Straight: The Significance of Being Lesbian* (New York: Routledge, 1996), 9–10.

13. Lauren Berlant and Michael Warner, "What Does Queer Theory Teach Us about X?" *PMLA* 110 (1995): 343–9.

14. Robyn Wiegman, "Queering the Academy," in Thomas Foster, Carol Siegel, and Ellen E. Berry eds., *Genders 26: The Gay '90s* (New York: New York University Press, 1997), 3–22.

15. Dale Bumpers, "Podium," *Independent* (26 January 1999), 9.

16. Quoted in Gore Vidal, "Birds and Bees and Clinton," *Nation* (28 December 1998): 5.

17. Sigmund Freud, "Negation" (1925) in *On Metapsychology*, Pelican Freud Library Volume 11 (Harmondsworth: Penguin, 1984), 439.

18. Vidal, "Birds and Bees and Clinton," 5.

NOTES TO THE INTRODUCTION

19. Walter Kirn, "When Sex Is Not Really Having Sex," *Time* (2 February 1998): 30.

20. Claudia Wallis, "Eager Minds, Big Ears," *Time* (9 February 1998): 67.

21. Barbara Kantrowitz, "Mom, What's Oral Sex?" *Newsweek* (21 September 1998): 38.

22. *Oregonian* (7 August 1998): D12.

23. *New Yorker* (9 February 1998): 31.

24. Pete Schulberg, "When It Comes to the Clinton Scandal, MSNBC Has Only One Thing on Its Mind," *Oregonian* (4 August 1998): C1, C8.

25. Madeleine Bunting, "Civic Spirit Is Still Strong. But It Doesn't Count for Much on Your CV," *Guardian* (21 September 1998): 16.

26. Michele Hanson, "Year of the Penis," *Guardian* G2 (21 September 1998): 7.

27. Charlotte Raven, "Is Sex Really The Best Thing Since Sliced Bread?" *Guardian* G2 (22 October 1998): 7.

28. Michel Foucault, *The History of Sexuality, Volume I: An Introduction* (London: Allen Lane, 1979), 56.

29. Plato, *The Republic*, trans. Desmond Lee (Harmondsworth: Penguin, 1974), 429, 438. In October 1999, the question of beds, aesthetics, and sexuality was returned to public consideration by the nomination of Tracey Emin's "My Bed" for Britain's Turner Prize. An installation including the artist's bed, soiled sheets, bloodied underwear, used condoms, empty vodka bottles, and other postcoital detritus, it immediately attracted critical debate and the satirical intervention of two performance artists, who were arrested for leaping upon the exhibit at the Tate Gallery in an attempt at "critical sex."

30. "The Wisdom of Solomon" (circa first century B.C.) 14. 18–27, in Bruce M. Metzger ed., *The Apocrypha of the Old Testament: Revised Standard Version* (New York: Oxford University Press, 1965), 119–20.

31. W. J. T. Mitchell, *Iconology: Image, Text, Ideology* (Chicago: University of Chicago Press, 1986), 197.

32. Sigmund Freud, "Leonardo da Vinci and a Memory of His Childhood" (1910), in *Art and Literature*, Pelican Freud Library Volume 14 (Harmondsworth: Penguin, 1985), 188.

33. Ibid., 186.

34. Ibid., 204.

35. Bumpers, "Podium," 9.

36. From *Outlook* 11 (Winter 1991) quoted in Cherry Smyth, *Lesbians Talk Queer Notions* (London: Scarlett Press, 1992), 17.

37. Robert M. Tipton, Kent G. Bailey, and Janet P. Obenchain, "Invasion of Males' Personal Space by Feminists and Non-Feminists," *Psychological Reports* 37 (1975): 99–102

38. Lisa Jardine, "Growing Up with Greer," *Observer* Review (7 March 1999): 11.

39. Freud, "Leonardo da Vinci," 176–7.

40. R. Muther, quoted in Freud, "Leonardo da Vinci," 200.

41. David Remnick, "Comment: Our Woman of Secrets," *New Yorker* (8 February 1999): 24.

Notes to Chapter 1

1. Terry Castle, *The Apparitional Lesbian: Female Homosexuality and Modern Culture* (New York: Columbia University Press, 1993), 241, fn. 6: "When Sam indeed begins 'speaking through' Oda Mae, professing his love, the effect is peculiarly homoerotic: as if Oda Mae were speaking for herself instead of the ghost. The fiction of ghostly return, in other words, somehow licenses an uncanny 'bodying forth'—onscreen— of female-female eroticism."

2. Judith Mayne, *Cinema and Spectatorship* (London: Routledge, 1993), 149–50.

3. Iain Johnstone, "Haunted by a Light Vessel," *Sunday Times* (7 October 1990): Section 7, 8–9.

4. William Parente, "Soul-Less Ghost," *Scotsman Weekend* (6 October 1990): III.

5. Mayne also describes Goldberg's function in *Ghost* as that of "mediator—between the audience and the improbability of the film, between the widely different stylistic reference points of the film," in *Cinema and Spectatorship,* 151.

6. Anton Antonowicz, "Ghostbuster," *Daily Mirror* (19 September 1990): 15.

7. Richard Dyer, *Heavenly Bodies: Film Stars and Society* (London: British Film Institute, 1987), 138–9: "Through slavery and imperialism, black people have been the social group most clearly identified by and exploited for their bodily labour. Blacks thus became the most vivid reminders of the human body as labour in a society busily denying it."

8. See Homi Bhabha, *The Location of Culture* (London: Routledge, 1994).

9. bell hooks, *Reel to Real: Race, Sex and Class at the Movies* (New York: Routledge, 1996), 94.

10. Michael Atkinson, "Video," *Guardian Guide* (7–13 December 1996): 115.

11. Michael Rogin, *Blackface, White Noise* (Berkeley: University of California Press, 1996), 9. But "Whoopi," as her profile often notes, also suggests the joke cushion and its simulated flatulence, an emission that is racialized in *Ghost* when "Rita Miller" tries to cover a fluffed line in the bank scene by explaining that she's got "gas."

12. Tania Modleski, *Feminism without Women: Culture and Criticism in a "Postfeminist" Age* (New York: Routledge, 1991), 131–3.

13. Mayne, *Cinema and Spectatorship*, 143.

14. Joseba Gabilondo, *Cinematic Hyperspace: New Hollywood Cinema and Science Fiction Film—Image Commodification in Late Capitalism* (Ph.D. diss., University of California, San Diego, 1991), 204.

15. Lotte Eisner, *The Haunted Screen* (Berkeley: University of California Press, 1969).

16. Gilberto Perez, *The Material Ghost: Films and their Medium* (Baltimore: Johns Hopkins University Press, 1998).

17. Maxim Gorky, as printed in the *Nizhegorodski Listok* newspaper (4 July 1896), and signed "I. M. Pacatus," trans. Leda Swan, in Jay Leyda ed., *Kino: A History of the Russian and Soviet Film* (London: George Allen & Unwin, 1960), 407.

18. See Jacques Derrida, *Specters of Marx: The State of the Debt, the Work of Mourning, and the New International*, trans. Peggy Kamuf (New York: Routledge, 1994), 10: "Let us call it a *hauntology*. This logic of haunting would not merely be larger and more powerful than an ontology or a thinking of Being. . . . It would harbor within itself, but like circumscribed places or particular effects, eschatology and teleology themselves."

19. Ian Christie, *The Last Machine: Early Cinema and the Birth of the Modern World* (London: British Film Institute, 1994), 18, argues that "filmmakers started offering their customers short interludes, often titled *A Kiss in the Tunnel*, to splice into the over-familiar phantom rides."

20. Rogin, *Blackface, White Noise*, 73.

21. Ibid., 75.

22. See also Miriam Hansen, *Babel and Babylon: Spectatorship in American Silent Film*

(Cambridge, Mass.: Harvard University Press, 1991), 39, for a commentary on this film.

23. See Terry Castle, *The Apparitional Lesbian*, especially 60–2, and Diana Fuss's "Introduction" to her edited collection, *Inside/Out* (New York: Routledge, 1991).

24. Jean-Joseph Goux, "The Phallus: Masculine Identity and the 'Exchange of Women,'" *differences* 4.1 (Spring 1992): 59.

25. Karl Marx, *A Contribution to the Critique of Political Economy* (New York: International Library, 1904), 168.

26. Jacques Lacan, "The Meaning of the Phallus," in Juliet Mitchell and Jacqueline Rose eds., *Feminine Sexuality* (London: Macmillan, 1982), 82.

27. Jean-Joseph Goux, "Numismatics," *Symbolic Economies* (Ithaca: Cornell University Press, 1990), 24.

28. Ibid., 18.

29. Ibid., 17–18.

30. Karl Marx, *Capital* (London: Lawrence & Wishart, 1974), 1:77.

31. Iain Johnstone, "Haunted by a Light Vessel," 8.

32. Mayne, *Cinema and Spectatorship*, 152.

33. See, in particular, *Falling Down* (1992), for its own elegiac treatment of the doomed white middle-class American male, and its own coin motif.

34. See Leo Braudy, *The Frenzy of Renown: Fame and Its History* (New York: Oxford University Press, 1986), 495–7.

35. Marx, *Capital*, 1:129.

36. Ibid., 105.

37. Jacques-Alain Miller ed., *The Seminar of Jacques Lacan, Book VII, The Ethics of Psychoanalysis, 1959–1960* (New York: W. W. Norton, 1992), 229.

38. Kaja Silverman, *Masculinity at the Margins* (New York: Routledge, 1992).

39. Goux, "The Phallus," 70.

40. Ibid., 67.

41. Gayatri Chakravorty Spivak, "Ghostwriting," *Diacritics* 25:2 (Summer 1995): 78, fn.25, denounces Freudo-Marxian "psychoanalytic radical chic" analogies, singling out the simile "money is like the phallus." In reply, I submit this *Ghost*.

42. Goux, "The Phallus," 68.

43. Ibid., 72.

44. Ibid., 73.

45. Tasha Colin, "Making Whoopi," *Daily Mail* (24 November 1992): 7.

46. Quoted in "Black Protest Fails to Disrupt Ceremony," *Evening Standard* (26 March 1996): 5.

Notes to Chapter 2

1. D. A. Miller, *Bringing Out Roland Barthes* (Berkeley: University of California Press, 1992), 6.

2. Richard Dyer, *Now You See It: Studies on Lesbian and Gay Film* (London: Routledge, 1990), 149.

3. Miller, *Bringing Out Roland Barthes*, 28.

4. D. N. Rodowick, "Reading the Figural," *Camera Obscura* 24 (1990): 10–15. The epigraph is from Michel Foucault, *This Is Not a Pipe* (Berkeley: University of California Press, 1983), 54.

5. Miller, *Bringing Out Roland Barthes*, 28.

6. Here, two incipient departures from this tradition should be saluted. In *The Optical Unconscious* (Cambridge: MIT Press, 1993), 276–7, Rosalind Krauss acknowledges Warhol's urinary emulation of Jackson Pollock in his *Piss* and *Oxidation* paintings as golden showers, a "homosexual decoding of the drip technique" motivated by "the erotics of aggressive rivalry." And in *The Cinematic Body* (Minneapolis: University of Minnesota Press, 1993), 237, Steven Shaviro argues that Warhol's films, "by taking 'deviance' for granted—which, among other things, was a way of articulating a gay style in those pre-Stonewall days . . . drown the postmodern technologies of power in a sea of limitless approbation, in the perverse excesses of their own exercise."

7. David E. James, *Allegories of Cinema: American Film in the Sixties* (Princeton: Princeton University Press, 1989), 59–67.

8. Emmanuel Cooper, *The Sexual Perspective* (London: Routledge & Kegan Paul, 1986), 267–8.

9. Camille Paglia, "The M.I.T. Lecture," in *Sex, Art, and American Culture* (London: Viking, 1992), 277.

10. Helen Vendler, "The Virtues of the Alterable," *Parnassus* (Fall–Winter 1972): 9.

11. Frank O'Hara, in Donald Allen ed., *The Collected Poems of Frank O'Hara* (New York: Knopf, 1971), 497.

12. Vendler, "The Virtues of the Alterable," 20.

13. Bruce Boone, "Gay Language as Political Praxis: The Poetry of Frank O'Hara," *Social Text* 1 (Winter 1979): 70.

14. Vendler, "The Virtue of the Alterable," 9.

15. Charles Altieri, "The Significance of Frank O'Hara," *Iowa Review* 4 (Winter 1973): 90–104.

16. Boone, "Gay Language as Political Praxis," 72.

17. Susan Sontag, "Notes on 'Camp,'" in *Against Interpretation and Other Essays* (New York: Farrar, Straus and Giroux, 1966), 291–2. In "Raiding the Icebox," in *Andy Warhol: Film Factory,* Michael O'Pray ed. (London: British Film Institute, 1989), Peter Wollen attempts to resolve the supposed opposition between Warhol's "minimalist aesthetic" and his "own voyeurism and love of sexual gossip" by the "literalism" of his early films, their "insistence on missing nothing, suppressing nothing" (25). Wollen also notes that the "Campbell" which Foucault repeats so mantrically at the end of *This Is Not a Pipe* can be deconstructed as "camp" and "belle" (27).

18. O'Hara, *Collected Poems*, 441–2.

19. Boone, "Gay Language as Political Praxis," 66.

20. Fredric Jameson, *Postmodernism, or, The Cultural Logic of Late Capitalism* (Durham: Duke University Press, 1991), 8.

21. Ibid., 7.

22. Martin Heidegger, "The Origin of the Work of Art," trans. Albert Hofstadter, in *Poetry, Language, Thought* (New York: Harper and Row, 1975), 32–4.

23. Jameson, *Postmodernism*, 8.

24. Heidegger, "The Origin of the Work of Art," 71.

25. Ibid., 33–4.

26. Jacques Derrida, *The Truth in Painting*, trans. Geoff Bennington and Ian McLeod (Chicago: University of Chicago Press, 1987), 255–382.

27. Bob Colacello, *Holy Terror: Andy Warhol Close Up* (New York: HarperCollins, 1990), 443.

28. Andy Warhol, in Pat Hackett ed., *The Andy Warhol Diaries* (New York: Warner Books, 1989), 306.

29. Jameson, *Postmodernism,* 8–9.

30. Fred Lawrence Guiles, *Loner at the Ball: The Life of Andy Warhol* (London: Black Swan, 1990), 354.

31. The phrase is Derrida's, who points out in *The Truth in Painting* 272–3, that "the pathos of the 'call of the earth' . . . was not foreign" to the Nazi ideology of the 1930s.

32. Heidegger, "The Origin of the Work of Art," 34, cited in Jameson, *Postmodernism*, 8.

33. Jesse Kornbluth, *Pre-Pop Warhol* (New York: Panache Press at Random House, 1988), 49.

34. Andy Warhol, *The Philosophy of Andy Warhol* (New York: Harcourt Brace Jovanovich, 1975), 54.

35. Heidegger, "The Origin of the Work of Art," 34.

36. Derrida, *The Truth in Painting*, 287.

37. Ibid., 265.

38. Ibid., 333.

39. Ibid., 267.

40. Stephen Koch, *Stargazer: Andy Warhol's World and His Films* (New York: Praeger, 1973), 122.

41. Jean Baudrillard, "Transpolitics, Transsexuality, Transaesthetics," in William Stearns and William Chaloupka eds., *Jean Baudrillard: The Disappearance of Art and Politics* (New York: St. Martin's, 1992), 19.

42. Jameson, *Postmodernism*, 9–10.

43. Derrida, *The Truth in Painting*, 370.

44. Patricia White, "Female Spectator, Lesbian Specter: The Haunting," in Diana Fuss ed., *Inside/Out: Lesbian Theories, Gay Theories* (New York: Routledge, 1991), 157. See also Tania Modleski, *Feminism without Women* (New York: Routledge, 1991), 131–4, for a related reading of the aptly titled *Ghost*.

45. Diana Fuss, "Inside/Out," in *Inside/Out*, 3.

46. Terry Castle, *The Apparitional Lesbian: Female Homosexuality and Modern Culture* (New York: Columbia University Press, 1993), 60–2.

47. Derrida, *The Truth in Painting*, 373.

48. Teresa de Lauretis, "Film and the Visible," in Bad Object Choices eds., *How Do I Look?* (Seattle: Bay Press, 1991), 251.

49. Severo Sarduy, "Writing/Transvestism," *Review* 9 (Fall 1973): 33.

50. Sarduy, ibid., cited in Marjorie Garber, *Vested Interests: Cross-Dressing and Cultural*

Anxiety (New York: Routledge, 1992), 150. Sarduy's argument is also crucial to the "Warhol's Bodies" chapter of Steven Shaviro's *The Cinematic Body*, 227–9.

51. Jameson, *Postmodernism*, 9.

52. Baudrillard, "Transpolitics, Transsexuality, Transaesthetics," 15–16.

53. Ibid., 11.

54. Ibid., 20.

55. Derrida, *The Truth in Painting*, 266.

56. Heidegger, "The Origin of the Work of Art," 78.

57. Paula Treichler, "AIDS, Homophobia, and Biomedical Discourse: An Epidemic of Signification," *Cultural Studies* 1:3 (October 1987): 263–305.

58. "[F]igure rather than ground, figure as ground, and as the calling into question of the possibility of ground"; see Garber, *Vested Interests*, 150.

Notes to Chapter 3

1. *Motion Picture Herald* 183:8 (26 May 1951): 861.

2. *Monthly Film Bulletin* 18:213 (1951): 347.

3. *Time* (25 June 1951).

4. Jeanine Basinger, *A Woman's View: How Hollywood Spoke to Women, 1930–1960* (New York: Knopf, 1993), 436.

5. Simone de Beauvoir, *The Second Sex* (1949), trans. and ed. H. M. Parshley (Harmondsworth: Penguin Books, 1972), 533.

6. Ibid., 583.

7. Ronnie Scheib, "Ida Lupino: Auteuress," *Film Comment* 16:1 (1980): 61.

8. Wendy Dozoretz, "The Mother's Lost Voice in Hard, Fast and Beautiful," *Wide Angle* 6:3 (1984): 52.

9. Theodor Adorno, *Minima Moralia: Reflections from a Damaged Life* (1951) trans. E. F. N. Jephcott (London: NLB, 1974), 38.

10. See Theodor Adorno, "Free Time," in J. M. Bernstein ed., *The Culture Industry: Selected Essays on Mass Culture* (London: Routledge, 1991), 164: "Just as the term 'show business' is today taken utterly seriously, the irony in the expression 'leisure industry' has now been quite forgotten."

11. Theodor Adorno, "Veblen's Attack on Culture," in *Prisms*, trans. Samuel and

Shierry Weber (Cambridge: MIT Press, 1981), 81. See also Adorno's "Free Time," 168: "The accepted reason for playing sport is that it makes believe that fitness itself is the sole, independent end of sport: whereas fitness for work is certainly one of the covert ends of sport."

12. Quoted in Billie Jean King with Cynthia Starr, *We Have Come a Long Way: The Story of Women's Tennis* (New York: McGraw-Hill, 1988), 41.

13. Quoted in ibid. Wills Moody's observation was made in the year that John R. Tunis published *Mother of a Champion.*

14. Michael Mewshaw, *Ladies of the Court: Grace and Disgrace on the Women's Tennis Tour* (London: Little, Brown, 1993), 204–5. Mewshaw also discusses the deleterious effects of parental ambition on players, particularly Jennifer Capriati and Mary Pierce. In today's multi-million-dollar game, however, the offending parents are usually *fathers.*

15. John Haylett and Richard Evans, *The Illustrated Encyclopedia of World Tennis* (Basingstoke: Marshall Cavendish, 1989), 229.

16. See *Saturday Review* (30 June 1951): "The shoestring budget keeps showing through, and the colorful backgrounds that might have been obtained for it with (I hate to say this) more money are simply not in evidence."

17. See Joan Riviere, "Womanliness as a Masquerade" (1929), in Victor Burgin, James Donald, and Cora Kaplan eds., *Formations of Fantasy* (London: Methuen, 1986), 35–44.

18. Sabrina Barton, in "'Crisscross': Paranoia and Projection in Strangers on a Train," *Camera Obscura* 25–26 (1991): 88, notes that in the famous tennis sequence in *Strangers on a Train*, a "reverse angle of the spectators' heads rhythmically following the back-and-forth movement of the ball invites the film audience to laugh at their coerced looking."

19. de Beauvoir, *The Second Sex,* 579.

20. Ibid., 233.

21. Ibid., 580.

22. Hank Whitemore, "My Life in Hollywood's Golden Age," *Parade Magazine* (20 February 1994): 14: "'See, Claire usually played the 'tough' girls.'"

23. Scheib, "Ida Lupino: Auteuress," 62.

24. Sigmund Freud, "Femininity" (1933 [1932]), in *New Introductory Lectures on Psychoanalysis* Pelican Freud Library Volume 2 (Harmondsworth: Penguin, 1977), 151.

25. Ibid., 155–7.

26. Dozoretz, "The Mother's Lost Voice," 56.

27. See Nancy Chodorow, *The Reproduction of Mothering: Psychoanalysis and the Sociology of Gender* (Berkeley: University of California Press, 1978).

28. Dozoretz cites a 28 March 1950 memo from producer William Fadiman to Gordon Youngman, insisting that "the screen play demands and requires a happy ending in which the heroine relinquishes any idea she might have had of turning professional and decides to marry the boy she has always loved."

29. *Commonweal* 54 (27 July 1951): 380.

30. E. Ann Kaplan, "Motherhood and Representation: From Postwar Freudian Figurations to Postmodernism," in E. Ann Kaplan ed., *Psychoanalysis and Cinema* (New York: Routledge, 1990), 128–42.

31. Sigmund Freud, "A Special Type of Choice of Object Made by Men" (1910), in *On Sexuality*, Pelican Freud Library Volume 7 (Harmondsworth: Penguin, 1977), 238.

32. This usage dates from at least the late nineteenth century, via the medieval meaning of "game" as "amorous sport or play" and "on the game" as an eighteenth-century phrase for robbery. See the *Oxford English Dictionary*.

33. For a discussion of this phrase, see Angela Carter, *The Sadeian Woman: An Exercise in Cultural History* (London: Virago, 1979), 134.

34. Mary Ann Doane, *Femme Fatales: Feminism, Film Theory, Psychoanalysis* (New York: Routledge, 1991), 265.

35. Walter Benjamin, "Central Park," *New German Critique* 34 (1985): 42.

36. Doane, *Femme Fatales*, 265.

37. See, for example, Basinger, *A Women's View*, 435.

38. That this is also the world of the film's director has not gone unremarked by Lupino's critics. See Barbara Koenig Quart, *Women Directors: The Emergence of a New Cinema* (New York: Praeger, 1988), 27:

> The anti-feminist content of her work becomes more explicit, and the gap between what Lupino herself did and the values she promulgated more dramatic. . . . The unambitious, decent ordinariness of the average loving American family is pitted against the pursuit of the best, the competitiveness that Hollywood itself was made of, that the directors of these films lived by—and the kind of drive a woman like Lupino would have had to have.

Notes to Chapter 4

1. John Stuart Mill, "The Spirit of the Age," *Examiner* (6 January–29 May 1831), reprinted in *Essays on Politics and Culture* (New York: Anchor Books, 1963), 1.

2. Reinhart Koselleck, *Futures Past: On the Semantics of Historical Time*, trans. Keith Tribe (Cambridge: MIT Press, 1985), 12.

3. Ibid., 18.

4. Jacques Derrida, *Specters of Marx: The State of the Debt, the Work of Mourning, and the New International,* trans. Peggy Kamuf (New York: Routledge, 1994), 125: "*Geist* can also mean specter, as do the words 'esprit' or 'spirit.' The spirit is also the spirit of spirits."

5. William Duff, *An Essay on Original Genius* [1767] (New York: Garland, 1970), 245.

6. Ibid., 179.

7. Ibid., 177.

8. The erectile responses described by both authors are intended to confine such visions to men, and Duff explicitly argues, in *Letters on the Intellectual and Moral Character of Women* (1807), that genius is a male attribute. This idea ultimately derives from the Latin origins of the term, which referred to the sacred procreative power of the male head of the family, or *gens*. See, in reply, Christine Battersby, *Gender and Genius: Towards a Feminist Aesthetics* (London: The Women's Press, 1989).

9. Terry Castle, *The Apparitional Lesbian: Female Homosexuality and Modern Culture* (New York: Columbia University Press, 1993).

10. Derrida, *Specters of Marx*, 10.

11. Ibid., 11.

12. Castle, *The Apparitional Lesbian*, 46–7.

13. Diana Fuss, "Inside/Out," in Diana Fuss ed., *Inside/Out: Lesbian Theories, Gay Theories* (London: Routledge, 1991).

14. Directed by Sheila McLaughlin, 1987, United States.

15. Teresa de Lauretis, "Film and the Visible," in Bad Object Choices eds., *How Do I Look?* (Seattle: Bay Press, 1991), 250–1.

16. Leo Bersani, *Homos* (Cambridge: Harvard University Press, 1995), 51.

17. See Mandy Merck, "Figuring Out Andy Warhol" in Jennifer Doyle, Jonathan Flatley, and José Estaban Muñoz eds., *Pop Out: Queer Warhol* (Durham: Duke University Press, 1996). Reprinted in this collection.

18. Terry Castle, *The Female Thermometer: Eighteenth-Century Culture and the Invention of the Uncanny* (Oxford: Oxford University Press, 1995).

19. Castle, *The Apparitional Lesbian*, 4.

20. Ibid., 13.

21. Judith Butler, "Imitation and Gender Insubordination," in Fuss ed., *Inside/ Out*, 15.

22. Castle, *The Apparitional Lesbian*, 14–15.

23. Derrida, *Specters of Marx*, 11.

24. Hugo von Hofmannsthal, cited in Gerd Uerkermann, "'Time Is a Strange Thing . . .': Past and Present in 'Der Rosenkavalier'" from the introduction to the libretto of the 1986 Decca production, conducted by George Solti, 23.

25. Lewis Lockwood, "The Element of Time in Der Rosenkavalier," in Bryan Gilliam ed., *Richard Strauss: New Perspectives on the Composer and his Work* (Durham: Duke University Press, 1992), 253.

26. Quoted by permisson from Boosey and Hawkes Music Publishers Limited and Schott and Co.

27. Cited in Uerkermann, "Time is a Strange Thing," 22.

28. Cited in ibid., 22.

29. Hugo von Hofmannsthal, cited in Norman del Mar, *Richard Strauss* Volume 1 (London: Barrie and Rocklift, 1962), 337.

30. Michel Poizat, *The Angel's Cry: Beyond the Pleasure Principle in Opera,* trans. Arthur Denner (Ithaca: Cornell University Press, 1992), 113.

31. William Mann, *Richard Strauss: A Critical Study of the Operas* (London: Cassell, 1964), 104.

32. See Bernd Urban, "Hofmannsthal, Freud und die Psychoanalyse," in *Europäische Hochshulschriften* (Frankfurt: Peter Lang, 1978).

33. Cited by James D. Steakley, "Iconography of a Scandal: Political Cartoons and the Eulenberg Affair in Wilhelmine Germany," in Martin B. Duberman, Martha Vicinus, and George Chauncey, Jr. eds., *Hidden from History: Reclaiming the Gay and Lesbian Past* (New York: Meridian, 1990), 256.

34. The *Oxford English Dictionary* traces this usage to 1895, and a reference in the *American Journal of Psychology* to "The Fairies" of New York, one of "the peculiar societies of inverts."

35. See Poizat, *The Angel's Cry*, 120–1.

36. Wayne Koestenbaum, *The Queen's Throat: Opera, Homosexuality and the Mystery of Desire* (London: Poseidon Press, 1993), 218.

37. See Karl Marx and Friedrich Engels, *Manifesto of the Communist Party* (1848): "Constant revolutionising of all production, uninterrupted disturbance of all social conditions, everlasting uncertainty and agitation distinguish the bourgeois epoch from all earlier ones." *Selected Works* (London: Lawrence and Wishart, 1968), 38.

38. Derrida, *Specters of Marx*, 123.

Notes to Chapter 5

The epigraphs are from Ivan Pavlov, "Experimental Psychology and Psychopathology in Animals," in *Selected Works* (Moscow: Foreign Languages Publishing House, 1955), 155; and *Cosmopolitan* (U.K. edition), April 1993, cover.

1. Tania Modleski, *Feminism without Women* (New York: Routledge, 1991), 5.

2. Catharine A. MacKinnon, *Only Words* (Cambridge: Harvard University Press, 1993), 17, 19.

3. Bernard Williams, "Drawing Lines," review of *Only Words*, by Catharine MacKinnon, *London Review of Books* (12 May 1994): 9; Marina Warner, "The Tongue Bites Deep," review of *Only Words*, by MacKinnon, *Independent on Sunday* (29 May 1994): Review Section, 32.

4. Williams, "Drawing Lines," 10. The irony here is that the reviewers didn't agree on what that argument was, with Williams maintaining that it was really about the incompatibility of current U.S. law on equality with that on freedom of speech.

5. Stanley Fish, "Introduction: Going Down the Anti-Formalist Road," *Doing What Comes Naturally* (Durham: Duke University Press, 1989), 18; Wendy Brown, "The Mirror of Pornography: MacKinnon's Social Theory of Gender" in *States of Injury: Power and Freedom in Late Modernity* (Princeton: Princeton University Press, 1995).

6. Quoted in Wendy Kaminer, "Feminists against the First Amendment," *Atlantic Monthly* (November 1992): 114.

7. Catharine A. MacKinnon, *Feminism Unmodified: Discourses on Life and Law* (Cambridge: Harvard University Press, 1987), 156.

8. Catharine A. MacKinnon, *Toward a Feminist Theory of the State* (Cambridge: Harvard University Press, 1989), 206.

9. MacKinnon, *Only Words*, 12.

10. Andrea Dworkin, *Pornography: Men Possessing Women* (New York: Perigee Books, 1979; London: Women's Press, 1981), 200–1.

11. A rhetorical strategy identified by Donald Alexander Downs, *The New Politics of Pornography* (Chicago: University of Chicago Press, 1989), 42.

12. MacKinnon, *Toward a Feminist Theory of the State*, 197.

13. See MacKinnon, *Feminism Unmodified*, 155, for relevant cases. MacKinnon herself writes, in *Sexual Harassment of Working Women* (New Haven: Yale University Press, 1979), 29: "Verbal sexual harassment can include anything from passing but persistent comments on a woman's body or body parts to the experience of an eighteen-year-old file clerk whose boss regularly called her in to his office 'to tell me the intimate details of his marriage and to ask what I thought about different sexual positions.' Pornography is sometimes used."

14. For the complete text of this ordinance, see Andrea Dworkin and Catharine A. MacKinnon, *Pornography and Civil Rights* (Minneapolis: Organizing Against Pornography, 1988), 99–105.

15. Quoted in *Off Our Backs* (June 1985): 12.

16. Mark Seltzer, *Bodies and Machines* (New York: Routledge, 1982), 94–5.

17. Jack London, "White Fang," in Earle Labor and Robert C. Leitz III eds., *The Call of the Wild, White Fang, and Other Stories* (Oxford: Oxford University Press, 1990), 94.

18. Ibid.

19. Seltzer, *Bodies and Machines*, 155.

20. Ivan Pavlov, *Lectures on Conditioned Reflexes*, trans. and ed. W. H. Gantt (New York: International Publishers, 1928), 1:38–9.

21. Pavlov, "Experimental Psychology," in *Selected Works*, 155.

22. Ibid.

23. Pavlov, "Physiology of the Higher Nervous Activity," in *Selected Works*, 271.

24. Pavlov, "Experimental Psychology," in *Selected Works*, 155.

25. See P. L. Broadhurst, "Abnormal Animal Behaviour," in W. H. Gantt, L. Pickenhain, and Ch. Zwingmann eds., *A Pavlovian Approach to Psychopathology* (Oxford: Pergamon Press, 1970), 177.

26. W. Horsley Gantt, "Psychosexuality in Animals," in W. H. Gannt et al. eds., *A Pavlovian Approach to Psychopathology*, 114.

27. Ibid., 112. Kinsey and his team did speculate on a possible neurological explanation for female "diversion" during coition. See Alfred C. Kinsey, Wardell B. Pomeroy, Clyde E. Martin, and Paul H. Gebhard, *Sexual Behavior in the Human Female* (Philadelphia: W. B. Saunders, 1953), 668–9.

28. Gantt, "Psychosexuality in Animals," 118.

29. H. J. Eysenck and P. K. B. Nias, *Sex, Violence, and the Media* (London: Paladin, 1980), 244.

30. Ibid., 237.

31. Edward Donnerstein, Daniel Linz, and Steven Penrod, *The Question of Pornography* (New York: Free Press, 1987), 14–5.

32. Edna F. Einseidel, "The Experimental Research Evidence," *The Attorney General's Commission on Pornography: Final Report, 1986* reprinted in Catherine Itzin ed., *Pornography: Women, Violence, and Civil Liberties* (Oxford: Oxford University Press, 1992), 249.

33. Andrea Dworkin, "Against the Male Flood: Censorship, Pornography, and Equality," in Itzin ed., *Pornography*, 520.

34. MacKinnon, *Toward a Feminist Theory of the State*, 148.

35. Dworkin, "Against the Male Flood," 522.

36. Ibid., 524.

37. MacKinnon, *Only Words*, 7.

38. Dennis Howitt, *Concerning Psychology* (London: Open University, 1991), 40.

39. John B. Watson, *Behaviorism* (1924) (New York: W. W. Norton, 1970), 8.

40. Andrea Dworkin, *Intercourse* (London: Secker & Warburg, 1987), 129.

41. Judith Butler, "Disorderly Woman," *Transition* 53 (1991): 91, describes MacKinnon's account of male domination as "the second nature produced by a systematic misogynist practice."

42. London, "White Fang," 94.

43. Jack London, "Eight Great Factors of Literary Success," quoted in Labor and Leitz eds., *Call of the Wild*, xii.

44. London, quoted in ibid., xv.

45. J. L. Austin, *How to Do Things with Words* (1962; reprint, Oxford: Oxford University Press, 1975), quoted in MacKinnon, *Only Words*, 121 n. 32.

46. MacKinnon, *Only Words*, 21.

47. I am indebted to Judith Butler for this observation. See Austin, *How to Do Things* *with Words,* esp. Lectures VIII, IX, and X; and Judith Butler, *Excitable Speech: A Politics of the Performative* (New York: Routledge, 1997).

48. Judith Butler, *Bodies That Matter* (New York: Routledge, 1993), 2.

49. MacKinnon, *Toward a Feminist Theory of the State,* 198.

50. MacKinnon, *Only Words,* 121.

51. Ibid., 21.

52. Perhaps because, as a 1990 report commissioned by the British government concluded,

> *Evidence of the adverse effects of pornography is far less clear cut than some earlier reviews imply. Inconsistencies emerge between very similar studies and many interpretations of these have reached almost opposite conclusions. . . . It is unlikely that pornography is the only determinant of sexual and other forms of violence and that pornography can be influential in the absence of other conducive factors.*

Dennis Howitt and Guy Cumberbatch, *Pornography: Impacts and Influences* (London: Home Office Research and Planning Unit, 1990), 94–5.

53. Nevertheless, "All rise," like "Get her," would be a perlocutionary rather than an illocutionary speech act.

54. MacKinnon, *Only Words,* 37.

55. *Report of the Committee on Obscenity and Film Censorship* (London: Her Majesty's Stationery Office, 1979), 103.

56. Ian Hunter, David Saunders, and Dugald Williamson, *On Pornography: Literature, Sexuality and Obscenity Law* (London: Macmillan, 1993), 184.

57. MacKinnon, *Only Words,* 17.

58. Eve Kosofsky Sedgwick, "Epidemics of the Will," in *Tendencies* (London: Routledge, 1994), 130–42.

59. Mark Seltzer, "Serial Killers (I)," *differences* 5.1 (1993): 111.

60. MacKinnon, *Only Words,* 16.

61. Dworkin, *Intercourse,* 119.

62. Seltzer, "Serial Killers," 111.

63. Bram Stoker, *Dracula* (1897) (New York: Bantam Books, 1981), 84.

64. W. Mischel, "A Social-Learning View of Sex Differences in Behavior," quoted in Stephen Frosh, *Psychoanalysis and Psychology: Minding the Gap* (New York: New York University Press, 1989), 173.

65. See Diana Fuss, *Essentially Speaking* (New York: Routledge, 1989), 2–6; and Judith Butler, *Bodies That Matter*, 4–12.

66. Sedgwick, "Epidemics of the Will," 138.

67. Toni Morrison, *Beloved* (New York: Signet, 1991), 33–4.

Notes to Chapter 6

1. For this account, I am indebted to Richard Boon, *Brenton: The Playwright* (London: Methuen Drama, 1991), and Philip Roberts, "The Trials of The Romans in Britain," in Ann Wilson ed., *Howard Brenton: A Casebook* (New York: Garland, 1992).

2. *New Society* (23 October 1980).

3. Mary Whitehouse, *Whatever Happened to Sex?* (Hove: Wayland, 1977), 67–8.

4. *Report of the Home Office Committee on Obscenity and Film Censorship* (London: Her Majesty's Stationery Office, 1979), 35.

5. Geoffrey Robertson and Andrew G. L. Nicol, *Media Law* (London: Sage Publications, 1984), 92.

6. Ibid., 87.

7. *Report of the Home Office Committee*, 130–1.

8. Quoted in Leslie J. Moran, *The Homosexuality of Law* (London: Routledge, 1996), 99.

9. John Marshall, "Pansies, Perverts and Macho Men: Changing Conceptions of Male Homosexuality," in Kenneth Plummer ed., *The Making of the Modern Homosexual* (London: Hutchinson, 1981), 139–40.

10. Jeffrey Weeks, *Coming Out: Homosexual Politics in Britain from the Nineteenth Century to the Present* (London: Quartet Books, 1977), 16.

11. Judith Walkowitz, *City of Dreadful Delights: Narratives of Sexual Danger in Late-Victorian London* (London: Virago, 1992), 278 n. 123. The legal connection between female prostitution and male homosexuality survived for seventy years, to be jointly considered in the 1950s by the Wolfenden Committee, concerned with the reregulation of sexual behavior in public. All three themes—public order, social dominance, and masculine sexuality—emerge in *The Romans in Britain*.

12. Richard Davenport-Hines, *Sex, Death and Punishment: Attitudes to Sex and Sexuality in Britain since the Renaissance* (London: Collins, 1990), 130–2.

13. Ed Cohen, *Talk on the Wilde Side* (New York: Routledge, 1993), 128–9.

14. Cited in ibid., 167.

15. *R. v. Howells* (1976), cited in Moran, *Homosexuality of Law*, 229 n. 14.

16. Howard Brenton, *The Romans in Britain* in *Plays:2* (London: Methuen Drama, 1989), 2.

17. Boon, *Brenton*, 181.

18. Brenton, *Plays:2*, viii.

19. Ibid., 2, vii–viii.

20. Quoted in Roberts, "The Trials of The Romans in Britain," 63–4.

21. Ibid., 64.

22. Ibid., 65.

23. Robertson and Nicol, *Media Law*, 94.

24. Ibid.

25. Robert F. Gross, "The Romans in Britain: Aspirations and Anxieties of a Radical Playwright," in Wilson, *Howard Brenton*, 76.

26. Brenton, *Plays:2*, 38.

27. Ibid., 34.

28. Petr Bogatyrev, "Semiotics in the Folk Theater" in Ladislav Matejka and Irwin R. Titunik eds., *Semiotics of Art* (Cambridge: MIT Press, 1978), 34.

29. *Report of the Home Office Committee*, 103.

30. Ibid., 122.

31. Ibid., 125.

32. Ian Hunter, David Saunders, and Dugald Williamson, *On Pornography: Literature, Sexuality and Obscenity Law* (London: Macmillan, 1993), 182–4.

33. Mandy Merck, "MacKinnon's Dog: Antiporn's Canine Conditioning," in Nancy Hewitt, Jean O'Barr, and Nancy Rosebaugh eds., *Talking Gender* (Chapel Hill: University of North Carolina Press, 1996), 78. Reprinted in this volume.

34. Judith Butler, *Excitable Speech: A Politics of the Performative* (New York: Routledge, 1997), 123.

35. The term is used in a subsequent congressional statute to indicate, in Butler's interpretation, "a natural teleology to homosexual status, whereby we are asked to understand such status as always almost culminating in an act." Ibid., 106.

36. Ibid., 125.

37. Conversely, she also attributed dangerous arousal to youth themselves, arguing that "this type of play could influence young people. There is a proven link between

NOTES TO CHAPTER 6

pornography and serious sex crimes. It is quite overwhelming society." Quoted in Boon, *Brenton*, 174.

Notes to Chapter 7

1. Quoted in Andrew Smith, "The New Coens," *Guardian* G2 (7 February 1997): 5.

2. From, respectively, Georgia Brown, "Fit to Be Tied," *Village Voice* (8 October 1996): 72; Geoff Brown, *Times* (27 February 1997): 37; Nick Bradshaw, "Bound," *Time Out* (26 February–3 March 1997): 73.

3. Victoria Stagg Elliott, *Diva* (October–November 1996): 3.

4. Judith Halberstam, "Gangster Dyke," *Girlfriends* (January—February 1997): 14.

5. Stagg Elliott, *Diva*, 3.

6. Halberstam, "Gangster Dyke," 14.

7. Amy Morissey, "The Gangster Film Unbound," *Gay Community News* 22:4 (Spring 1997): 33.

8. Halberstam, "Gangster Dyke," 14.

9. Jean Noble, "Bound and Invested: Lesbian Desire and Hollywood," *Film Criticism* 12:3 (Spring 1998): 16.

10. Radclyffe Hall, *The Well of Loneliness* (1928) (London: Virago, 1982), 143, 187–8, 271, 227, 219, 233, 316, 300, respectively. For this account of the significance of the hand in the novel, I am indebted to Wren Sidhe, "Radclyffe Hall's Lesbian Digits: Writing the Body of the Invert in The Well of Loneliness," unpublished paper for the Anatomy, Identity, Hegemony Conference at Cheltenham and Gloucester College of Higher Education, 10 April 1999.

11. Joanne Winning, "Mother Love: Psychoanalysis and the Lesbian Love Story," *Archive of the Self: Reading Lesbian Modernism Through Dorothy Richardson's Pilgrimage* (University of Wisconsin Press, forthcoming). I am indebted to Winning for this account of manual imagery in Richardson's writing.

12. Dorothy Richardson, *Backwater* (1916), *Pilgrimage* (London: Virago, 1979), 1:282–3.

13. Richardson, *The Tunnel* (1919), *Pilgrimage* (London: Virago, 1979), 2:262.

14. Richardson, *Backwater*, 283.

15. Richardson, *Pointed Roofs* (1915), *Pilgrimage*, 1:56.

16. Richardson, *Backwater*, 283.

17. Ibid.

18. Dr. Emily L. Sisley and Bertha Harris, *The Joy of Lesbian Sex* (New York: Simon and Schuster, 1977), 40, quoted in Noble, "Bound and Invested," 11.

19. Zoe Schramm-Evans, *Making Out: The Book of Lesbian Sex and Sexuality* (London: Pandora, 1995), 159.

20. Ibid., 113. Writing about sex between lesbians and gay men, Pat Califia, *Public Sex: The Culture of Radical Sex* (Pittsburgh: Cleis Press, 1994) observes (184–5): "In fisting the emphasis is not on the genitals. . . . more often than straight sex, gay sex assumes that the use of hands or the mouth is as important as genital-to-genital contact. . . . When penetration does happen, dildos and fingers are as acceptable as (maybe preferable to) cocks."

21. Michèle Aina Barale, "Below the Belt: (Un)Covering the Well of Loneliness," in Diana Fuss ed., *Inside/Out: Lesbian Theories, Gay Theories* (New York: Routledge, 1991), 237.

22. Ibid., 249–50.

23. Judith Roof, *A Lure of Knowledge: Lesbian Sexuality and Theory* (New York: Columbia University Press, 1991), 54.

24. Ibid., 63.

25. See Mandy Merck, "Dessert Hearts" in Martha Gever, John Greyson, Pratibha Parmar eds., *Queer Looks: Perspectives in Lesbian and Gay Film and Video* (New York: Routledge, 1993), 377.

26. Judith Roof, *A Lure of Knowledge*, 64.

27. Sigmund Freud, "Fetishism" (1927), in *On Sexuality,* Pelican Freud Library Volume 7 (Harmondsworth: Penguin Books, 1977), 354.

28. Teresa de Lauretis, *The Practice of Love: Lesbian Sexuality and Perverse Desire* (Bloomington: Indiana University Press, 1994), 243.

29. Judith Butler, *Bodies That Matter* (New York: Routledge, 1993), 89.

30. Ibid., 88–9.

31. Louise Allen, *The Lesbian Idol* (London: Cassell, 1997), 71–2.

32. Ibid., 115. Emphasis in original.

33. Ibid., 117.

34. Eve Kosofsky Sedgwick, "Is the Rectum Straight?" *Tendencies* (Routledge: London, 1994), 98.

35. Ibid., 101–2.

36. *Variety* (December 18, 1968).

37. Vito Russo, *The Celluloid Closet: Homosexuality in the Movies* (New York: Harper and Row, 1981), 173.

38. Compare this defiant response with the obliging explanation of vaginal fisting provided by the bisexual heroine of *Chasing Amy* (1997).

39. Noble, "Bound and Invested," 4.

40. Mark Salisbury, "Twisted Sister," *Premiere* (U.K. edition) (February 1997): 80, quotes Jennifer Tilly saying "I tried to get my hands in every shot because the Wachowskis were very taken by my nail polish."

41. Denis Diderot, "Les bijoux indiscrets" (1748), J. Assezat ed., *Oeuvres complètes de Diderot,* volume 4 (Paris: Kraus, 1966), discussed in Linda Williams, *Hard Core: Power, Pleasure and the "Frenzy of the Visible"* (London: Pandora, 1990), 1–3.

42. Georgia Brown, "Fit to Be Tied," 72.

43. Unsigned review of "Bound," *Independent* (1–7 March 1997): "The Eye," 8.

44. Andreas Laurentius, *Historia anatomica humani corporis* (1599), translated by Helkiah Crooke, *Microcosmographia: A Description of the Body of Man* (London: William Jaggard, 1615), 729. See also Katherine Rowe, "'God's handy worke,'" in David Hillman and Carla Mazzio eds., *The Body in Parts: Fantasies of Corporeality in Early Modern Europe* (New York: Routledge, 1997), 285–309.

45. Hieronymus Fabricus, *De visione voce auditu,* Venice 1600. See William Schupbach, *The Paradox of Rembrandt's "Anatomy of Dr. Tulp"* (London: Wellcome Institute for the History of Medicine, 1982), 19–20.

46. Aristotle, *On the Parts of Animals,* cited in William Schupbach, *The Paradox of Rembrandt's "Anatomy,"* 58. For a discussion of this debate, see Jonathan Goldberg, *Writing Matters: From the Hands of the English Renaissance* (Stanford: Stanford University Press, 1990), 85–6.

47. Frederick Engels, "The Part Played by Labour in the Transition from Ape to Man" (1895–6), in Karl Marx and Frederick Engels, *Selected Works* (London: Lawrence and Wishart, 1968), 357.

48. Ibid., 355. Emphasis in original.

49. John Bulwer, in James W. Cleary ed., *Chirologia: or the Natural Language of the Hand and Chironomia: or the Art of Manual Rhetoric* (Carbondale: Southern Illinois University Press, 1974), 50.

50. John Donne, "Elegie XIX: To His Mistris Going to Bed," in Charles M. Goffin ed.,

The Complete Poetry and Selected Prose of John Donne (New York: Modern Library, 1952), 83–4.

Notes to Chapter 8

1. Douglas Crimp, "AIDS: Cultural Analysis/Cultural Activism," *October* 43 (Winter 1987): 15.

2. Jan Zita Grover, "AIDS: Keywords," *October* 43 (Winter 1987): 19; emphasis in original.

3. Suki Ports, "Needed (For Women and Children)," *October* 43 (Winter 1987): 169–76.

4. Simon Watney, *Policing Desire: Pornography, AIDS and the Media* (Minneapolis: University of Minnesota Press, 1987), 12.

5. Ibid., 126.

6. Ibid., 28.

7. Leo Bersani, "Is the Rectum a Grave?" *October* 43 (Winter 1987): 206.

8. Ibid., 222.

9. Jean Laplanche, *Life and Death in Psychoanalysis* (Baltimore: Johns Hopkins University Press, 1985), 87. Laplanche is commenting on Freud's theory of the "propping" of the sexual drive on a nonsexual function in the *Three Essays on the Theory of Sexuality* (1905).

10. Ibid., 97.

11. Leo Bersani, *The Freudian Body* (New York: Columbia University Press, 1986), 62–3; emphasis in original.

12. Georges Bataille, *Erotism: Death and Sensuality*, trans. Mary Dalwood (San Francisco: City Lights Books, 1986), 17.

13. Ibid.

14. Bersani, "Is the Rectum a Grave?" 218, fn. 25.

15. Bersani, *The Freudian Body*, 144.

16. Bataille, *Erotism*, 18.

17. Michel Foucault, *The Use of Pleasure* (New York: Vintage Books, 1986), 72–7.

18. Cited by Bernard-Henri Levy, "Foucault: Non au sexe roi," *Le Nouvel Observateur* (12 March 1977): 98, trans. David M. Halperin, *Saint Foucault* (New York: Oxford University Press, 1995), 78.

19. James Miller, *The Passion of Michel Foucault* (New York: Simon and Schuster, 1993).

20. Aiskhines, *Prosecution of Timarkhos*, cited by K. J. Dover, *Greek Homosexuality* (London: Duckworth, 1978), 20.

21. Dover, *Greek Homosexuality*, 106

22. Ibid., 104.

23. Foucault, *The Use of Pleasure*, 215.

24. Bersani, "Is the Rectum a Grave?" 211. Emphasis in original.

25. Ibid., 212.

26. Leo Bersani, *Homos* (Cambridge: Harvard University Press, 1995), 164. My emphasis.

27. In *The Use of Pleasure*, Foucault notes Plato's reluctance to describe proscribed sexual acts, instead offering euphemisms such as "to grant one's favours" or "to do the thing," and claims that "the Greeks would have found it improper that someone would call by name, in a set speech, things that were only vaguely alluded to even in polemics and law court addresses," 209. Conversely, Dover cites a wealth of ceramic illustrations and inscriptions representing homosexual acts, as well as literary examples such as Theocritus's lines in which the goatherd Kamatos recalls to the shepherd Lakon, "Don't you remember when I got stuck into you and you grinned and moved your tail to and fro very nicely and held onto that oak-tree?" *Greek Homosexuality*, 104.

28. Dover moves out of the Greek to observe that "Vulgar idiom in many languages uses 'buggered' or 'fucked' in the sense 'defeated,' 'worsted,'" *Greek Homosexuality*, 105. And describing the political philosophy of Catharine MacKinnon, Drucilla Cornell writes "The female condition is the condition of subordination, what is manifested within it carries the taint of our violation. The 'base' is that we are fucked; the superstructure, the ideology that we like it." *Beyond Accommodation* (New York: Routledge, 1991), 126.

29. Bersani, "Is the Rectum a Grave?" 212–13.

30. Catharine A. MacKinnon, *Feminism Unmodified: Discourses on Life and Law* (Cambridge: Harvard University Press, 1987), 3, 172; cited in Bersani, "Is the Rectum a Grave?" 213.

31. Bersani, "Is the Rectum a Grave?" 215. Emphasis in original. See, for example, Andrea Dworkin, *Intercourse* (London: Secker and Warburg, 1987).

32. Ibid.

33. Leo Bersani, *The Culture of Redemption* (Cambridge: Harvard University Press, 1990), 1974.

34. Bersani, "Is the Rectum a Grave?" 219.

35. Ibid., 221.

36. Jonathan Dollimore, "Sex and Death," *Textual Practise* 9.1 (1995): 31.

37. The reference is not to Oscar, but to the term used in media discussion of the notorious 1988 attack on a woman jogger in New York's Central Park by a "pack" of teenage boys. The term's linking of primitivism, violence, and misogyny is discussed by Mark Seltzer in *Bodies and Machines* (New York: Routledge, 1992), 217, fn. 8.

38. Bersani, *The Freudian Body*, 24, 42.

39. Bersani, *The Culture of Redemption*, 30.

40. Biddy Martin, "Extraordinary Homosexuals and the Fear of Being Ordinary," in *Femininity Played Straight* (New York: Routledge, 1996), 46. The association of femininity with domesticity has, of course, its (ostensible) obverse, in which women are seen as closer to nature than men. For an account of the complexities of this presumption, see Sherry Ortner's famous article, "Is Female to Male as Nature Is to Culture?" in Michelle Zimbalist Rosaldo and Louise Lamphere eds., *Woman, Culture and Society* (Stanford: Stanford University Press, 1974), 67–87.

41. I am indebted to Naomi Segal for this observation. See also Carole-Anne Tyler, "Boys Will Be Girls: The Politics of Gay Drag," in Diana Fuss ed., *Inside/Out* (New York: Routledge, 1991), 40: "Gay men [in 'Is the Rectum a Grave?'] are the better women, represented as better equipped to undo identity."

42. Bersani, "Is the Rectum a Grave?" 208.

43. Jonathan Dollimore, "Desire Is Death," in M. De Grazia ed., *Material Culture in the Early Modern Period* (Cambridge: Cambridge University Press, 1996), 369.

44. Jonathan Dollimore, "Sex and Death," *Textual Practice* 9:1 (1995): 27.

45. Ibid., 35.

46. Ibid., 48.

47. Ibid., 33.

48. Oscar Moore, *A Matter of Life and Sex* (first published in 1991 under the pseudonym Alec F. Moran by Paper Drum; subsequently London: Penguin Books, 1992). Moore's posthumous article, "Rites of Fatality" (*Guardian*, 21 September 1996, Weekend Section, 16–23) is a virtual compendium of the themes under criticism here: gay men knowingly courting death through sex; fatality as the inevitable concomitant of pleasure; promiscuity as the cause of AIDS. In the typical style of the *memento mori*, it is illustrated with "before" and "after" pictures of the stricken author.

49. Rupert Haselden, "Gay Abandon," *Guardian* (7 September 1991): 14–15.

50. Douglas Crimp, "How to Have Promiscuity in an Epidemic," *October* 43 (Winter 1987): 253, fn. 17 in Dollimore, "Sex and Death," 50–l.

51. John Rechy, *The Sexual Outlaw* (London: W. H. Allen, 1978), 301, cited in Dollimore, "Sex and Death," 31.

52. Dollimore, "Sex and Death," 36.

53. Jeff Nunokawa, "'All the Sad Young Men': AIDS and the Work of Mourning," in Diana Fuss ed., *Inside/Out* (New York: Routledge, 1991), 316.

54. Dollimore, "Sex and Death," 27.

55. Ibid., 31.

56. Ibid., 32, citing Michael Rumaker, *A Day and Night at the Baths* (California: Grey Fox Press, 1979).

57. Dollimore, "Sex and Death," 49.

58. The reference is to Paula A. Treichler, "AIDS, Homophobia and Biomedical Discourse: An Epidemic of Signification" *Cultural Studies* 1.3 (October 1987), reprinted in *October* 43 (Winter 1987): 31–70.

59. Cyril Collard, *Savage Nights*, trans. William Rodarmor (London: Quartet Books, 1993), 8. The French original is *Les nuits fauves* (Paris: Flammarion, 1989).

60. Ibid., 12.

61. Ibid., 15.

62. Ibid., 53. See also 27: "My savages are short, solid and muscular. They lean against walls, one leg bent, one foot flat against the cement, their slightly turned heads bowed, eyes looking up. Or, more rarely, they're girls, always in movement." As this passage suggests, "girls" can be found on the wild side of this novel, so long as they're as exotic, juvenile, and persecutory as Laura, with her endless scenes and answerphone threats, proves to be.

63. Ibid., 84.

64. Ibid., 8.

65. Ibid., 147.

66. On the correlation of male masochism and political dominance, see Kaja Silver-

man, "White Skin, Brown Masks: The Double Mimesis, or with Lawrence in Arabia," in *Male Subjectivity at the Margins* (New York: Routledge, 1992).

67. Mandy Rose, quoted in Melissa Benn, "Adventures in the Soho Skin Trade," *New Statesman* (11 December 1987): 23. Emphasis in original.

68. Cornell, *Beyond Accommodation*, 152.

69. Ibid., 153.

70. MacKinnon, *Feminism Unmodified*, 39, cited in Cornell, *Beyond Accommodation*, 154.

71. Wendy Brown, *States of Injury: Power and Freedom in Late Modernity* (Princeton: Princeton University Press, 1995), 90–1.

72. Bersani, *Homos*, 64.

73. Bersani, "Is the Rectum a Grave?" 218.

74. Carole-Anne Tyler, "Boys Will Be Girls," 40, argues that in "Is the Rectum a Grave?" "promiscuous anal sex has exactly a phallicizing function, swelling the ego of the theoretical impersonator (as 'feminine masochist') at the expense of women." Kaja Silverman, *in Male Subjectivity at the Margins*, 350, claims that "for Bersani . . . the defining feature of the gay man is that he narcissistically loves the phallic attributes of other male bodies." Finally, in "The Psychoanalysis of AIDS," *October* 63 (Winter 1993): 114, Tim Dean maintains that "Is the Rectum a Grave?" paradoxically re-enshrines "the gay ego as an agent of mastery. . . . [A]ny appeal to the ego, even an appeal for it to solicit its own shattering, must count as a nonpsychoanalytic solution, for in seeking to eliminate the significance of the unconscious, Bersani's recommendation implicitly advocates a redemption of subjectivity—if not selfhood—as such."

75. Guy Hocquenghem, *Homosexual Desire* (London: Allison & Busby, 1978), 89. See also Eve Kosofsky Sedgwick, "A Poem Is Being Written," in *Tendencies* (London: Routledge, 1994), 204: "Although there is no reason to suppose that women experience, in some imaginary quantitative sense 'less' anal eroticism than men do, it can as far as I can determine almost be said as a flat fact that, since classical times, *there has been no important and sustained Western discourse in which women's anal eroticism means*. Means anything." Emphasis in original.

76. Bersani, "Is the Rectum a Grave?": 211; emphasis in original.

77. Cora Kaplan, "Wild Nights: Pleasure, Sexuality, Feminism," in *Sea Changes: Culture and Feminism* (London: Verso, 1986), 34.

78. Mary Wollstonecraft, in Carol H. Poston ed., *A Vindication of the Rights of Women*, 2d ed. (New York: W. W. Norton, 1988), 11.

79. Compare MacKinnon's *Toward a Feminist Theory of the State*, 130:

> *So many distinctive features of women's status as second-class—the restriction and constraint and contortion, the servility and the display, the self-mutilation and requisite presentation of self as a beautiful thing, the enforced passivity, the humiliation—are made into the content of sex for women. Being a thing for sexual use is fundamental to it. This approach identifies not just a sexuality that is shaped under conditions of gender inequality but reveals this sexuality itself to be the dynamic of the inequality of the sexes.*

And Mary Wollstonecraft, *A Vindication of the Rights of Women*, 117:

> *Every thing that they see or hear serves to fix impressions, call forth emotions, and associate ideas, that give a sexual character to the mind. False notions of beauty and delicacy stop the growth of their limbs and produce a sickly soreness, rather than delicacy of organs. . . . This cruel association of ideas, which every thing conspires to twist into all their habits of thinking, or, to speak with more precision, of feeling, receives new force when they begin to act a little for themselves; for they then perceive that it is only through their address to excite emotions in men that pleasure and power are to be obtained.*

80. Kaplan, "Wild Nights," 56.

81. Ibid., 32.

82. See also Cora Kaplan, "Pandora's Box: Subjectivity, Class and Sexuality in Socialist Feminist Criticism," in *Sea Changes*, 147–76.

83. Kaplan, "Wild Nights," 55.

84. Bersani, *Homos*, 87.

85. Ibid., 90.

86. Ibid., 88.

87. Ibid., 89.

88. Ibid., 105, citing David M. Halperin, *One Hundred Years of Homosexuality and Other Essays on Greek Love* (New York: Routledge, 1990), 30.

89. Ibid., 106. My emphasis. With the publication of Simon Goldhill, *Foucault's Virginity: Ancient Erotic Fiction and the History of Sexuality* (Cambridge: Cambridge University Press, 1995), the absolutism of this ancient ordinance has been challenged. See James Davidson's review of Goldhill, "Cures for Impotence," *London Review of*

Books (19 October 1995): 22, on Foucault's debt to Dover's citation of homosexually submissive positions in primate power relations:

> *Even Foucault, who would not normally allow a monkey within a hundred miles of his philosophy, is quite happy to refer to Dover's bestiary as evidence for ancient attitudes to penetration. His followers have tended to follow suit, producing a curious blend of primatology and psychoanalysis, treating the penis as a transcendental signifier and reading the meanings of making love without reference to cultural conventions. A theory which claims to challenge universalising notions of sexuality depends on universalising interpretations of sex.*

See, further, letters in response in the 2 November 1995, 30 November 1995, 14 December 1995, and 4 January 1996 issues of the *London Review of Books*.

90. Jacqueline Rose, *The Haunting of Sylvia Plath* (London: Virago, 1991), 209.

91. Ibid., 235.

92. Ibid.

93. Bersani, *Homos*, 106–7.

94. Ibid., 140.

95. Ibid., 59.

96. Sigmund Freud, "From the History of an Infantile Neurosis" (1918), in *Case Histories II*, Pelican Freud Library Volume 9 (Harmondsworth: Penguin, 1984), 327.

97. Ibid., 301.

98. Bersani, *Homos*, 112.

99. Bersani, "Is the Rectum a Grave?" 222.

100. Any association of the phallus with an actual man risks the naturalization of male privilege which both Bersani and MacKinnon so constantly contest and concede.

101. For a discussion of Wilson's work, see Cherry Smyth, *Damn Fine Art* (London: Cassell, 1996), 109–13.

102. Winifred Woodhull, *Transfigurations of the Maghreb: Feminism, Decolonization and Literatures* (Minneapolis: University of Minnesota Press, 1993), 57.

103. Ibid., 75.

104. Kaplan, "The Indefinite Disclosed: Christina Rossetti and Emily Dickinson," in *Sea Changes*, 112.

105. Wollstonecraft, *Vindication of the Rights of Woman*, 57.

Notes to Chapter 9

1. Paul de Man, "Autobiography as De-Facement," in *The Rhetoric of Romanticism* (New York: Columbia University Press, 1984), 75. Emphasis in original.

2. Howard Eilberg-Schwartz, "Introduction: The Spectacle of the Female Head," in Howard Eilberg-Schwartz and Wendy Doniger eds., *Off with Her Head! The Denial of Women's Identity in Myth, Religion, and Culture* (Berkeley: University of California Press, 1995), 1, 2.

3. Allison Pearson, "It's the Women He Treats Like Cotton Pickin' Slaves . . . ," *Evening Standard* (11 February 1998): 13.

4. See Cynthia Chase, *Decomposing Figures: Rhetorical Readings in the Romantic Tradition* (Baltimore: Johns Hopkins University Press, 1986), 84.

5. See David Sylvester, *Magritte* (London: Thames and Hudson, 1992), 207–8.

6. Sigmund Freud, "Medusa's Head" (1922) in *Sexuality and the Psychology of Love* (New York: Collier Books, 1963), 212.

7. The association of Magritte's *Le viol* with this sexual practice is demonstrated in the use of the 1934 version to illustrate Paul Ableman, *The Mouth and Oral Sex* (London: Christopher Kypreos/Running Man Press, 1969), 95.

8. Linda Williams, *Hard Core: Power, Pleasure and the "Frenzy of the Visible"* (London: Pandora, 1990), 98–9.

9. The representation of women "in postures of sexual submission or sexual servility" is one of nine possible characteristics of "pornography" as defined in the ordinance that Dworkin and MacKinnon drafted for the city of Minneapolis, Minnesota, in 1983. See Donald Alexander Downs, *The New Politics of Pornography* (Chicago: University of Chicago Press, 1989), 44.

10. Cited in Varda Burstyn ed., *Women against Censorship* (Douglas & MacIntyre: Vancouver, 1985), 24.

11. Catharine A. MacKinnon, *Feminism Unmodified: Discourses on Life and Law* (Cambridge: Harvard University Press, 1987), 11.

12. Ibid., 7.

13. *Final Report of the Attorney General's Commission on Pornography* (Nashville: Rutledge Hill Press, 1986), 439. This commercially published edition of the report is flagged with warnings of "sexually explicit material" in an apparent attempt to attract readers on that basis.

14. Carl Bernstein and Bob Woodward, *All the President's Men* (New York: Simon and Schuster, 1974), 71.

15. Ibid., 77–8.

16. Ibid., 260.

17. Ibid., 131.

18. A "knowledgeable source" quoted in Evan Thomas and Matthew Cooper, "Extracting a Confession," *Newsweek* (31 August 1998): 33.

19. Catharine A. MacKinnon, *Sexual Harassment of Working Women* (New Haven: Yale University Press, 1979), 55.

20. Jeffrey Toobin, "Terms of Impeachment," *New Yorker* (14 September 1998): 38.

21. Quoted in Katharine Viner, "Look Forward in Anger," *Guardian* G2 (26 February 1998): 4.

22. Sigmund Freud, "Civilization and Its Discontents" (1930), in *Civilization, Society and Religion*, Pelican Freud Library Volume 12 (Harmondsworth: Penguin, 1985), 288–9, fn. 1.

23. Sigmund Freud, "Fragment of an Analysis of a Case of Hysteria" ("Dora") (1905), in *Case Histories I*, Pelican Freud Library Volume 8 (Harmondsworth: Penguin, 1977), 59.

24. Ibid., 60.

25. Ibid., 86. But see also Sigmund Freud, "Three Essays on Sexuality" (1905), in *On Sexuality*, Pelican Freud Library Volume 7 (Harmondsworth: Penguin, 1977), 64:

> *The limits of such disgust are, however, often purely conventional: a man who will kiss a pretty girl's lips passionately, may perhaps be disgusted at the idea of her toothbrush. . . . But there is no doubt that the genitals of the opposite sex can in themselves be an object of disgust and that such an attitude is one of the characteristics of all hysterics, and especially of hysterical women.*

26. Sigmund Freud, "Analysis of a Specimen Dream" (1900) in *The Interpretation of Dreams*, Pelican Freud Library Volume 4 (Harmondsworth: Penguin, 1976), 180–99.

27. Jacques Lacan, "The Dream of Irma's Injection," in Jacques Alain-Miller ed., *The Ego in Freud's Theory and the Technique of Psychoanalysis, 1954–1955*, The Seminar of Jacques Lacan Book II (Cambridge: Cambridge University Press, 1988), 158.

28. See Jeffrey Moussaieff Masson, *Freud: The Assault on Truth* (London: Faber and Faber, 1984), 55–106. While accepting the likelihood of Freud's guilt in this matter and its influence on the dream of Irma's injection, I am not persuaded by Masson's theory of its relationship to the renunciation of the seduction theory.

29. See Carla Mazzio, "Sins of the Tongue," in David Hillman and Carla Mazzio eds., *The Body in Parts: Fantasies of Corporeality in Early Modern Europe* (New York: Routledge, 1997), 59–60.

30. See Katharine Park, "The Rediscovery of the Clitoris," in Hillman and Mazzio eds., *The Body in Parts,* 176.

31. G. J. Barker-Benfield, *The Horrors of the Half-Known Life: Male Attitudes toward Women and Sexuality in Nineteenth-Century America* (New York: Harper and Row, 1976), 91–4.

32. Scott Capurro, "Hell's Belle," *Guardian* (17 August 1998): 9.

33. Camille Paglia, "Oral Sexual Personae," reprinted from the online magazine *Salon,* 22 January 1998, in *Harper's Magazine* (May 1998): 20.

34. John (Johann) Caspar Lavater, *Essays on Physiognomy: Designed to Promote the Knowledge and Love of Mankind,* trans. Thomas Holcroft (London: William Tegg, 1860), 11.

35. Ibid., 9.

36. Ibid., 44.

37. Ibid., 15.

38. Judith Wechsler, *A Human Comedy: Physiognomy and Caricature in Nineteenth Century Paris* (London: Thames and Hudson, 1982), 24.

39. Leslie A. Zebrowitz, *Reading Faces: Window to the Soul?* (Boulder: Westview Press, 1997), 9.

40. Ibid., 47.

41. Ibid., 87.

42. Ibid., 22.

43. Lavater, *Essays on Physiognomy*, 475.

44. Pearson, "It's the Women," 13.

45. Carole Malone, "Get Out the Strait Jacket . . . Bill's Hormones Are Running Wild," *Sunday Mirror* (1 February 1998): 25.

46. Genevieve Fox, "Monica, an Icon for Modern Women," *Independent*, Tuesday Review (25 August 1998): 9. Lewinsky's use of her mouth for speech *and* sex is a vivid reply to Catharine MacKinnon's question in *Feminism Unmodified*, 193: "Even if she can form words, who listens to a woman with a penis in her mouth?"

47. Lewinsky's access to the presidential personage was described by White House senior adviser Barry Toiv as "face time." See Kenneth W. Starr (with analysis by the staff of the *Washington Post*), *The Starr Report* (New York: Public Affairs, 1998), 50. Subsequently, a novel by Erik Tarloff on the theme of a married president who has an affair with a White House aide was published with the title *Face-Time* (New York: Crown Publishers, 1998).

48. "Monica's Secrets," *Newsweek* (23 February 1998): 27.

49. Andy Lines, "President Pinocchio," *Mirror* (11 September 1998):1.

50. http: //www.netwebsites.com/impeach/:6 October, 1998.

51. Barbara Ehrenreich, "The Ultimate Phallusy," *Guardian* (15 August 1998): 3. This Lacanian interpretation could be extended to the 1 February 1998 cover image of the Italian newsweekly *Panorama*, which pictured a miniature Clinton crucified on a woman's crotch. An adaptation of the poster for *The People vs. Larry Flynt* (which itself reverses Magritte's 1943 *L'océan* by reducing the man's body, rather than the woman's, to the figure of the erect penis), the image transforms the president from the masculine subject who has the phallus to the feminine one who *is* it. The coverline for this issue is "Sesso e Potere"—"Sex and Power."

52. Marina Warner, "Is There Another Place from Which the Dickhead's Self Can Speak?" *London Review of Books* (1 October 1998): 8.

53. *Time* (2 February 1998): 12, 31.

54. Andy Lines, "Is Clinton Going Down?" *Mirror* (29 July 1998): 1.

55. Peter Bradshaw, "You're Never Alone with a Cigar—Especially in the White House," *Evening Standard* (25 August 1998): 22.

56. Freud, "Fragment of an Analysis of a Case of Hysteria," 99.

57. Ibid., 109.

58. Ibid., 108.

59. Bradshaw, "You're Never Alone with a Cigar," 22.

60. *The Starr Report*, 62.

61. Bradshaw, citing www.drudgereport.com, "You're Never Alone with a Cigar," 22.

62. Andy Lines, "Have A Cigar, Monica," *Mirror* (24 August 1998): 7, citing www.drudgereport.com.

63. On the day after its release, it was reported that

> the Starr Report is expected to break all previous records for web access. . . . Judging by the length of time taken to download, the sections relating to Monica Lewinsky,

chapters II (Initial Sexual Encounters), III (Continued Sexual Encounters), and VI (Resumption of Sexual Encounters), were proving the most popular. . . . CNN recorded over 20 million hits on the first day of Mr. Clinton's testimony to the grand jury. The official Royal Family site recorded 35 million accesses in the fortnight following the death of Diana, Princess of Wales."

Paul Kelso, "Frenzy and Frustration Add up to Webwars," *Guardian* (12 September 1998): 7.

64. Sigmund Freud, "Three Essays on Sexuality" (1905), in *On Sexuality*, Pelican Freud Library Volume 7 (Harmondsworth: Penguin Books, 1977), 62.

65. De Man, "Wordsworth and the Victorians," *The Rhetoric of Romanticism*, 90.

66. Akin Ojumu, "Taking the Lewinsky Name in Vain," *Observer* "Screen" (17 October 1999): 8.

Index

ABOUT THE AUTHOR

Mandy Merck is Professor of Media Arts at Royal Holloway, University of London. She is the author of *Perversions: Deviant Readings*, editor of *After Diana*, and co-editor of *Coming Out of Feminism?*